Second Edition

AQA French
Higher

Marie-Thérèse Bougard

Lol Briggs

Séverine Chevrier-Clarke

Jean-Claude Gilles

Oliver Gray

Steve Harrison

Ginny March

Nelson Thornes

D0265934

First edition published in 2009 by Nelson Thornes Ltd

This edition published in 2013 by:
Nelson Thornes Ltd
Delta Place
27 Bath Road
CHELTENHAM
GL53 7TH
United Kingdom

13 14 15 16 17 / 10 9 8 7 6 5 4 3 2 1

A catalogue record for this book is available from the British Library

ISBN 978 1 4085 2170 0

Cover photograph: Chase Jarvis/Getty
Illustrations by Kathy Baxendale, Russ Cook, Mark Draisey, Robin Edmunds, Stephen Elford,
Tony Forbes, Celia Hart, Abel Ippolito and Andy Keylock
Page make-up by Hart McLeod, Cambridge
Printed and bound in Spain by GraphyCems

Contents

Context – Lifestyle, Topic 1 – Health

1.1 You are what you eat   1.2 Healthy and unhealthy lifestyles
1.3 Dealing with ailments, tobacco, alcohol and drugs

Context – Lifestyle, Topic 2 – Relationships and choices

2.1 Relationships with family and friends   2.2 Future plans regarding marriage / partnership
2.3 Social issues: family, friends and society

Context – Home and environment, Topic 5 – Home and local area
5.1 Home   5.2 My local area   5.3 Routine and celebrations

Context – Home and environment, Topic 6 – Environment
6.1 Current problems facing the planet   6.2 Local issues and actions

Reading

Learning vocabulary

Writing

Getting ready for the exam

Building grammar knowledge

Listening

Developing exam strategies

Speaking

Understanding how the exam works

The AQA GCSE French exam is divided into four main subject areas, called **Contexts**. This book is divided up in the same way, with colour-coding to help you know where you are. Each Context is divided into two **Topics**, making a total of eight Topics to study during the course.

Lifestyle	Leisure	Home and environment	Work and education

The exam is divided up according to the four **Language Skills**: Listening, Speaking, Reading and Writing. Each one of these has its own separate exam, either in the form of an end-of-course paper or as a Controlled Assessment.

Writing (30%) (Controlled Assessment)

Listening (20%) (Exam)

Reading (20%) (Exam)

Speaking (30%) (Controlled Assessment)

AQA GCSE French

📖 Reading

The Student Book contains plenty of French reading material on the kind of subjects that come up in the GCSE exam. A headphones icon means the texts are also recorded so that you can compare the spoken and written word. The activities that follow the reading passages are similar to the types of questions you'll encounter in the exam.

🎧 Listening

Some activities only have a headphones icon. This means they're for developing listening skills and you won't see the words written down. The recordings are available from the Kerboodle book – just click on the icon next to the activity. A few of these recordings also exist as video, to help to bring the French language alive.

🗨 Speaking

Your ability to speak in French accounts for 30% of your final mark. In every Topic there are activities that are designed to build up the skills you need for your Speaking Controlled Assessment while using the language you have just learnt.

✏ Writing

Many students think that Writing is the hardest part of the exam, but it doesn't have to be if you are properly prepared. Each Topic contains carefully structured tasks that will help you to develop the skills you need to maximise your grade.

V Learning vocabulary

You can't get away from the fact that vocabulary has to be learnt in order to do well in the exam, so we are giving you help with this in various different ways.

- Vocabulary lists – For each section where new language is introduced there is a list of up to 20 useful words that come up in the tasks. There are also recordings to help you learn to pronounce each word correctly. Why not start by learning these?

- Vocabulary tasks – Every Foundation spread starts with a vocabulary activity. You might w

on these together as a class, or you can use them for practice and revision at home.

- Context lists – AQA have made lists of words that come up in their exams, one for each of the four subject areas or Contexts. We have put these lists in Kerboodle and added English translations.

- Interactive activities – If you learn well by getting instant feedback, why not try out the vocabulary builder in Kerboodle?

G Building grammar knowledge

Understanding grammar is the key to building your own phrases. AQA GCSE French helps you to consolidate your grammar knowledge in a logical way.

- Grammar boxes outline the grammar points you need to know for the exam.

- Activities next to the boxes provide instant practice, before you have had time to forget what you have just read.

- Interactive grammar activities in Kerboodle give you more practice.

- There is a Grammar section with verb tables at the back of the Student Book, to refer to whenever you need to.

Using *avoir mal à*

To say something hurts, use the correct part of *avoir* followed by *au, à la, à l'* or *aux* and the name of the part of the body:

J'ai mal au pied. – My foot hurts.

Grammaire page

Language structure boxes

These tables provide the scaffolding you need to construct different sentences for Speaking and Writing. On Kerboodle you will find editable versions matched to most of the Student Book Topics, allowing you to get creative by adding your own ideas and vocabulary items.

Je mange	souvent / rarement / quelquefois / régulièrement
Je fais	
Je me couche	assez / très
Je me lève	
Pour me relaxer, je	lis / fais du sport / regarde la télé.

 **Lien** ### Accessing Groundwork Student Book pages

Where you see this link icon in your book, this means you can access Groundwork pages, offering more basic activities and grammar practice for revision or catch-up work, directly from your Higher Kerboodle Book.

Developing exam strategies

Getting a good grade at GCSE French is not just about how much you know; it is also about how you apply this knowledge in the exam. Throughout the book you will find strategy boxes that are linked to exam-type activities. Read them carefully and use the suggestions to help you improve your grade.

> ### Use pictures to help you focus
>
> The pictures in questions 1 and 2 tell you whereabouts in the advert to focus. The fact that for both questions there is a (3) means that each time there is only one item that is not mentioned. Make sure you write down three letters each time.
>
> *Stratégie 1a*

Getting ready for the exam

At the end of each Context, you will find an Exam Practice section. There are four of these in the book. They give you:

- further practice in the sort of Reading and Listening questions you will meet in the exam
- recaps on Reading and Listening strategies, plus a few new ones
- some sample tasks for Speaking and Writing Controlled Assessments, with example answers
- exam technique advice to explain everything you need to know about AQA Controlled Assessments
- some Grade boosters to tell you what you need to do to push up your grade.

> ### Grade booster
>
> #### To reach grade A, you need to ...
>
> - Write 40 to 50 words per bullet point, conveying a lot of relevant information clearly, e.g. for bullet point 1, you could give a lot of details. Limit yourself to 40–50 words and focus on quality of communication.

Kerboodle offers an innovative, blended range of products to help engage teachers and students alike. It can be purchased as a whole learning solution or in parts, depending on the needs of each school, college, department and learner.

Kerboodle for AQA GCSE French includes differentiated resources focused on developing key grammar, vocab, listening, reading and writing skills. These engaging and varied resources include videos of native speakers, self-marking tests, listening activities with downloadable transcripts, interactive vocabulary builders, practice questions with study tips and comprehensive teacher support.

Our AQA GCSE French Kerboodle resources are accompanied by online interactive versions of the Student Books. All your Kerboodle resources are embedded to open directly from the book page.

Where appropriate there are links to support Groundwork and Higher activities.

Find out more at www.kerboodle.com

Log into Kerboodle at live.kerboodle.com

Numbers 1–20, ages, days of the week and seasons

1 📖 🎧 **G** Match the phrases with the correct photos.

1 J'ai trois ans. 3 Il a un an.
2 J'ai vingt ans. 4 Il a quinze ans.

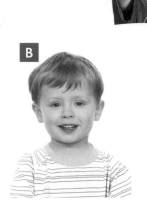

1	un	11	onze
2	deux	12	douze
3	trois	13	treize
4	quatre	14	quatorze
5	cinq	15	quinze
6	six	16	seize
7	sept	17	dix-sept
8	huit	18	dix-huit
9	neuf	19	dix-neuf
10	dix	20	vingt

Saying your age

Grammaire   page 187

Remember you need to use *avoir* when saying how old you are.

Tu as quel âge? How old are you?

J'ai quinze ans. I am fifteen.

Elle a seize ans. She is sixteen.

Il a dix-huit ans. He is eighteen.

2 💬 Work with a partner. Take turns to read out the phone numbers on the screen. Note that in French, phone numbers are said in pairs of digits, as they are shown: if the figure 27 is part of a phone number, you would say *vingt-sept*, <u>not</u> *deux, sept*.

4-19-07-15-11
2-03-18-12-20
8-16-13-05-09
5-01-14-06-17
7-19-15-02-08
9-05-17-20-12

3a 🖊 Solve the anagrams to find the correct days of the week.

1 dinlu   3 diuje
2 madichen   4 drinvede

3b 🖊 The letter 'e' has been deleted throughout the word snake. Divide it into the four seasons, as shown in the *Vocabulaire,* and add the missing letters, with accents if required.

nhivrauprintmpsnautomnnt

lundi	Monday	*vendredi*	Friday	*au printemps*	in spring
mardi	Tuesday	*samedi*	Saturday	*en été*	in summer
mercredi	Wednesday	*dimanche*	Sunday	*en automne*	in autumn
jeudi	Thursday			*en hiver*	in winter

Months, birthdays and time

1

Marion:	Mon anniversaire, c'est au mois de décembre.
Pierre:	Le vingt-cinq décembre?
Marion:	Non, le quinze décembre. Et toi?
Pierre:	Moi, c'est le dix janvier.

2

Charles:	Mon anniversaire, c'est le quatorze avril. Et toi?
Chloé:	Euh … Moi, c'est le premier octobre.
Charles:	Le premier octobre? C'est aujourd'hui! Bon anniversaire!

janvier	January
février	February
mars	March
avril	April
mai	May
juin	June
juillet	July
août	August
septembre	September
octobre	October
novembre	November
décembre	December
Bon anniversaire!	Happy birthday!

1a 📖 🎧 **G** Look at the two conversations above and write the four dates digitally, for example 25/12, in the order they occur.

1b 📖 🎧 💬 Read the conversations in pairs. Then have a similar conversation about your own birthdays.

2 📖 🎧 Match each sentence with the corresponding clock.

1 Il est cinq heures.
2 Il est midi moins cinq.
3 Il est huit heures vingt.
4 Il est une heure et demie.
5 Il est trois heures et quart.
6 Il est onze heures moins le quart.

> ### Dates in French
> To say dates in French, use:
> *le* + number + month.
> *le six janvier*
> (literally) the six January
> The only exception is for the first day of each month:
> *le premier avril*
> (literally) the first April
>
> **Grammaire** *page 192*

A B C D E F

3a 📖 🎧 **G** Reorganise the sentences below into chronological order, and write the times digitally (1–6).

Exemple: **6** 07h15

1 Le soir, nous mangeons vers dix-neuf heures quarante-cinq.
2 Les cours finissent généralement à dix-sept heures.
3 Je prends mon petit déjeuner à sept heures vingt.
4 En général à vingt-deux heures trente, je dors.
5 J'arrive au collège à huit heures trente.
6 Je me lève à sept heures quinze.

et quart	quarter past	*midi*	midday
et demi(e)	half past	*minuit*	midnight
heures	o'clock, hours	*moins le quart*	quarter to

> ### Time
> ■ To ask the time, you can say:
> *Quelle heure est-il?* (formal)
> *Il est quelle heure?*
> *Quelle heure il est?*
> ■ A typical reply is:
> *Il est midi / deux heures et demie.*
> ■ To say when something happens / is happening, use *à* to introduce the time:
> *Je me lève à sept heures.*
>
> **Grammaire** *page 192*

3b ✏️ Adapt the sentences in activity 3a to describe your own typical school day. Write them in the correct order.

Classroom equipment and colours

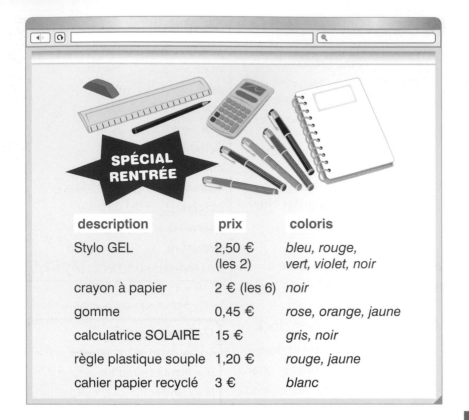

description	prix	coloris
Stylo GEL	2,50 € (les 2)	bleu, rouge, vert, violet, noir
crayon à papier	2 € (les 6)	noir
gomme	0,45 €	rose, orange, jaune
calculatrice SOLAIRE	15 €	gris, noir
règle plastique souple	1,20 €	rouge, jaune
cahier papier recyclé	3 €	blanc

SPÉCIAL RENTRÉE

blanc(he)	white
bleu(e)	blue
un cahier	notebook
un crayon	pencil
une calculatrice	calculator
un dictionnaire	dictionary
une gomme	eraser
gris(e)	grey
jaune	yellow
un livre	book
noir(e)	black
une règle	ruler
rose	pink
rouge	red
un stylo	pen
une trousse	pencil case
vert(e)	green
violet(te)	purple

1a 📖🎧 Can these items be bought from the catalogue above?

  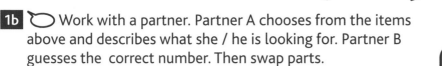

1b 💬 Work with a partner. Partner A chooses from the items above and describes what she / he is looking for. Partner B guesses the correct number. Then swap parts.

Exemple: A   Je voudrais un crayon jaune et un stylo gris.
                 B   C'est le numéro 3.

2a ✏️ **G** Copy the text and fill in each of the gaps with *un*, *une* or *des*. Make the adjectives agree when necessary.

Je voudrais _____ calculatrice gris_____, _____ cahier et _____ dictionnaire. Je vais aussi commander _____ stylos (_____ stylo bleu_____ et _____ stylo rouge_____), _____ trousse jaune_____, _____ règle vert_____, _____ crayons et _____ gommes.

2b ✏️ Adapt the text above to say what you would like to order.

Saying 'an' or 'some'

- How to say 'a(n)'/'some':

  un stylo   a pen
  une gomme   an eraser
  des crayons   (some) pencils

Although you can leave out 'some' in English, you have to include *des* in French.

- When using adjectives, make them agree with the nouns when necessary.

  un stylo vert   a green pen
  une gomme verte   a green eraser

Grammaire page 174

Numbers and dates

1a 📖 🎧 **G** Replace the following digits with words from the vocabulary list. Translate the sentences into English.

◄ | Q | [   ] | 🔍

Mon père a 53 ans.
J'ai économisé 99 euros ...
Ma grand-mère a 84 ans!
Il y a 27 élèves dans ma classe.
Mon nouveau jean a coûté 68 euros.
Mon frère a regardé 75 matchs de foot.

1b 🗨 Work with a partner. Partner A reads one of the numbers from the posts above. Partner B reads the corresponding sentence. Then swap parts.

Exemple: **A** Vingt-sept.

B Il y a 27 élèves dans ma classe.

2 📖 🎧 Read the text in the bubble, then complete the quantities required for each ingredient – using digits.

Pour ce gâteau, il faut cinq cents grammes de pommes, deux cent cinquante grammes de farine, cent vingt-cinq grammes de beurre et cent grammes de sucre.

1 **2** **3** **4**

3a ✏ Rewrite the following years using digits.

1 deux mille quatorze
2 mille neuf cent soixante-huit
3 mille neuf cent quarante-cinq
4 mille sept cent quatre-vingt-neuf
5 mille neuf cent quatre-vingt-seize

3b 🗨 Work out how to say the year you were born in French.

Je suis né en _____ . | Je suis née en _____ .

Grammaire page 192

Numbers

70 is literally 60, 10 (*soixante-dix*)
71 is literally 60 and 11 (*soixante et onze*)
72 is literally 60, 12 (*soixante-douze*)
And so on.
80 is literally 4 20s (*quatre-vingts*)
81 is literally 4, 20, 1 (*quatre-vingt-un*)
And so on.
Use *mille* (the word for 1000) when saying years in French.
1995: *mille neuf cent quatre-vingt-quinze*
2013: *deux mille treize*

27	vingt-sept
30	trente
40	quarante
50	cinquante
53	cinquante-trois
60	soixante
68	soixante-huit
70	soixante-dix
71	soixante et onze
75	soixante-quinze
80	quatre-vingts
81	quatre-vingt-un
84	quatre-vingt-quatre
90	quatre-vingt-dix
91	quatre-vingt-onze
99	quatre-vingt-dix-neuf
100	cent
999	neuf cent quatre-vingt-dix-neuf
1000	mille
2000	deux mille

French pronunciation

🎧 It is not hard to produce the correct sounds for a good French accent.

Remember that vowel sounds in French are not all exactly like English, and can change if they have an accent. You also need to know how some combinations of vowels sound. Vowels may have more than one sound depending on the word. Where this occurs below we have given examples.

a	chat, grand
e	sept, le, entrer
é	café
è	crème
ê	fête
i	dix
î	gîte
ie	géographie
o	dommage, poser
ô	drôle
oi	toi
u	tu
au or eau	beau
eu	deux
ou	rouge
œu	sœur
ui	puis

Vowels followed by n have a nasal sound, e.g. sans, gens, fin, bon, train, bien.

🎧 Then there are some patterns of letters which make these sounds:

ç or ce or ci (soft c)	garçon, morceau, cinéma
ch (like English 'sh')	chaussure
ge or gi (the g is soft)	géographie, gîte
gn (sounds like 'nyuh')	espagnol
h (silent)	hôtel, huit, thé
ill (sounds like 'y')	billet, bouteille
qu (sounds like 'k')	quel

r / rr	growled slightly in the back of your throat, e.g. Robert, marron
s or t	at the end of a word these are usually silent, e.g. gris, petit, mais
ail (at the end of a word)	travail
ain (at the end of a word)	demain
ais or ait (at the end of a word)	mais, fait
an or am; en or em	grand, chambre; sens, temps
im or in	impossible, international

1 Now try saying these well known French-speaking places with the correct accent.

Paris   Bordeaux   Marseille   Belgique   Avignon

🎧 **The alphabet sounds**

A	ah	B	beh		C	seh
D	deh	E	euh		F	eff
G	zheh	H	ash		I	ee
J	zhee	K	kah		L	ell
M	emm	N	enn		O	oh
P	peh	Q	koo*		R	err
S	ess	T	teh		U	oo*
V	veh	W	doobluh veh	X	eeks
Y	eegrek	Z	zed			

* oo pronounced with your lips pushed forward

Typing French accents and punctuation
One way to type letters with accents is to click on: Insert > symbol > then find the letter and accent you want.

Alternatively you can hold down the ALT key and type these numbers. Make sure that the Number Lock is on. It may be different for laptops.

131 = â	133 = à	135 = ç	130 = é	136 = ê	0156 = œ
138 = è	140 = î	147 = ô	150 = û	151 = ù	0128 = €

Using a dictionary

French > English

- Make sure that you find the meaning that makes sense for the particular sentence you are translating. Many French words have more than one meaning, e.g. *le temps* = 'time' or 'weather'.

- If you are trying to work out the meaning of a verb, you will have to find the infinitive in the dictionary (ending in *-er, -re* or *-ir*) and then look at the verb ending to work out the person and tense of the verb, e.g. *mangez* > *manger* – 'to eat'.

English > French

- Make sure you know if the word you need is a noun (a person, place or thing), a verb (usually an action) or an adjective (describes a noun).

- Sometimes the word in English can be the same when written, even though you pronounce it differently.

Example of dictionary layout

Ignore the words in [ ]. They are there to show French speakers how to pronounce the English word.

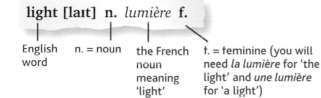

light [laɪt] n. *lumière* **f.**

| English word | n. = noun | the French noun meaning 'light' | f. = feminine (you will need *la lumière* for 'the light' and *une lumière* for 'a light') |

light [laɪt] adj. *léger* **(not heavy)**; *clair* **(colour)**

adj. = adjective — the French adjectives for 'light' (two meanings)

light [laɪt] vt. *allumer*

vt. / vi. = verb — the French verb 'to light' (i.e. 'to light a candle')

It is very important to understand that a dictionary will help you to find individual words, but you have to use your knowledge of how the French language works in order to put a sentence together. Very often the way a phrase is said is completely different from the English, e.g. *le chien de Paul* literally means 'the dog of Paul', but we would say 'Paul's dog'.

The most common mistake people make when using a dictionary is thinking that they can translate something literally word for word, without realising whether the French they have looked up is a noun, verb or adjective. The result can be quite funny for an English speaker who knows French, but a French speaker won't understand anything.

1 See if you can work out what this student wanted to say, then try to produce the correct version.

Je boîte une pièce de théâtre football.

Je ('I') – at least this word is correct!
boîte ('can') – noun, e.g. a can of drink
une pièce de théâtre ('play') – noun, e.g. a play at the theatre
football (football) – noun – this word is also correct.
Correct version: *Je peux jouer au football.*
je peux ('I can' – irregular verb, present tense); *jouer* (infinitive of verb 'to play'); *au football* (*au* needed after *jouer* + sport).

2 Try to find the correct translations for these words.

1 a match (to light a candle)
2 a case (for clothes)
3 fair (as in fair hair)
4 move (as in move house)
5 fly (as in fly in a plane)
6 left (as in the past tense of leave)

1.1 F   Des régimes différents

Je ne suis pas végétarienne car je mange du poulet, mais je n'aime pas d'autres viandes. Je préfère le poisson. Mon père, Bernard, ne mange pas de desserts sucrés parce qu'il est diabétique, mais ma mère, Adrienne, adore les gâteaux et le chocolat. Elle essaie d'y résister. Elle ne veut pas être grosse, mais c'est difficile.

Mon frère, Christophe, travaille tard le soir, et achète souvent du fast food pour son dîner, mais il sait que c'est mauvais pour la santé. Ma sœur, Amélie, aime faire la cuisine et elle adore les fruits.

Quelquefois, le dimanche, nous mangeons ensemble, et Amélie prépare un poulet rôti et une salade de fruits. C'est bien car toute la famille peut en manger et c'est un repas sain.

1a 📖🎧 Read Caroline's blog about her and her family's eating habits. Match the names to the pictures.

Caroline   Bernard   Adrienne   Christophe   Amélie

1b 📖 🎧 Read Caroline's blog again. Who …

1 does not eat red meat?
2 cooks chicken for the family?
3 can eat cakes but tries not to?
4 eats late in the evening?
5 has a diet affected by a medical condition?

2 **ⓖ** Choose the correct form of the verb to complete these sentences.

1 Elle **bois / boit / boire** souvent du jus d'orange.
2 Vous **aime / aimes / aimez** le fast food?
3 Tous les soirs, ils **mange / manges / mangent** de la viande.
4 J'**adore / adores / adorer** les fruits.
5 Ils **boire / boit / boivent** trop de vin.
6 Nous **déteste / détestons / détestez** les légumes.
7 Je **prend / prends / prenez** du café au petit déjeuner.

3a 🎧 Listen to Section A. Match the countries to the topics mentioned.

1	Canada	a	a diet lacking variety
2	Niger	b	a spicy stew
3	Ivory Coast	c	obesity
4	Morocco	d	malnutrition

3b 🎧 Listen to Section B. Lucie is talking about her eating habits in Guadeloupe. Which three sentences are true?

1 Traditional cooking in Guadeloupe is generally healthy.
2 Her father is a fisherman.
3 She says that she has coffee for breakfast.
4 She has a banana every day for lunch.
5 They usually eat rice with their evening meal.
6 She often chooses a healthy dessert.

4 🖊 Write a short paragraph about your eating habits and those of three other people you know. Give reasons.

J'	aime	les fruits		c'est bon pour la santé.
Je	n'aime pas	les légumes		c'est mauvais pour la santé.
Mon père	adore	la viande	car	c'est un plat sain.
Ma mère	déteste	le chocolat	parce que	c'est délicieux.
Mon frère	préfère	les frites		je suis / il est / elle est végétarien(ne).
Ma sœur		les pizzas		
Mon ami(e)		les boissons sucrées		ça a un goût horrible.

Present tense of -er verbs, boire and prendre

Most French verbs are -er verbs and follow the same pattern as *aimer*.

aimer = to like

singular	plural
j'aime	nous aimons
tu aimes	vous aimez
il / elle / on aime	ils / elles aiment

Boire (to drink) and *prendre* (to take) are irregular verbs and do not follow this pattern. Look them up in the verb tables on pages 193–197 and make a table similar to the one above for each of them.

Also revise how to say 'some' in French.
See page 28 ➡

Grammaire

Adding variety to your written language

Try to vary your language so as to not overuse certain words. As well as the words in the table, you can include language that is used in the other activities on these pages: *je prends, je bois, il achète, en général, souvent*, or words from the vocabulary on page 28.

Stratégie 4

Lien

1.1 Groundwork is available in the Foundation book.

1.1 H — On mange sain?

Trois jeunes nous parlent de leur régime alimentaire

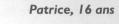

A Je suis végétarienne depuis deux ans parce que je pense que manger de la viande est cruel et barbare. Je mange beaucoup de fruits et de salades, mais en général je n'aime pas tellement les légumes. Mes copines aiment manger des hamburgers, mais moi, je refuse de les accompagner quand elles vont au McDo. Je déteste boire des boissons sucrées. Je mange de temps en temps du chocolat et des bonbons, mais je sais que c'est mauvais pour la santé.

Floriane, 15 ans

B Je fais attention à ce que je mange parce que je suis allergique aux noix. J'évite les biscuits, le chocolat et les gâteaux parce qu'ils peuvent me rendre très malade. En général, je préfère la cuisine étrangère, surtout les pâtes et les pizzas. Je bois beaucoup d'eau. Le steak-frites est mon plat préféré. Je mange du fast food mais avec modération. Les légumes sont bons pour la santé mais j'en mange rarement. Je n'aime pas le goût.

Patrice, 16 ans

C Je ne mange jamais de porc parce que c'est interdit aux musulmans. Hier, j'ai mangé de l'agneau et j'ai bu de l'eau. J'adore les légumes, surtout les haricots verts et les petits pois. J'ai horreur du fast food parce qu'il y a trop de graisse et de sucre dedans. En revanche, je prends souvent des desserts. Je ne peux pas résister aux petits gâteaux que ma mère prépare. J'en mange presque tous les jours. J'aime boire du thé à la menthe.

Halima, 14 ans

1a 📖 Find in the texts the French for these words and phrases.

Floriane:

| 1 vegetarian | 2 sweet drinks | 3 from time to time |

Patrice:

| 4 I avoid | 5 my favourite dish | 6 the taste |

Halima:

| 7 forbidden | 8 especially | 9 too much fat |

1b 📖 🎧 Read the texts. Decide whether these sentences are true (**T**), false (**F**) or not mentioned (**?**).

1 Floriane hates the idea of eating animals.
2 She sometimes goes to McDonald's.
3 She never drinks coffee.
4 Patrice doesn't eat cakes due to a health problem.
5 He likes Italian food.
6 Halima often eats fish.
7 She never eats meat.
8 Her mother doesn't like cooking.

📖 **Tackling reading activities**

When approaching a reading text, look out for clues to help you understand the main messages, such as the layout, the title, the typeface and any photos or drawings. Start by picking out the words you know already, and then look at words whose meaning you can easily work out, such as words that are the same or similar in English (e.g. *végétarienne*, *pizzas*).

Stratégie 1b

2 **G** Copy the sentences and fill in each gap with the correct form of the infinitive in brackets.

1 Ma mère _____ (**préférer**) faire la cuisine le soir pendant que je _____ (**commencer**) à faire mes devoirs.

2 Nous _____ (**manger**) vers sept heures et puis nous _____ (**ranger**) la cuisine.

3 Nous _____ (**acheter**) la plupart de nos provisions au supermarché. Est-ce que vous _____ (**préférer**) le supermarché ou le marché?

4 Le samedi je _____ (**promener**) le chien dans le parc avec mes amis. Nous _____ (**commencer**) avec un jeu de balle.

5 Nous _____ (**lancer**) la balle et le chien l'attrape. Après ça, mes amis _____ (**acheter**) des boissons au **café**.

3a 🎧 Listen to Section A. Choose the correct word or phrase to complete each sentence.

1 In Senegal, the sea is never **too far / cold / rough**.

2 Fish is an **expensive / important / rare** part of the diet in Senegal.

3 Meat is usually eaten **every day / once a week / on special occasions**.

4 A typical meal consists of cereals, fish and **salad / a spicy sauce / vegetables**.

3b 🎧 Listen to Section B. Match the beginnings and endings of the sentences.

1 Le plat préféré d'Hamidou contient	a	suffisamment.
2 Il mange rarement	b	à l'extérieur.
3 On mange régulièrement	c	du riz.
4 Chez Hamidou, on mange	d	à table.
5 La famille ne mange pas	e	du poulet.
6 La plupart des Sénégalais mangent	f	du doussa.

4 🗨 Work with a partner. Prepare answers to the following questions, then take turns to ask and answer.

■ Est-ce que tu aimes le fast food? Pourquoi?

■ Tu aimes manger des fruits et des légumes?

■ Tu manges souvent des sucreries?

■ Tu es végétarien(ne)? Pourquoi (pas)?

■ Quel est ton plat préféré?

■ Est-ce que tu prends toujours un petit déjeuner?

■ Qu'est-ce que tu as mangé et bu hier soir?

Est-ce que tu aimes le fast food? Pourquoi?

Oui, je pense que le fast food est pratique, délicieux et ce n'est pas cher.

Moi, je n'aime pas le fast food parce que c'est mauvais pour la santé.

Grammaire *page 193*

Some awkward *-er* verbs

You should be able to conjugate any regular *-er* verb. Watch out for a few that use the regular endings but change the stem slightly.

A stem ending in *g*, like *manger*, adds an *e* in the *nous* form of the present tense, so that the *g* is still pronounced as a soft sound: *nous mangeons*.

The *c* becomes *ç* in the *nous* form of verbs like *commencer*, again to keep the soft sound. *commençons*.

Other verbs lose or change an accent in the *nous* and *vous* forms:

j'achète, nous achetons

je préfère, nous préférons

This indicates a different pronunciation in each case.

Also learn how to use *au, à la, à l', aux* with adjectives and verbs.

See page 29 ➡

1.2 F   Le bien-être

Objectifs

Describing a healthy lifestyle

Present tense of *faire* and *dormir*

Using negatives

1 🅥 Sort the words and phrases below into the four groups shown in the grid.

se coucher	se relaxer	l'activité physique	un régime équilibré

courir sur place   dormir   boire de l'eau régulièrement   le gymnase   le sommeil

faire la grasse matinée   les jeux vidéo   éviter les sucreries   lire un magazine

une alimentation saine   écouter de la musique   la natation

Avez-vous la forme?

A

B

C

1

Deux semaines au Centre Blairot pour 20 euros. Offre spéciale d'introduction.

Deux visites par semaine à notre gymnase, c'est exactement ce qu'il vous faut pour vous aider à garder la forme. Ici, pendant une visite d'une heure, vous pouvez faire du cyclisme, comme sur la photo, et aussi courir sur place.

2

3 paquets de sachets "Relax" pour le prix de 2 paquets. Offre spéciale jusqu'à vendredi.

Vous ne dormez pas très bien? Vous avez peut-être une vie stressante? Chaque nuit, avant de vous coucher, il faut boire une tasse de notre infusion. Pour garder la forme, nous recommandons huit heures de sommeil par nuit. Notre boisson va vous aider à dormir, et à vous réveiller le matin plein d'énergie.

3

L'auteur va signer cette nouvelle bible anti-stress. Venez dans notre magasin entre 10 et 11 heures samedi!

Voilà sept idées pour éliminer le stress:

- Pour me relaxer, je joue de la guitare ou de la flûte.
- De temps en temps, je lis un bon livre.
- Le week-end, je fais souvent des promenades à la campagne.
- Je fais la grasse matinée de temps en temps.
- Tous les jours, je me lève à la même heure, parce que la routine est importante pour moi.
- Je mange équilibré et j'évite les matières grasses et les sucreries.
- Moi, je cours dans le parc, comme ça je reste en forme.

Achetez le livre *Mille idées pour éliminer le stress* et trouvez des possibilités qui vont transformer votre vie et vous aider à vous relaxer.

2a 📖📖 🎧 Read the adverts 1–3 and match them to the photos A–C.

2b 📖 🎧 In which adverts are the following mentioned?

a   une boisson chaude
b   se lever tard
c   faire du vélo
d   manger sain
e   deux heures d'exercice par semaine
f   une solution quand on est stressé.

Using the vocabulary lists

Refer to the vocabulary (pages 30–31) to help with new words.

The lists of words on those pages are the ones that are likely to be in the reading and listening exams, so you need to learn them!

You might like to download the audio file to help you with the pronunciation. Try covering the English words and testing yourself, or asking a friend to test you.

Stratégie 2b

3 🄶 Work with a partner. Choose *faire* or *dormir* to fill each gap, then decide what the verb ending should be. Write down the missing word.

1   Il est sportif. Il _____ du sport tous les jours.
2   Je me couche à dix heures et je _____ huit heures.
3   De temps en temps, elles vont au centre commercial où elles _____ du shopping.
4   Vous êtes fatigué! Est-ce que vous _____ bien?
5   Ma sœur et moi, nous _____ dans la même chambre.
6   Tu _____ ton lit le matin?

Present tense of *faire* and *dormir*

Faire is an irregular verb.

faire = to make or do

singular	plural
je fais	nous faisons
tu fais	vous faites
il / elle / on fait	ils / elles font

Dormir is also irregular. Find it in the verb tables on page 195 and draw a table like the one above to help you learn it.

Also learn about adverbs of frequency.

See page 28 ➡

Grammaire   page 195

4a 🎧 Listen to Section A of Docteur Bernard's advice. Copy the sentences and fill in each gap with the correct word.

1   C'est une bonne idée de faire du sport _____.
2   Si vous n'aimez pas le sport, vous pouvez faire des _____.
3   Le sport vous aide à éviter les _____ cardiaques.
4   Pour combattre le stress, il est important de bien _____.
5   Il ne faut pas se _____ trop tard.

promenades
coucher
maladies
régulièrement
dormir
copains

4b 🎧 Listen to Section B. Which items in the list does the doctor mention as potentially positive (**P**) or negative (**N**)? Which ones does she not mention (**?**)?

1   blogs
2   conversation
3   salt
4   fruit
5   alcohol
6   drinking water
7   playing sport

5 🗨 How healthy is your lifestyle? Work with a partner. Prepare answers to the following questions, then take turns to ask and answer.

■   Tu fais souvent de l'exercice?
■   Qu'est-ce que tu fais pour te relaxer?
■   Est-ce que tu dors bien?
■   À ton avis, es-tu en bonne forme?

Tu fais souvent de l'exercice?

Oui, je fais de la natation. Et toi?

Using negatives

To develop your speaking, you can use negative forms. In other words, you can say what you don't eat and so on: *je ne mange pas de viande, je ne dors pas bien, je ne me couche pas de bonne heure.*

Stratégie 5

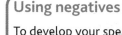 **Lien**

1.2 Groundwork is available in the Foundation book.

1.2 H — Pour garder la forme

Objectifs

Saying whether you are fit or unfit

Some useful adverbs of frequency

Referring to the past

Les jeunes: comment gardent-ils la forme?

Carole, 14 ans, est en bonne forme parce qu'elle mène une vie active. Par exemple, elle s'entraîne au gymnase deux fois par semaine pour faire de la musculation. Le week-end, elle fait souvent des randonnées à la campagne. Ça lui fait du bien de respirer l'air pur.

Henri, 15 ans, trouve qu'il est essentiel de se détendre parce que le lycée est très stressant, et il n'aime pas trop travailler, les devoirs l'épuisent. Après ses devoirs, il passe toujours une heure à écouter de la musique ou à jouer de la guitare ou de la flûte. De temps en temps, il lit un bon livre. Le samedi, il fait toujours la grasse matinée.

Audrey, 16 ans, n'a pas envie d'être en mauvaise santé. Elle mange équilibré et elle évite de manger des matières grasses et des sucreries. Elle nous avertit qu'il faut dormir huit heures par nuit, sinon on risque de se sentir fatigué au lycée. Tous les jours, elle se lève à la même heure et elle prépare le petit déjeuner pour tout le monde. La routine est importante pour elle.

Christian, 15 ans, est rarement en bonne forme. Il dit que le sport lui cause des douleurs dans les jambes. Il a beaucoup de devoirs et il se couche très tard parce qu'il veut réviser pour ses examens. Ses parents insistent pour qu'il travaille dur et il veut les rendre heureux.

1a 📖 Find in the text the French for these words and phrases.

1 she trains
2 weight training
3 fresh air
4 to relax
5 he has a lie in
6 she avoids
7 to feel tired
8 pains

1b 📖 🎧 Read the text and write down the name of the person who best fits these statements.

1 takes regular exercise
2 works late in the evening
3 finds school work stressful
4 reads to relax
5 thinks it is important to get plenty of sleep
6 tries to please his parents
7 likes outdoor activities
8 helps the family in the morning

2 🅖 🗨 Work with a partner. Prepare answers to the following questions, then take turns to ask and answer. In each of your answers, use a different adverb of frequency.

1 Tu manges de la viande?
2 Tu dors bien?
3 Tu vas souvent au centre sportif?
4 Tu manges souvent des frites?
5 Tu manges souvent du poisson?
6 Tu fais de la natation?

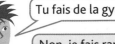

Tu fais de la gymnastique?

Non, je fais rarement de la gymnastique.

Non, je ne fais jamais de gymnastique.

Ⓖrammaire page 177

Some useful adverbs of frequency

To add variety to your language, learn these adverbs of frequency: *quelquefois, une fois par semaine, deux fois par semaine, parfois, encore, régulièrement, généralement, rarement.*

Also revise the present tense of *finir* and other *-ir* verbs.

See page 29 ➡

3a 🎧 Listen to Section A, where Olivier is talking about Yannick Agnel. Choose the correct English word to complete these sentences.

1 Yannick is Olivier's **friend / hero / brother**.
2 He won his gold medals in **London / Bejing / Athens**.
3 Yannick lives in the **north / west / south** of France.
4 At university, he studies the environment in the **oceans / mountains / deserts** as well as training in the pool.
5 Olivier wants to **study at the same university as / be a champion swimmer like / study the same subject as** Yannick.

3b 🎧 In Section B, Olivier is describing his training routine. Answer the questions in English.

1 How often does he go to the pool early in the morning?
2 When does he have breakfast?
3 Why is he more likely to eat frequent small meals than two large ones?
4 Which two activities does he mention other than training at the pool?
5 What does Stéphane do at the swimming club?
6 How is Sunday different from the rest of the week for Olivier?

4 🖋 Write a few paragraphs about your own lifestyle. Include answers to these questions.

- What do you drink and how often?
- How often do you do physical exercise?
- How do you relax? What did you do last weekend to avoid stress?
- How many hours do you sleep?
- How much time do you spend on homework?
- What do you eat and how often?

> **Referring to the past**
>
> You can improve your grade by referring to more than one time frame. In this writing activity you need to use a past tense for the third bullet point. It is also often possible to refer to the future: *Demain, je vais jouer au tennis.*
>
> **Stratégie 4**

Je mange / bois / prends	souvent / rarement / quelquefois	des frites / boissons sucrées / de la viande rouge.
Je fais	régulièrement / de temps en temps	des randonnées / de la natation / du sport.
Je joue		au foot / au basket / au rugby.
Je dors	toujours / normalement	huit heures par nuit.
Je me couche		de bonne heure / tôt / tard / à la même heure.
Je travaille	dur / trop / deux heures tous les soirs.	
Pour me détendre, je	lis / fais du sport / regarde la télé.	
Le week-end dernier, j'ai	lu un bon livre / écouté de la musique.	

1.3 F On parle de l'alcool, du tabac et de la drogue

cigarettesbièrefumeurcidrealcooldroguesdurestabacnon-fumeurcannabiscomprimédroguesdoucesvin

1 **V** Separate the words in the snake. Sort them into three groups: *boire*, *se droguer* or *fumer*. Add the English meanings.

Les opinions des jeunes

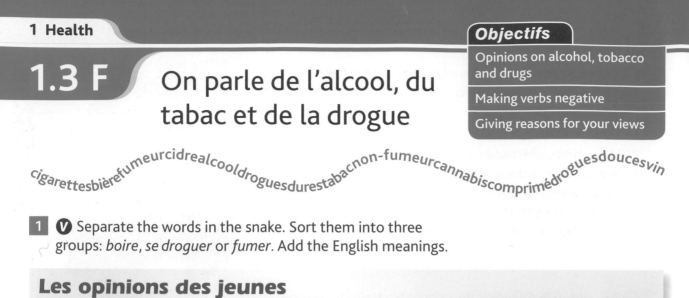

Georges, 17 ans

On commence avec des cigarettes et de la bière. Plus tard on essaie le whisky, la vodka et les drogues dures. L'alcool et les drogues sont dangereux parce que c'est trop facile de devenir dépendant.

Fatima, 17 ans

Je ne bois pas d'alcool parce que c'est contre ma religion. J'ai essayé les cigarettes, mais je n'ai pas aimé le goût. Ça ne me dit rien.

Pauline, 16 ans

L'alcool est une drogue mais c'est une drogue légale et il est facile d'acheter du cidre dans les supermarchés. Je bois avec mes copines pour être sociable. Il est plus facile de parler aux garçons quand on a bu, on est moins timide.

Victor, 16 ans

Je bois pour oublier mes problèmes au lycée. Je me sens très stressé en ce moment à cause des examens. Quand je bois de la bière, je me relaxe et je me sens bien. Je sais que c'est mauvais pour la santé mais je ne peux pas résister à l'alcool, surtout le samedi soir quand je suis avec mes amis.

2a Read Georges' and Fatima's opinions. Who mentions:

1 low and high strength alcohol?
2 having tried cigarettes?
3 the taste of tobacco?
4 hard drugs?
5 addiction?

2b Read Pauline's and Victor's opinions, then copy and complete these sentences in English.

1 Pauline thinks it's easy to get hold of _____.
2 She drinks with her _____.
3 After drinking, she finds that she becomes less _____.
4 Victor drinks to forget his problems at _____.
5 When he drinks he feels _____.

3 🇬 💬 Work with a partner. Partner A reads out a sentence and Partner B gives the negative version, using the expression in brackets. Then swap roles.

1 Je fume. (**ne … jamais**)
2 Mon père boit beaucoup d'alcool. (**ne … plus**)
3 Je bois du Coca quand je suis avec mes amis. (**ne … que**)
4 J'aime le goût du vin. (**ne … pas**)
5 Le tabac aide à combattre le stress. (**ne … personne**)
6 Être en bonne santé coûte cher. (**ne … rien**)

4a 🎧 Listen to Section A. Decide if these six people drink alcohol (**A**), use drugs (**D**) or express a negative opinion (**N**).

1 ___ 2 ___ 3 ___ 4 ___ 5 ___ 6 ___

4b 🎧 Listen to Coralie and Félix in Section B. Choose the correct English sentence for each speaker.

1 **Coralie**
   a I am a heavy smoker.
   b Cigarettes calm my nerves.
   c My parents don't know I smoke.

2 **Félix**
   a I still smoke from time to time.
   b I think my friends smoke to appear more grown-up.
   c I think cigarettes are very expensive.

5 🖊 You are taking part in a survey on an online forum. Write your answers to the questions, giving reasons for your views.

Qu'est-ce que tu en penses?

1 Est-ce que c'est un problème si on fume cinq cigarettes par jour?
2 Est-ce qu'il est facile d'arrêter de fumer?
3 Est-ce que l'alcool est mauvais pour la santé?
4 Boire une ou deux bières avec des amis, c'est sociable ou stupide?
5 Est-ce que le cannabis est dangereux?

À mon avis, c'est	un problème	parce que / qu'	il est facile de devenir dépendant.
Je pense / crois que c'est	facile	car	après on risque d'essayer les drogues dures.
	difficile		on le fait pour être comme les autres / être adulte / se relaxer.
	dangereux		on peut devenir violent.
	stupide		
	sociable		toutes les drogues sont dangereuses.

Making verbs negative 🇬 Grammaire page 188

Put *ne* (or *n'*) before the verb and a negative word after it.

Je ne fume pas. – I don't smoke.

Je ne fume plus. – I don't smoke any more.

Les fumeurs ne respectent personne. – Smokers don't respect anyone.

Je ne fume jamais. – I never smoke.

Ça ne me dit rien. – That does not interest me.

Je ne fume que cinq cigarettes par jour. – I only smoke five cigarettes a day.

Also learn about expressions with *avoir.*   See page 28 ➡

Giving reasons for your views Stratégie 5

Always try to justify your opinion by using a connective such as *parce que* or *car*.

If you want to qualify your view, you can say 'I know that …': *Je sais que l'alcool est dangereux.*

You could also say 'I think that … but …': *Je pense que l'alcool est dangereux, mais j'aime le goût.*

🔗 **Lien**
1.3 Groundwork is available in the Foundation book.

1.3 H Les risques de l'alcool, du tabac et des drogues

L'ivresse du samedi soir

A Voici le témoignage de Patrick, 15 ans:

«J'ai besoin de boire. Je suis réservé et l'alcool m'aide à être sociable. Mais je sais que boire est dangereux, surtout quand on boit pour essayer d'oublier quelque chose, pour cacher les réalités difficiles. Par exemple, pour moi, l'alcool m'aide à oublier mes problèmes avec ma famille et avec mon travail scolaire. J'ai peur de ne pas réussir. L'alcool du samedi soir ne m'a pas rendu dépendant, mais j'ai quelquefois peur de boire trop d'alcool. Je pense que je peux arrêter si je veux. Mais se passer d'alcool, est-ce que ça va être aussi facile que ça? Je n'en sais rien.»

B La consommation excessive d'alcool le samedi soir par les adolescents (ce que les Anglais appellent le «binge-drinking», c'est-à-dire la cuite du samedi soir) est maintenant habituelle. Les jeunes sont exposés à des risques importants: accidents de voiture, violences et maladies (vomissements, perte de connaissance, coma). Les risques à long terme sont bien connus: l'alcoolisme, les maladies sérieuses du foie et les crises cardiaques. On risque de gâcher sa vie. Lors d'une fête, l'alcool aide à mettre une bonne ambiance et renforce le sentiment de faire partie d'un groupe. Les jeunes consomment de plus en plus de bière au taux d'alcool élevé (11°) et des cocktails d'alcool fort très sucrés, vendus à bas prix dans les supermarchés. Est-ce qu'on va voir de plus en plus d'alcooliques dans l'avenir?

Est-ce que tu t'es vu quand tu es ivre?

1a Find these words and phrases in the texts. Write down their English meanings.

1 j'ai besoin de
2 j'ai peur de
3 se passer de
4 perte de connaissance
5 les maladies du foie
6 gâcher sa vie
7 la bière au taux d'alcool élevé
8 vendus à bas prix

1b Read the texts, then match the beginnings and endings of the sentences.

1 Patrick boit pour
2 Il dit que certains boivent pour
3 Il pense qu'il peut
4 Quand on boit trop, on risque
5 L'alcool peut provoquer
6 Les cocktails sucrés

a vivre sans alcool.
b des maladies graves.
c de devenir victime d'un accident.
d combattre sa timidité.
e ne sont pas chers.
f échapper à la réalité.

Asking questions

The easiest way to ask a question is to put *est-ce que* at the start: *Est-ce que tu bois de la bière?* (Do you drink beer?).

You can also form a question by inverting the subject and the verb: *Bois-tu du vin?* (Do you drink wine?).

If you need a question word it can be used with either question form: *Quand as-tu commencé à boire?* or *Quand est-ce que tu as commencé à boire?* (When did you start drinking?)

For a list of question words, see the grammar section.

Also learn about *devoir* + infinitive. *See page 29*

Grammaire pages 188–189

2 Choose the correct question word to fit each question.

1 **Comment / Combien / Où** de verres vas-tu boire?
2 **Où / Qui / Combien** vas-tu ce soir?
3 **Qui / Combien / Pourquoi** est-ce que tu bois de l'alcool?
4 **Comment / Quoi / Combien** as-tu arrêté de fumer?
5 **Quoi / Quand / Qui** est-ce que tu vas sortir?
6 **Est-ce que / Pourquoi / Comment** tu es dépendant?

3a 🎧 Listen to Section A. Choose the correct sentence for each speaker.

1 Maika

   a Je suis accro aux cigarettes.

   b Le tabagisme passif m'inquiète.

   c Ma mère est en bonne santé.

2 Olivier

   a Certains jeunes fument pour faire comme leurs amis.

   b Il est facile pour les jeunes d'arrêter de fumer.

   c Personne ne fume dans mon école.

Stratégie 3a

Focusing on key points

Before you attempt Activity 3a, make sure you understand the written statements. Think about which parts of the statements are likely to be different from the audio, so that you can focus on the key points when you listen.

3b 🎧 Listen to the information in Section B. Correct the mistakes in these sentences.

1 Paul has been an addict for five years.
2 He started taking drugs at home.
3 It's a habit he finds easy to kick.
4 He will have rehabilitation next year.
5 He wants to quit the habit by the end of the month.

4 🗨 Work with a partner. Prepare answers to the following questions, then take turns to ask and answer. Use the language structure box to help, but use your own ideas as well.

1 Pourquoi est-ce que les jeunes boivent de l'alcool?
2 Est-ce que tu bois souvent de l'alcool? Où? Avec qui?
3 Est-ce que tu as déjà fumé?
4 Combien de tes amis fument?
5 À ton avis, est-ce que le cannabis est dangereux?

Stratégie 4

Using phrases to give opinions

Use a variety of phrases to give your opinions, e.g. *je pense que* … (I think that …). A list of different opinion phrases is given in the vocabulary section on page 31.

Also try to say what you don't do or think, to show that you can use the negative.

> À quel âge est-ce que tu as commencé à boire de l'alcool?

> J'ai commencé il y a deux ans, à l'âge de quinze ans.

> Je bois pour être sociable et parce que mes amis boivent.

À mon avis, les jeunes boivent pour	être sociables / faire comme les autres / se relaxer.
Je bois / ne bois pas souvent parce que	ça me relaxe / je n'aime pas le goût.
Je bois	chez moi / chez des amis / avec ma famille.
Je n'ai jamais fumé parce que	le tabac cause des maladies graves / est dégoûtant.
J'ai fumé une fois mais	je n'ai pas aimé ça / le goût.
Je fume le soir pour	faire adulte / me calmer les nerfs.
Ils ne fument jamais	car c'est mauvais pour la santé / ils sont sportifs.
Un ou deux fument de temps en temps	quand ils sont avec des amis / stressés.
Je pense que c'est / ce n'est pas dangereux parce que	les drogues douces posent moins de risques.
	on risque d'essayer les drogues dures.

(G) Health

1 For each of the items pictured, write a sentence starting with *Je voudrais* (I would like) followed by *du*, *de la*, *de l'* or *des* and the name of the item. Use the word snake to help you.

Grammaire page 174

How to say 'some'
The French words for 'some' or 'any' are *du* (masculine), *de la* (feminine), *de l'* (before vowels) and *des* plural). Note that most food nouns ending in e are feminine, and that 'pasta' is always plural: *des pâtes*.

Exemple: *Je voudrais de la soupe.*

eaufraisesgâteaupâtespouletsaladesoupe

2 Put the sentences (1–6) in order, from the least to the most frequent. Copy the expression of frequency in each case.

1 Je fais de temps en temps la grasse matinée.
2 Je mange tous les jours des légumes.
3 Je mange rarement des gâteaux.
4 J'écoute toujours mes parents.
5 Je fais souvent du sport.
6 Je ne fume jamais.

Grammaire page 177

Adverbs of frequency
The most common adverbs of frequency are:

de temps en temps – from time to time
ne … jamais – never
rarement – rarely
souvent – often
toujours – always
tous les jours – every day

3 Choose the correct form of *avoir* or *être* to complete each sentence. Then translate the sentences into English.

1 Je n' **ai / est / a** pas d'alcool chez moi, car je **ai / suis / est** musulman.
2 Tu n' **as / es / et** pas d'énergie, parce que tu **ai / es / est** fatigué.
3 Elle **a / ai / est** très malade, elle **a / est / ont** le cancer du poumon.
4 Nous **avons / ont / sommes** trop de travail et nous **avons / êtes / sommes** très stressés.
5 Vous n' **avez / est / êtes** pas en bonne santé et vous **a / avez / êtes** mal au cœur.
6 Elles **avons / ont / sont** envie de prendre des drogues, mais les drogues **est / ont / sont** dangereuses.

Grammaire page 187

Expressions with *avoir*
Avoir normally means 'to have': *j'ai beaucoup d'énergie* (I have lots of energy), but in certain expressions it can mean 'to be': *j'ai faim* (I am hungry). Learn the expressions below:

avoir … ans – to be … years old
avoir froid / chaud – to be cold / hot
avoir faim – to be hungry
avoir soif – to be thirsty
avoir raison – to be right / correct
avoir envie de – to want (to do something)

4 Copy the sentences and fill in each the gap with the correct form: *au, à la, à l'* or *aux*.

1 Ma sœur est allergique _____ lait de vache et _____ farine de blé.

2 Le sucre est défendu _____ garçon car il est diabétique.

3 J'essaie de résister _____ crème, parce que c'est mauvais pour la santé.

4 Il demande _____ enfants de lui donner un bonbon.

5 La purée plaît _____ bébés car c'est facile à manger.

6 Le médecin dit que les cigarettes sont interdites _____ homme qui a un cancer du poumon.

Grammaire *page 189*

Using *au, à la, à l', aux* with adjectives and verbs

These words are used to describe contents and flavours of foods: *les sauces à la crème, les boissons frappées aux fruits*. They are also used after some adjectives and verbs.

*Il est **allergique aux** noix.* – He is allergic to walnuts.

*Le porc est **interdit / défendu aux** musulmans.* – Pork is forbidden to Muslims.

(Note two different ways of saying 'forbidden'. You may come across either.)

*Ce repas **plaît aux** enfants.* – The children enjoy this meal.

*Elle essaie de **résister aux** gâteaux.* – She tries to resist cakes.

*La fille **demande** à la dame de l'aider.* – The girl asks the lady to help her.

---

5 Replace each infinitive with the correct form of the present tense.

1 Au restaurant, vous `finir` toujours le repas avec un bon dessert?

2 Non! Mon copain Arthur `choisir` souvent un énorme dessert au chocolat, mais pas moi!

3 Au supermarché, comment `remplir` -vous votre panier?

4 On voit beaucoup de gens qui `remplir` leurs paniers de nourriture très grasse, mais nous, nous `choisir` surtout des fruits et des légumes.

5 Est-ce que tu `choisir` les frites à la cantine?

6 Oui, de temps en temps, mais je `finir` le repas avec un yaourt ou une pomme.

Grammaire *page 182*

Present tense of *finir* and other *-ir* verbs

Finir and a few other *-ir* verbs such as *remplir* (to fill), *choisir* (to choose) and *réussir* (to succeed) follow a regular pattern in the present tense. Remove the *-ir* and then add the endings (underlined) below.

finir = to finish

singular	plural
je fin<u>is</u>	nous fin<u>issons</u>
tu fin<u>is</u>	vous fin<u>issez</u>
il / elle / on fin<u>it</u>	ils / elles fin<u>issent</u>

Some *-ir* verbs, such as *dormir* (to sleep) are irregular. You can look these up in the verb tables on pages 194–197. Another one to check is *faire* (to make or do). Many of these verbs follow the pattern of endings -s, -s, -t in the singular.

---

6 Make a table for the present tense of *devoir*. Then replace the English in brackets with the correct French.

1 Je (**mustn't eat**) trop de frites.

2 Ils (**mustn't**) se coucher trop tard.

3 Il (**must learn**) à aimer les légumes.

4 On (**mustn't smoke**) dans les lieux publics.

5 Elle (**mustn't buy**) de boissons alcoolisées.

6 Nous (**must**) faire attention à notre poids.

7 Tu (**must stop**) de fumer.

8 Vous (**must say**) «non» à la drogue.

Grammaire *page 187*

Devoir + infinitive

Use *devoir* to say what you must and must not do. Remember it is followed by an infinitive. To check how to conjugate *devoir* in the present tense, go to the verb table on page 194.

(V) Health

Topic 1.1 You are what you eat

1.1 F Des régimes différents ➡ *pages 16–17*

la	boisson	drink
	bon(ne)	good
la	cuisine	cooking
	cultiver	to cultivate, to grow
	délicieux(-euse)	delicious
le	dîner	dinner
	ensemble	together
	épicé(e)	spicy
	essayer	to try
le	goût	taste
	gros(se)	fat
	malade	ill
	mauvais(e)	bad
	pauvre	poor
le	plat	dish
le	poisson	fish
	quelquefois	sometimes
le	repas	meal
le	riz	rice
	rôti(e)	roast
	sain(e)	healthy
la	santé	health
	sucré(e)	sweet
	végétarien(ne)	vegetarian
la	viande	meat

1.1 H On mange sain? ➡ *pages 18–19*

l'	agneau (m)	lamb
l'	alimentation (f)	diet
	allergique	allergic
le	citron vert	lime
la	crème	cream
	dehors	outside
	équilibré(e)	balanced
	étranger(-ère)	foreign

	éviter	to avoid
	faire attention	to pay attention
	favori(te)	favourite
la	fête	festival / celebration
la	graisse	fat
	interdit(e)	forbidden
la	menthe	mint
le	musulman	Muslim
les	noix (f)	nuts, walnuts
la	nourriture	food
l'	oignon (m)	onion
	par terre	on the ground
les	pâtes (f)	pasta
la	pêche	fishing
	résister à	to resist
	salé(e)	salty

Topic 1.2 Healthy and unhealthy lifestyles

1.2 F Le bien-être ➡ *pages 20–21*

se	coucher	to go to bed
	courir	to run
	de temps en temps	from time to time
	dormir	to sleep
la	grasse matinée	lie-in
au	lieu de	instead of
la	maladie	illness
	même	same
le	régime	diet
	régulièrement	regularly
le	sel	salt

le	sommeil	sleep
	souvent	often
les	sucreries (f)	sweet things
	tard	late
	tous les jours	every day

1.2 H Pour garder la forme ➡ *pages 22–23*

	avertir	to warn
	avoir envie de	to want to
se	détendre	to relax
la	douleur	pain
	encore	still
s'	entraîner	to train
l'	entraîneur (m)	trainer
	épuiser	to exhaust
	faire partie de	to belong to
	gagner	to win
le	héros (m)	hero
la	médaille	medal
	mener	to lead
la	musculation	weight training
	parfois	sometimes
la	randonnée	walk / hike
	rarement	rarely
	respirer	to breath
se	sentir	to feel
	utiliser	to use
la	vie	life

Topic 1.3 Dealing with ailments, tobacco, alcohol and drugs

1.3 F On parle de l'alcool, du tabac et de la drogue ➡ *pages 24–25*

l'	alcool (m)	alcohol
	arrêter	to stop
la	bière	beer
	cher(-ère)	dear, expensive
le	cidre	cider
	combattre	to combat, to fight
	contre	against
	coûter	to cost
	dangereux(-euse)	dangerous

	dépendant(e)	addicted
	devenir	to become
	doux(-ce)	soft
la	drogue	drug
se	droguer	to take drugs
	dur(e)	hard
	facile	easy
	fumer	to smoke
le	(non-)fumeur	(non-)smoker
	grave	serious
le	poumon	lung
le	problème	problem
le	tabac	tobacco

1.3 H Les risques de l'alcool, du tabac et des drogues ➡ *pages 26–27*

	à mon avis	in my opinion
	avoir besoin de	to need
	avoir peur de	to be afraid of
	bas(se)	low
	cacher	to hide
la	consommation	consumption
	consommer	to consume
	dégoûtant(e)	disgusting
	échapper	to escape
le	foie	liver
	fort(e)	strong
la	fumée	smoke
	gâcher	to waste, to spoil
	ivre	drunk
	je crois que …	I believe that …
	je pense que …	I think that …
	je trouve que …	I find that …
	oublier	to forget
se	passer de	to do without
la	pression	pressure
	provoquer	to provoke
	renoncer à	to give up
	réussir	to succeed
le	risque	risk
le	taux	rate, level

2 Relationships and choices

2.1 F   Ma famille et mes amis

Objectifs

Getting on with others

Reflexive verbs (singular)

Including adjectives

1 ⓥ Match the adjectives below with their translations. Decide whether each one is in its masculine form (**m**) or its feminine form (**f**). If it does not change, write (**m or f**).

casse-pieds	gentil	shy	kind
compréhensive	sympa	lazy	sad
mignonne	timide	annoying	older
jaloux	aînée	nice	numerous
triste	paresseux	alone, lonely	funny
seule	drôle	jealous	understanding
nombreux		sweet	

◀ ↻   🔍

On s'entend bien ou mal?

Pierre

Mon meilleur ami s'appelle Paul. Je m'entends bien avec lui. Nous avons beaucoup de choses en commun et nous aimons la même musique et les mêmes films. Paul est toujours sympa et très calme.

Amélie

Ma sœur aînée m'énerve. Elle est très égoïste et paresseuse. On se dispute souvent à cause de la télé car nous n'aimons pas les mêmes émissions. Elle n'aide pas à la maison et mes parents ne la grondent pas. Ce n'est pas juste!

Julien

En ce moment, je me dispute souvent avec mes parents. Ils ne me laissent pas sortir les soirs de semaine avec mes copains car j'ai des devoirs. Ma mère est plus compréhensive mais mon père est très strict. Je préfère sortir avec mes copains plutôt que rester à la maison.

Estelle

J'aime bien un garçon de ma classe mais je suis trop timide pour lui parler. Il est gentil et très drôle mais il est toujours avec un groupe de garçons désagréables. Je pense que nous avons des choses en commun mais il est difficile de lui parler.

2a 📖 🎧 Read the four blog entries. Write the name of the correct person for each statement.

1 _____ argues with his / her parents about going out on weekday evenings.

2 _____ and her sister argue about television programmes.

3 _____ thinks a boy in her class is kind and funny.

4 _____ has a lot in common with his best friend.

5 _____'s mother is more understanding than his father.

6 _____ can't talk to a boy she likes because she is too shy.

 Lien

2.1 Groundwork is available in the Foundation book.

2b 📖 🎧 Match the beginnings and endings of the sentences.

1   Pierre et son ami Paul …
2   Amélie et sa sœur …
3   Julien pense que son père …
4   Estelle pense qu'un garçon de sa classe …
5   La sœur d'Amélie est …
6   Estelle est …

a   égoïste.
b   s'entendent bien.
c   est trop strict.
d   est gentil.
e   trop timide.
f   se disputent souvent.

3 Ⓖ Work with a partner. Partner A says the sentence, filling in the missing reflexive pronoun, and Partner B translates the sentence into English. Swap over for each sentence.

1   Ma meilleure amie _____ appelle Morgane.
2   Je _____ entends bien avec mon frère.
3   On _____ dispute tout le temps.
4   Mon beau-frère _____ appelle Jean-Claude.
5   On _____ intéresse aux mêmes choses.
6   Tu ne _____ entends pas bien avec tes parents.

> **Grammaire** — *page 183*
>
> **Reflexive verbs (singular)**
>
> These verbs always have **reflexive pronouns** (*me, te, se*) before them. If the verb begins with a vowel, shorten the pronoun to *m', t'* or *s'*. Here are two examples:
>
> *se disputer avec* (to argue with) and *s'entendre bien avec* (to get on well with).
>
> Use *elle* and *lui* at the end of a sentence:
>
> *je m'entends bien avec elle* – I get on well with her
>
> *tu te disputes avec lui* – you are arguing with him
>
> Also revise adjective agreement.
>
> *See page 44* ➡

4a 🎧 🎬 Listen to and / or watch the video. Choose two words or expressions to describe the members of each person's family.

1   Florence   2   Jean-Jacques   3   Abdul   4   Liliane

a   lovable
b   divorced
c   sense of humour
d   annoying
e   critical
f   understanding
g   separated
h   strict

4b 🎧 🎬 Listen to and / or watch the video again. Decide who is being referred to.

1   Her parents are divorced.
2   His parents are separated.
3   His parents think he is lazy.
4   Her father has remarried.
5   She can talk to her mother.
6   He doesn't see his mother any more.

5 ✏ You are working as part of the scriptwriting team for a TV soap and you are describing a new family. In a group, decide who is in the family. Then each person describes one member of the family.

■ Who is in the new family?
■ What are they like?
■ How do they get on with each other and why?
■ What do they argue about?

> **Stratégie 5**
>
> **Including adjectives**
>
> When writing French, always try to include adjectives in your work in order to make it more individual and interesting.
>
> Remember that most adjectives in French follow the noun and you need to check you have added the correct ending (Is it masculine or feminine? Is it singular or plural?):
>
> *Elle se dispute avec sa <u>grande</u> sœur. Il est toujours avec un groupe de garçons <u>désagréables</u>.*

2.1 H Comment sont-ils?

Une famille nombreuse

Aminata habite au Cameroun en Afrique.
Elle nous parle de sa famille.

A Depuis l'âge de quatre ans, moi, ma mère et mes deux frères habitons avec une belle-mère, c'est-à-dire la deuxième femme de mon papa. Quand j'avais huit ans, mon père s'est marié pour la troisième fois: j'ai donc une seconde belle-mère. Et maintenant, j'ai aussi cinq demi-frères et quatre demi-sœurs. Au total, douze enfants, trois femmes et un mari vivent ensemble dans une petite maison au nord de Yaoundé, la capitale.

B Les mères préparent les repas à tour de rôle. Pendant les repas, nous mangeons tous ensemble. Mon père ne veut pas de division dans la famille. Quand j'étais petite, je me disputais beaucoup avec mes demi-frères et sœurs. Mais avec le temps, nous avons appris à être plus tolérants.

C Vous savez, pour un Africain, le fait de vivre en concubinage, comme ça arrive en France, c'est choquant. La règle pour habiter ensemble au Cameroun, c'est le mariage. Il ne faut pas oublier que la communauté est très importante dans mon pays, plus importante que l'individu.

Aminata

D Et puis en France, la monogamie ne semble pas toujours être un bon modèle. Les séparations sont devenues très fréquentes. Combien de femmes, par exemple, se retrouvent seules et sans argent après un divorce? Combien d'enfants sont déprimés à cause de la séparation de leurs deux parents? Et combien de pères ne voient pas leurs enfants qu'ils aiment? Je crois que la famille au Cameroun est plus stable que la famille en France.

1a 📖 Find in the text the correct word to match each of these definitions.

a la deuxième femme de mon père

b le fils de ma belle-mère et de mon père

c vivre avec quelqu'un sans être marié

d être marié à une seule femme ou un seul mari

e les parents n'habitent plus ensemble

f le couple n'est plus marié

1b 📖🎧 Read the article and choose a suitable title for each paragraph.

1 The distress caused by divorce and separation

2 Arrangements for meal times

3 Living together is frowned upon

4 A very large family

1c 📖🎧 Answer the questions in English.

1 How many people are there in Aminata's family? (Give details.)

2 What does she say about meal times?

3 How has her relationship with her half-brothers and sisters changed?

4 What does she think about couples living together outside marriage?

5 How does she explain the importance of marriage in Cameroon?

6 What three consequences of divorce does she mention?

Using cognates to help you

Stratégie 1a

Cognates are words that are the same, or nearly the same, in different languages. Some of these are easy to recognise because they are exactly the same (except sometimes for an accent): *séparation, stable* and *divorce*.

Sometimes one or more letters are added (e.g. *seconde*), or subtracted (e.g. *individu*). Sometimes you have to change a letter (e.g. *enfant* → 'infant').

Use this technique whenever you are trying to make sense of a new piece of text.

2 🄖 🗨 Work with a partner. Partner A says the sentence with the missing pronoun and verb ending. Partner B translates the sentence into English. Swap over for each sentence.

1 Elles _____ habill_____ comme moi.
2 Vous ne _____ entend_____ pas bien avec votre frère.
3 Nous _____ disput_____ tout le temps.
4 Elles _____ parl_____ souvent au téléphone.
5 Ils _____ confi_____ souvent à leur mère.
6 Vous voulez _____ reposer avant de sortir?

3a 🎧 Listen to the descriptions of five people. Choose the correct adjective to describe each of them (1–5).

sincere	dynamic	intelligent	sporty
funny	selfish	hardworking	quiet

3b 🎧 Listen again and correct these sentences.

1 Girls don't like Thomas.
2 François is a shy boy.
3 Georges is kind.
4 Delphine likes telling sad stories.
5 Caroline is interested in films.

4 🗨 Work with a partner (not your best friend). Prepare answers to the following questions, then take turns to ask and answer.

■ Quelles sont tes qualités?
■ Comment s'appelle ton meilleur ami / ta meilleure amie?
■ Tu t'entends toujours bien avec lui / elle?
■ Quelles sont les qualités importantes d'un bon ami / d'une bonne amie?
■ Tu as un petit ami / une petite amie?

Quelles sont tes qualités?

On dit que je suis assez amusante, mais de temps en temps je suis un peu timide.

On dit que je suis	(très / un peu) sympa / amusant(e).	
Je m'entends bien avec lui / elle parce que / qu'	nous nous intéressons aux mêmes choses.	
	il / elle est amusant(e) / fidèle.	
Un(e) bon(ne) ami(e) doit être	loyal(e) / compréhensif(-ve).	
J'ai un petit ami / une petite amie	et il / elle est vraiment sympa.	
Je n'ai pas de petit(e) ami(e)	parce que	je suis trop jeune / je veux passer mes examens avant de sortir avec quelqu'un.

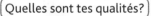

Grammaire page 183

Reflexive verbs (plural)

These verbs are used:

■ When people carry out an action that involves themselves: *nous nous levons à sept heures*

■ To talk about interactions between people: *ils se disputent souvent.*

The plural reflexive pronouns are *nous*, *vous* and *se*. Don't forget to shorten *se* before a vowel.

Examples:
nous nous entendons bien.

vous vous disputez souvent?

ils se lèvent à sept heures.

elles s'entendent bien avec leurs parents.

Also revise possessive adjectives.
See page 44 ➡

2.2 F Est-ce que je vais me marier?

Objectifs

Talking about future relationships

Aller + infinitive

Adding opinions when writing

1 🅥 Find the pairs. Some are opposites and some have similar meanings.

Lien

2.2 Groundwork is available in the Foundation book.

1	un mari	a	une famille monoparentale
2	les parents	b	les enfants
3	avoir des enfants	c	un partenaire
4	une famille avec deux parents	d	divorcer
5	se marier	e	la belle-mère
6	le beau-père	f	ne pas avoir d'enfants

On parle de la vie familiale

1

Maintenant: J'apprécie la solitude. Je passe beaucoup de temps dans ma chambre devant mon ordinateur, mais je fais du baby-sitting quelquefois et ça me plaît. J'aime aussi faire des promenades toute seule. Je n'ai pas beaucoup d'amis de mon âge, mais j'aime les enfants.

A

B

C

2

Maintenant: Mes parents sont divorcés. J'habite avec ma mère et mes sœurs. Ma mère trouve que le mariage n'est pas nécessaire, et je suis d'accord avec elle. À mon avis, il n'est pas important de se marier pour avoir une famille. Je pense que la famille idéale, c'est une mère, un père, une fille et un garçon.

3

Maintenant: Pour moi, la religion est importante. J'ai une petite amie, et on sort ensemble depuis un an. Elle habite chez ses parents. Je ne veux pas vivre avec elle sans être marié. Je n'aime pas les enfants – ils m'énervent!

a

Le futur: Je vais trouver un partenaire très sympa et loyal, et on va vivre ensemble. On va tous les deux avoir un bon travail, donc on va avoir assez d'argent pour acheter une belle maison. Je voudrais avoir deux enfants, mais je ne vais pas rester à la maison, je vais payer quelqu'un pour les garder.

b

Le futur: Je vais me marier à l'église, peut-être dans trois ou quatre ans. Je trouve que la cérémonie du mariage est très romantique. Ça va être une journée très spéciale pour nous deux, et un bon souvenir pour toute la vie. Nous n'allons pas avoir d'enfants.

c

Le futur: Je vais acheter un appartement en ville. Je vais inviter mes amis de temps en temps, mais généralement je vais être seule. Je ne vais pas me marier, mais je vais peut-être avoir un enfant. À mon avis, une famille monoparentale n'est pas une mauvaise idée.

2a 📖📖 🎧 Match the different views on family life (1–3) with the plans for the future (a–c) and the correct pictures (A–C).

2b 📖 🎧 Read the views on family life and plans for the future again. Who says the following? Write the correct combination (1–3, a–c, A–C).

1 I intend to live with my partner without getting married.
2 I want to live alone.
3 I want to get married quite young.
4 I don't want children.
5 It's not important to get married before having children.
6 I like the idea of being a single parent.

3 🅖 Transform the following sentences into the immediate future tense using *aller*.

Exemple: Il voyage en Australie. →
            Il <u>va voyager</u> en Australie.

1 Elle trouve l'amour!
2 Je me marie à l'âge de vingt-cinq ans.
3 Elle sort avec son petit ami.
4 J'ai deux enfants.
5 Tu es riche et célèbre?
6 J'adore ma femme.

> **Aller + infinitive**
>
> Use the verb *aller* (to go) in the present tense followed by an infinitive (e.g. *travailler*) to express future plans.
>
> *Je vais travailler.*   I am going to work.
>
> *Elle va se marier.*   She is going to get married.
>
> If you have forgotten the present tense of *aller*, look it up in the verb tables (page 194).
>
> Also revise *devoir*, *pouvoir* and *vouloir* (present tense).
>
> *See page 44* ➡
>
> *Grammaire* *page 185*

4a 🎧 Listen to the three speakers. Select the correct phrase to complete each sentence.

1 Malika's parents are going to choose …
   a her future husband.
   b her boyfriend.
   c her wedding dress.
2 Maxime would like to …
   a get married and have children.
   b get married because it's important.
   c have children without getting married.
3 Stéphanie would like …
   a to get married in church.
   b to have one child.
   c a quiet husband.
4 Stéphanie thinks that …
   a religion is not important.
   b the wedding ceremony is romantic.
   c having children is not important.

4b 🎧 Listen again. Decide who thinks the following: Malika, Maxime or Stéphanie?

1 I don't intend to get married.
2 I don't know him.
3 Religion is important.
4 I'd like to have one or two children.
5 My ideal partner is loyal.
6 I'd like to have lots of children.

5 🖊 Write a reply to this email. Give details about your life now and your plans for the future.

> Salut!
>   En ce moment, j'habite avec ma mère car mes parents sont divorcés. C'est un peu triste. Plus tard, j'aimerais avoir ma maison et habiter avec ma copine. J'ai l'intention de me marier et d'avoir trois enfants. Pour moi, le mariage, c'est important. Ma femme idéale va être généreuse et sympa.
>   Et toi? Avec qui habites-tu? Est-ce que tu voudrais te marier? Aimerais-tu avoir des enfants?

> **Adding opinions when writing**
>
> When writing, try to include opinions as often as you can.
>
> In the present tense, you can use *c'est* followed by an adjective to give a simple opinion: *c'est sympa, c'est intéressant, c'est ennuyeux.*
>
> In the future, you can use *ça va être …* (it's going to be …): *Ça va être super.*
>
> *Stratégie 5*

2.2 H Seul, marié ou en concubinage?

A Je trouve que le mariage n'est pas nécessaire et plus tard, je vivrai en concubinage avec ma copine. On achètera une maison en ville et on aura peut-être des enfants. À mon avis, il n'est pas important de se marier pour avoir des enfants. Ma copine sera sympa et marrante.
Alexandre

B Moi, j'espère que dans cinq ou six ans, j'habiterai avec quelqu'un que j'aime. Nous nous marierons et nous aurons des enfants plus tard. Le mariage est important pour la sécurité. À mon avis, une famille monoparentale n'est pas une bonne idée.
Élodie

C Moi, j'aimerais habiter seul mais j'aime bien voir des amis de temps en temps. Plus tard, j'achèterai un appartement et j'irai souvent au cinéma ou à des spectacles avec des amis. J'aurai un travail que j'aime. Je ne me marierai pas et je n'aurai pas d'enfants. Ils m'énervent.
Simon

1a 📖 🎧 Read three people's views on future relationships. Match the expressions (1–3) with their definitions (a–c).

1 vivre en concubinage
2 une famille monoparentale
3 habiter seul

a vivre seul
b vivre avec quelqu'un sans être marié
c une famille avec un seul parent (le père ou la mère)

1b 📖 🎧 Answer the questions in English.

1 What are Alexandre's views on marriage?
2 What does he think about having children?
3 Will Élodie get married to her boyfriend? Why? / Why not?
4 What is her opinion of single-parent families?
5 Why will Simon not get married?
6 Why won't he have any children?

2 🅖 Transform the following sentences so they are in the future tense.

1 Ils vont fêter leurs fiançailles.
2 Je vais sortir avec ma petite amie ce soir.
3 Elle va répondre à ma demande en mariage.
4 Je vais tomber amoureuse à l'âge de vingt-cinq ans.
5 Vous allez vivre ensemble?
6 Nous allons nous marier à l'église.
7 Est-ce que tu vas rester à la maison avec les enfants?
8 Il va habiter avec sa petite amie.

The future tense *Grammaire* (page 185)

To form the future tense for -er and -ir verbs, use the infinitive as the stem and add the following endings: -ai, -as, -a, -ons, -ez, -ont.

If the infinitive ends in -re, remove the -e before adding the endings: elle attendra.

Revise phrases such as je voudrais, j'aimerais, j'ai l'intention de + infinitive to express future intentions.

Also learn some common irregular verbs in the future tense. *See page 45* ➡

3a 🎧 Listen to the three speakers. Choose three qualities that each person would like in his / her ideal partner.

1 Chloé   **2** Vincent   **3** Patricia

a	musical	d	clever	g	quiet	j	rich
b	self-confident	e	good-looking	h	average height	k	fond of children
c	shy	f	funny	i	generous		

3b 🎧 Listen again. Complete the sentences by selecting a, b or c each time.

1 Chloé's ideal partner will work …
  a in the medical sector.
  b in business.
  c in education.

2 Chloé's partner will often give her …
  a books and chocolates.
  b flowers and jewellery.
  c flowers and chocolates.

3 Vincent's partner will be …
  a famous.
  b kind.
  c a musician like him.

4 Vincent and Marie-Laure will …
  a travel and play music.
  b have children.
  c travel with their children.

5 Patricia doesn't like men who are …
  a lazy.
  b selfish.
  c intelligent.

4 🗨 Conduct a survey on the qualities people would like in their future ideal partner. Here are some possible questions but you could invent more of your own. Ask the questions to each person in your group.

■ Comment sera ton / ta partenaire idéale?
■ Qu'est-ce qu'il / elle aimera faire de son temps libre?
■ Est-ce qu'il / elle aimera les enfants?
■ Qu'est-ce qu'il / elle fera dans la vie?
■ Tu te marieras avec lui / elle?
  – Si tu réponds «oui» à cette question, où et quand?
  – Si tu réponds «non» à cette question, pourquoi pas?

Mon / Ma partenaire idéal(e) sera	gentil(le) / sympa / généreux(-euse).
Il / elle aimera	faire du sport / aller au ciné / écouter de la musique / danser / faire du cyclisme.
Il / elle aimera les enfants / n'aimera pas les enfants	parce qu'ils sont (souvent) adorables / mignons / casse-pieds / méchants.
On se mariera	à l'âge de …ans / à l'église / dans un château.
Je vivrai avec mon / ma partenaire sans me marier	parce que (pour moi) le mariage n'est pas important / essentiel.

Answering unprepared questions

Part of your examination will involve answering questions for which you have not prepared. If, for example, you are talking about your future plans, you may be asked if you want to get married.

Also think of the likely follow-up questions, such as: How old will you be? Describe your ideal partner. Do you want children?

Stratégie 4

Qu'est-ce ton partenaire idéal aimera faire de son temps libre?

Il aimera écouter de la musique.

2.3 F On n'a pas les mêmes chances

Objectifs

Discussing poverty and social issues

Present tense of *-ir* verbs and *-re* verbs

Key words (reading)

1 **V** Match each phrase with its English translation.

1 sans domicile fixe (SDF)
2 un logement
3 une organisation caritative
4 des cartons
5 un sac de couchage
6 au chômage
7 les choses indispensables
8 un quartier défavorisé

a carboard boxes
b a charity
c a sleeping bag
d homeless
e the necessities
f a deprived area
g unemployed
h accommodation

Qu'est-ce qu'on peut faire pour aider les personnes défavorisées?

Léon habite à Paris, où il y a environ 5 000 hommes et femmes sans domicile fixe dans les rues. Il travaille pour une organisation qui s'occupe des personnes qui n'ont pas de maison. Ces personnes sont presque toujours sans travail, elles ont faim et elles n'ont pas de logement. Voici ce que dit Léon: «Mon travail, c'est d'offrir de la soupe et une tranche de pain à chaque personne malheureuse qui arrive au centre.»

Thomas travaille pour une organisation caritative. Il remplit des cartons de toutes sortes de choses pour les SDF, par exemple des sacs de couchage, du shampooing et du savon. Comme ils sont au chômage, ils n'ont pas assez d'argent pour acheter les choses indispensables de la vie. Thomas dit «Ces pauvres gens attendent avec impatience notre arrivée.»

Jules est volontaire dans un groupe sportif qui aide les jeunes des quartiers défavorisés. Il passe cinq heures par semaine à faire du sport dans les centres de loisirs d'un quartier de Paris où il y a beaucoup de familles pauvres. Grâce au sport, ces adolescents ont la chance d'avoir une vie meilleure. «La première fois, il n'y avait que cinq garçons et trois filles, mais ils ont parlé à leurs voisins et maintenant on a trente jeunes dans notre groupe. On est très populaires!» explique Jules.

2a 📖 🎧 Read the article and write the name of the appropriate person for each picture (A–C).

2b 📖 🎧 Which four of these sentences are true?

1 The people who come to Léon are usually unemployed.
2 Léon helps by giving the people money to buy soup and bread.
3 Thomas's charity helps by providing basic necessities for the homeless.
4 The homeless people are always happy to see the volunteers.
5 Jules earns money by working for his charity.
6 Sport gives hope to these young people.

Key words (reading)

Searching for key words can save time and lead you to the answer more quickly. For example, if you are asked the question 'when?' you would look for a time, a date, a month, a day, etc. If you are asked about the advantages of something, you would look for positive words, such as *utile* or *intéressant*.

Stratégie 2a–2b

3a ⓖ Copy and complete the grid for the verbs *remplir* (to fill) and *attendre* (to wait for). Follow the model in the grammar box.

remplir = to fill	singular	plural
	je _____	nous _____
	tu _____	vous remplissez
	il /elle / on remplit	ils / elles _____

attendre = _____	singular	plural
	j'_____	nous _____
	_____ attends	vous _____
	il / elle / on _____	_____ _____

3b ⓖ Copy the sentences and fill in the gaps. First decide which verb you need from the list, then choose the correct ending.

1 Je _____ des cartons de toutes sortes de choses à manger et à boire.
2 Les gens du village _____ l'arrivée du docteur de Médecins Sans Frontières.
3 Nous _____ des cartes d'anniversaire au marché pour collecter de l'argent pour une école au Congo.
4 Nathalie commence son travail avec les SDF à huit heures du soir, et elle _____ à minuit.
5 On ne _____ pas d'être sans domicile fixe: ça peut arriver parce qu'on n'a pas de travail.

vendre　attendre　choisir
remplir　finir

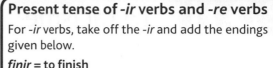

Present tense of -ir verbs and -re verbs

Grammaire page 182

For -*ir* verbs, take off the -*ir* and add the endings given below.

finir = to finish

singular	plural
je finis	*nous finissons*
tu finis	*vous finissez*
il / elle / on finit	*ils / elles finissent*

Find the pattern for -*re* verbs (e.g. *vendre*) in the verb tables (page 193) and make a similar table to help you learn it.

Also learn about patterns of endings for masculine and feminine nouns. *See page 44* ➡

Lien
2.3 Groundwork is available in the Foundation book.

4a 🎧 Listen to Simon and Marie discussing various social issues. Complete the sentences by selecting a, b or c.

1 Marie thinks that the homeless people are in a difficult situation because they …
　a have no family.　c have no help.
　b are unemployed.
2 Simon believes that the homeless must find …
　a a job.　b a house.　c some food.
3 Marie thinks that homeless people also have …
　a feelings.　c other problems.
　b rights.
4 Simon gives the example of …
　a heart condition.　c disability.
　b alcoholism.

4b 🎧 Listen again and decide who said the following.

1 Charities do an excellent job.
2 Homeless people are in a difficult situation.
3 It's difficult to find a job when you are homeless.
4 Homeless people need to look for a job.
5 They have alcohol dependency issues.
6 They can suffer from a mental illness.

5 🗩 Work with a partner. Discuss these statements, saying whether you agree or not.

■ Les organisations caritatives doivent aider les SDF.
■ Les SDF doivent chercher du travail.
■ Les SDF choisissent d'habiter dans la rue.
■ Il est difficile de trouver du travail quand on est SDF.

Agreeing / disagreeing in a discussion

Stratégie 5

To agree use: *c'est vrai / tu as raison / je suis d'accord / exactement / justement.*

To disagree use: *c'est faux / tu as tort / je ne suis pas du tout d'accord / certainement pas.*

2.3 H Le racisme

Les immigrés en France

A Il y a plus de sept millions d'immigrés en France. La plupart de ces immigrés viennent d'Afrique du Nord (la Tunisie, le Maroc ou l'Algérie). Ils habitent surtout dans les grandes villes industrielles. Ils sont venus en France principalement pour des raisons économiques, pour trouver du travail. Les immigrés ont influencé la musique, la cuisine et la culture françaises.

B Halima, 15 ans, parle de son expérience …

«Mes parents sont arrivés de Tunisie il y a trente ans parce qu'ils voulaient trouver du travail et une meilleure vie. Nous habitons dans la banlieue parisienne dans un appartement au sixième étage d'un grand immeuble. Je suis née en France et je suis française, mais je suis fière de la culture tunisienne. J'aime la cuisine tunisienne et j'écoute de la musique populaire d'Afrique du Nord. Mes parents m'ont dit qu'ils ont surtout rencontré des gens racistes quand ils cherchaient du travail. Mais moi, je crois que les gens sont plus tolérants maintenant. Ce qui me plaît, c'est que tout le monde s'entend bien dans mon collège.

En revanche, je ne peux pas porter le foulard islamique quand je vais au collège. Je trouve cette loi inacceptable.»

1a 📖 Find in the text the French for the following words and expressions.

a immigrants
b have influenced music
c a better life
d the suburbs
e a tall tower block
f I am proud of
g racist people
h the Muslim headscarf

1b 📖🎧 Decide whether the statements are true (**T**), false (**F**) or not mentioned (**?**) in the article. Read Section A for statements 1–3 and Section B for statements 4–9.

1 Tunisia is a North African country.
2 A lot of immigrants came to France to be with their families.
3 The immigrants have influenced French cuisine.
4 Halima's family live in the centre of Paris.
5 Halima was born in Tunisia.
6 Halima's parents work in a factory in Paris.
7 They have been victims of racial discrimination.
8 Halima wants to wear the Islamic scarf at school.
9 She wants to become a teacher.

2 **G** Copy the sentences and fill in each gap with the correct infinitive.

1 Elle ne peut pas _____ le foulard islamique au collège.
2 Ses parents voulaient _____ une meilleure vie.
3 Je sais _____ des plats tunisiens.
4 Nous devons _____ du travail.
5 Ils doivent _____ leur pays.
6 Tu voudrais _____ au centre-ville?

| cuisiner | trouver | quitter |
| habiter | avoir | porter |

3a 🎧 Listen to the five news reports (**a**–**e**) and match these headlines with the correct news items.

1 Vandalism of graves
2 Racist incident in school
3 A racist mugging
4 Campsite owner guilty of racism
5 Racism in a stadium

3b 🎧 Listen again and correct the mistakes in these statements.

1 L'élève musulmane était absente parce qu'on ne lui permettait pas de porter le foulard islamique.
2 On a agressé l'homme parce qu'il était riche.
3 Un incident raciste a eu lieu pendant un match de basket-ball.
4 On a trouvé des graffitis sur des tombeaux chrétiens.
5 La propriétaire du camping a refusé un emplacement aux deux sœurs parce qu'elles étaient en retard.

4 ✏️ Write an account for a newspaper about a racist incident you have witnessed or read about, giving your views on the subject.

■ Where and when did the incident take place?
■ What happened?
■ How did it make you feel?
■ What do you think should happen as a result?

L'incident a eu lieu	samedi / il y a un mois / la semaine dernière	dans la rue / dans un bus / au stade.
Un homme a Un groupe de jeunes ont	agressé … / insulté …/ refusé de …	
Cet incident m'a	attristé(e) / déprimé(e) / fâché(e) / enragé(e).	
Ce qui me choque / surprend, c'est …		
Ce que j'aime, c'est … / Ce que je n'aime pas, c'est …		
À mon avis, il faut On devrait	punir les coupables / supprimer … / interdire …	

Grammaire page 181

Verbs followed by an infinitive

All verbs of liking, disliking and preferring (such as *aimer*, *adorer*, *préférer*, *détester*) are followed by the infinitive. The same applies to *savoir* and to modal verbs: *vouloir*, *pouvoir* and *devoir*.

J'aime danser. – I like dancing.

Je dois travailler. – I have to work.

Elle ne peut pas porter le foulard. – She can't wear the scarf.

Ils veulent trouver du travail. They want to find some work.

Also revise verbs that are followed by *à* or *de* and an infinitive.   *See page 45* ➡

Stratégie 4

Checking written work

Check your written work, using a dictionary and the grammar section (pages 172–192) as needed.

■ Masculine words need *le, un* or *du*, feminine words *la, une* or *de la* (*dans la rue, dans un bus*).

■ With feminine or plural words, adjectives with the nouns will also have to change (*des joueurs noirs*).

■ Check accents (*à mon avis, un homme a été agressé*).

■ Check verb endings, using the verb tables (pages 193–197).

Relationships and choices

1 Choose the correct adjectives to complete the following sentences.

1 Sa mère est **bavard / bavarde**, mais elle n'est pas **méchant / méchante**.

2 Ta grand-mère est **triste / tristes** parce qu'elle est **seul / seule**.

3 Il a des parents **riche / riches** et **célèbre / célèbres**.

4 J'ai une copine très **gentil / gentille** mais **timide / timides**.

5 Mon **grand / grands** frère est **paresseux / paresseuses**.

6 Ses **petits / petites** sœurs sont **pénible / pénibles**.

7 Mon frère **aîné / aînée** est très **égoïste / égoïstes**.

8 Elle a des grands-parents **pauvre / pauvres** mais très **gentils / gentilles**.

Grammaire — pages 174–175

Adjective agreement

Adjectives have different endings depending on whether they describe masculine, feminine, singular or plural nouns. Add -e if the noun is feminine, and add -s if it is plural. They usually go after the noun:

une fille intelligente	a clever girl
des enfants gentils	kind children

If the adjective already ends in -e, there is no need to add another one:

un garçon timide	a shy boy
une fille timide	a shy girl

Some adjectives, including *petit*, *grand* and *joli* usually go before the noun:

ma grande sœur	my big sister

2 Choose the correct form of *devoir*, *pouvoir* and *vouloir* each time. Then find the correct translation and complete it.

1 Je ne **veux / voulons** pas me marier avec lui.

2 Tu ne **dois / doit** pas être méchant avec ton copain.

3 Il ne **devez / doit** pas bavarder avec ses copains.

4 Elle ne **veut / veux** pas habiter chez sa mère.

5 Nous ne **veulent / voulons** pas divorcer.

6 Vous ne **peut / pouvez** pas vous entendre.

7 Ils ne **peuvent / pouvons** pas avoir d'enfants.

a _____ can't get on.

b _____ can't have children.

c _____ don't want a divorce.

d _____ don't want to marry him.

e _____ doesn't want to live with her mother.

f _____ mustn't be mean to your friend.

g _____ mustn't gossip with his friends.

Grammaire — page 187

Devoir, *pouvoir* and *vouloir*: present tense

devoir = to have to

singular	plural
je dois	*nous devons*
tu dois	*vous devez*
il / elle / on doit	*ils / elles doivent*

pouvoir = to be able to

singular	plural
je peux	*nous pouvons*
tu peux	*vous pouvez*
il / elle on peut	*ils / elles peuvent*

vouloir = to want (to)

singular	plural
je veux	*nous voulons*
tu veux	*vous voulez*
il / elle / on veut	*ils / elles veulent*

3 Masculine or feminine? Find the odd one out in each set.

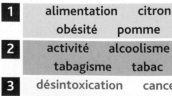

1 alimentation   citron   obésité   pomme

2 activité   alcoolisme   tabagisme   tabac

3 désintoxication   cancer   relaxation   spécialité

Grammaire — page 173

Masculine and feminine nouns

When learning a new noun, always learn whether it is masculine or feminine. There are patterns to help you remember the correct gender.

All words ending in *-isme* are masculine: *l'alcoolisme*, *le tabagisme*.

Most fruit items ending in -e are feminine:

la banane, la cerise, la fraise, la poire, la pomme.

Words ending in *-tion* are usually feminine: *l'alimentation*, *la dégustation*.

Words ending in *-ité* are usually feminine: *l'obésité*, *la spécialité*.

4 Copy the sentences and fill in each gap with the correct French word, as indicated in brackets.

1 Elles ont des problèmes avec _____ parents. (**their**)
2 _____ amis sont tout le temps ici. (**your**, *pl.*)
3 _____ enfants ne sont pas très aimables. (**her**)
4 Nous allons rendre visite à _____ grand-mère. (**our**)
5 Est-ce que _____ mère est stricte? (**your**, *sing.*)
6 Ils vont dormir chez _____ oncle. (**their**)

Possessive adjectives

	masculine singular	feminine singular	plural (m and f)
my	*mon*	*ma*	*mes*
your	*ton*	*ta*	*tes*
his / her	*son*	*sa*	*ses*
our	*notre*	*notre*	*nos*
your (pl.)	*votre*	*votre*	*vos*
their	*leur*	*leur*	*leurs*

Nos *parents sont divorcés.* **Votre** *père est strict.* **Leur** *cousin s'appelle David.*

Grammaire pages 176–177

5 Match the future tense forms with the present tense forms of the same verb. The subject pronoun may be different in each case.

1 il faudra
2 tu verras
3 ils sauront
4 elle viendra
5 il pourra
6 vous voudrez
7 je serai
8 nous irons
9 il aura
10 vous ferez

a je sais
b tu veux
c nous pouvons
d elles viennent
e vous voyez
f il faut
g nous avons
h ils font
i tu es
j elle va

Irregular future forms

Most verbs use the infinitive to form the future tense, but some irregular verbs use a different stem. Here are some common irregular future forms that are worth learning by heart.

être → ser-	je serai	I shall be
savoir → saur-	je saurai	I'll know
avoir → aur-	il aura	he will have
pouvoir → pourr-	je pourrai	I'll be able to
aller → ir-	nous irons	we shall go
vouloir → voudr-	je voudrai	I'll want to
faire → fer-	ils feront	they will do
voir → verr-	je verrai	I'll see
venir → viendr-	je viendrai	I'll come

il faut → il faudra – it will be necessary to

Grammaire page 185

6 Copy the text and fill in each gap with *à* or *de / d'* as appropriate.

Jules explique le but de son groupe sportif:

«On essaie **1** _____ aider les jeunes des quartiers défavorisés. On a décidé **2** _____ organiser des activités sportives dans des centres de loisirs. Ça marche bien: les jeunes continuent **3** _____ venir nombreux et ils apprennent **4** _____ jouer ensemble et **5** _____ bien s'entendre. Ils commencent **6** _____ être trop nombreux et on cherche d'autres volontaires pour nous aider **7** _____ nous occuper du groupe. Moi, je ne vais pas arrêter **8** _____ faire ce travail, ça me plaît énormément. »

Verbs that take à or de

These verbs need à to introduce the infinitive that follows:

aider à	to help	*commencer à*	to start
apprendre à	to learn	*continuer à / de*	to continue
arriver à	to manage	*réussir à*	to succeed

J'apprends à nager. I am learning to swim.

These verbs need *de* (or *d'*) before the infinitive that follows:

arrêter de	to stop	*s'occuper de*	to look after
décider de	to decide	*oublier de*	to forget
essayer de	to try	*refuser de*	to refuse

Il s'occupe des SDF. He looks after homeless people.

Grammaire page 181

Relationships and choices

Topic 2.1 Relationships with family and friends

2.1 F Ma famille et mes amis ➡ pages 32–33

	aîné(e)	older
	casse-pieds	infuriating / a pain
	célibataire	single
les	choses en commun (f)	things in common
	compréhensif(-ve)	understanding
	désagréable	unpleasant
se	disputer	to argue
	égoïste	selfish
	énerver	to annoy
	s'entendre bien / mal avec	to get on well / badly with
	gronder	to reprimand
	jaloux(-ouse)	jealous
	mignon(ne)	cute, sweet, pretty
	paresseux(-euse)	lazy
	seul(e)	alone
	souvent	often
	timide	shy
	tranquille	quiet, calm
	triste	sad

2.1 H Comment sont-ils? ➡ pages 34–35

	bouger	to move
	cadet(te)	younger
	choquant(e)	shocking
le	concubinage	living together (without being married)
se	confier à	to confide to
	déprimé(e)	depressed
	extraverti(e)	extrovert, outgoing
la	famille nombreuse	large family
	fidèle	loyal, faithful

l'	individu (m)	individual
le	mari	husband
le / la	meilleur(e) ami(e)	best friend
la	monogamie	monogamy
	réservé(e)	reserved, quiet
le	sens de l'humour	sense of humour

Topic 2.2 Future plans regarding marriage / partnership

2.2 F Est-ce que je vais me marier? ➡ pages 36–37

l'	amour (m)	love
la	belle-mère	stepmother
	devenir	to become
	être d'accord avec	to agree with
la	famille monoparentale	single-parent family
	rencontrer	to meet
la	solitude	solitude, being on one's own
le	souvenir	memory

2.2 H Seul, marié ou en concubinage? ➡ pages 38–39

la	bague	ring
des	bijoux (m)	jewellery
	embrasser	to kiss
	épouser	to marry (someone)
	faire du cyclisme	to go cycling
les	fiançailles (f)	engagement (to be married)
se	mettre en colère	to get angry
	musclé(e)	muscular
	tomber amoureux(-euse)	to fall in love
	vivre	to live

Topic 2.3 Social issues: family, friends and society

2.3 F On n'a pas les mêmes chances
➡ *pages 40–41*

l'	*alcoolisme (m)*	alcoholism
l'	*automobiliste (m)*	car driver
	avoir raison	to be right
	avoir tort	to be wrong
le	*carton*	cardboard box
	choisir	to choose
le	*chômage*	unemployment
	défavorisé(e)	deprived
	déprimé(e)	depressed
l'	*équipe (f)*	team
le	*logement*	accommodation
la	*maladie*	illness
	malheureux(-euse)	unhappy, unfortunate
	meilleur(e)	better
l'	*organisation caritative (f)*	charity
le	*quartier*	area, district
	remplir	to fill
	résoudre	to solve
le	*sac de couchage*	sleeping bag
le	*SDF (sans domicile fixe)*	homeless person
le	*trottoir*	pavement
la	*vie*	life
le	*voisin*	neighbour

	enrager	to infuriate
la	*fête de l'Aïd el-Kebir*	Eid Ul-Fitr festival
	fier / fière	proud
le	*foulard*	scarf, headscarf
l'	*immeuble (m)*	block of flats
l'	*immigré(e)*	immigrant
	influencer	to influence
	juif(-ve)	Jewish
la	*loi*	law
	pauvre	poor
	permettre	to allow
	pire	worse
le	*plat*	dish
	principalement	mainly
	punir	to punish
le	*racisme*	racism
	raciste	racist
	refuser	to refuse
	surtout	especially
la	*tombe, le tombeau*	grave
l'	*usine (f)*	factory

2.3 H Le racisme ➡ *pages 42–43*

	agresser	to attack, to assault
la	*banlieue*	suburbs
le	*cimetière*	cemetery
	chrétien(ne)	Christian
le	*coupable*	culprit
l'	*emplacement (m)*	place, site
l'	*emploi (m)*	job
	emprisonner	to put in prison

Higher – Exam practice

Pavel – bon fils, bon frère

A Je m'appelle Pavel. J'habite avec mon père et ma sœur, Sonia. Elle a six ans et elle est handicapée. Mon père est veuf depuis trois ans. Sa vie est difficile car il travaille dans un hôpital, mais il doit aussi s'occuper de ma sœur. Moi, je m'entends bien avec mon père et ma sœur.

B Comme mon père travaille, je passe beaucoup de temps avec Sonia. Le matin, je l'aide à se laver et à s'habiller. Normalement, elle passe la journée à l'école primaire et moi, je vais au collège. À trois heures et demie, je vais chercher Sonia et je m'occupe d'elle avant la rentrée de papa.

C S'il fait beau, nous allons au parc. Elle adore donner du pain aux oiseaux sur le lac et en été, si j'ai de l'argent, j'achète des glaces au kiosque. Le trajet du parc à la maison peut être difficile car les trottoirs de notre ville ne sont pas bien adaptés aux fauteuils roulants et souvent les automobilistes ne sont pas très patients quand nous traversons la rue.

D Hier, nous avons parlé des vacances d'été. Nous allons passer une semaine dans un hôtel à la campagne. Ce sera la première fois depuis la mort de ma mère que nous allons partir en vacances car papa ne gagne pas beaucoup d'argent. C'est ma grand-mère qui a réservé les chambres et elle va nous accompagner.

E Pour moi, c'est difficile de sortir avec mes copains ou de faire du sport en semaine, à cause de ma sœur, mais le samedi, ma grand-mère passe la journée chez nous. Elle reste avec ma sœur et range un peu la maison. Ça permet à mon père de faire du shopping et je peux aller au centre sportif. Je joue au basket et j'aime nager. J'adore ma sœur, mais j'aime aussi beaucoup le samedi car je suis avec mes copains.

F Je passe la plupart des dimanches à la maison, mais dimanche dernier, j'ai joué dans un tournoi de basket, et l'après-midi, papa et Sonia sont venus voir le dernier match. C'était bien parce que notre équipe a gagné.

1a 📖 Read the article and choose a suitable title for each paragraph.

1 Work at home and at school
2 Plans for a family holiday
3 A family outing to the sports centre
4 A small family with big responsibilities
5 Time outdoors – worth the effort!
6 Sport on Saturday

Total = 6 marks

1b 📖 Read the article in detail and answer the questions in English.

1 When did Pavel's mother die?
2 What does Pavel do at 3.30pm?
3 What does Sonia especially like to do at the park?
4 What two difficulties does Pavel mention about the walk home from the park?
5 Why has Pavel not had a holiday recently?
6 Why is Saturday important to Pavel?

Total = 7 marks

Dealing with a long text

The type of task in Activity 1b refers to the whole article, but usually the questions roughly follow the order of the text. It is unlikely that you will need to read the whole passage six times to find the answers.

Stratégie 1b

2a 🎧 Listen to five participants speaking on a radio phone-in programme about discrimination related to work. From the choices below, identify what each person is complaining about.

1 **Élodie**
a The attitude of the men she works with
b The quality of refreshments in the office
c The rude manners of her boss

2 **Dolorès**
a Her colleagues at work
b Her working hours
c Conditions in the nursery

3 **Thierry**
a The type of work he had to do
b The behaviour of colleagues towards him
c The behaviour of colleagues towards another employee

4 **Graziella**
a The number of people she has to supervise
b The amount she earns in comparison to others
c The amount of work she has to do

5 **Jean-François**
a The conditions where he works
b Having to give up playing rugby when he starts his new job
c The attitude of his friends towards his job

Total = 5 marks

2b 🎧 Listen again to all the speakers. Match the statements to the speakers. Write **E** (Élodie), **D** (Dolorès), **T** (Thierry), **G** (Graziella) or **JF** (Jean-François).

1 _____ is talking about a new job he / she is about to start.
2 _____ works for a construction company.
3 _____ witnessed racism at work.
4 _____ has difficulties with childcare arrangements.
5 _____ earns less than a man who does the same work.

Total = 5 marks

Total for Reading and Listening = 23 marks

Using clues in the questions – a reminder

Activity 2b is an example of a task where you need to think about what clues there are in the questions that might help you with the answer. For example, question 1 refers to an event in the future, while question 3 refers to the past, so you need to listen for people using the appropriate tense.

Stratégie 2b

Higher – Speaking

Une vie saine

You are talking to your French friend Adrien about your lifestyle.
He wants to know:

1 if you are in good health
2 if you eat healthily
3 if you exercise regularly
4 if you have a stressful lifestyle
5 if you smoke
6 if you drink alcohol.
7 !

! Remember, you will have to respond to
something that you have not yet prepared.

> **info**
>
> **Important information:**
> This sample task is for practice
> purposes only and should not
> be used as an actual assessment
> task. Study it to find out how to
> plan your Controlled Assessment
> efficiently to gain maximum
> marks and / or work through it
> as a mock exam task before the
> actual Controlled Assessment.

1 If you are in good health

- Say that you are usually in good health and in good shape.
- Mention the last time you weren't well. Say what was wrong and how long it lasted.
- Say what you and others did about it.
- Say what you will do to avoid a recurrence of the problem.

> **Stratégie**
>
> Start your plan. Write a maximum of six words
> for each of the bullet points 1–7. Here are some
> suggested words for bullet point 1 of this sample task:
> *bonne santé, rhume, symptômes, solution.*
> Remember that the maximum number of words
> allowed in your plan is 40.
> Use the imperfect tense to describe your symptoms:
> *j'avais de la fièvre.* Use the perfect tense to say how
> long it lasted and what was done about it: *ça a duré …*
> Use the immediate future or the future tense to say
> what you will do. See Exam technique S11.

2 If you eat healthily

- Say what you like to eat and drink and whether it is good for your health.
- Say whether you follow a particular diet and say why / why not.
- Say what you think people should do to avoid obesity.
- Say what you think is an ideal diet, mentioning all three meals.

> **Stratégie**
>
> Suggested words for your plan: *repas – sains?, régime, éviter – obésité, idéalement.*
> Use *Pour éviter l'obésité, il faut / il ne faut pas …*
> Start the last sub-division of bullet point 2 with *Pour un régime idéal, on devrait / on ne devrait pas* + verb in the infinitive.
> Use different phrases to express your opinion: *je pense / je trouve / je crois que … / à mon avis / selon moi,* etc.

3 If you exercise regularly

- Say which sports you play, when, where and who with.
- Explain the benefits of playing a sport (stay in good shape, sleep better, a way of meeting people, etc.).
- Say how much walking and cycling you do (how far, how long for, how frequently).
- Say how fit you are and say what you intend to do to get fitter.

> **Stratégie**
>
> Suggested words for your plan: *sports, bienfaits, marche, vélo, forme – intentions.*
> To explain the benefits of playing a sport, start with *Quand on fait du sport, on …*
> Start the last sub-division of bullet point 3 with *Pour être plus en forme, je vais / j'ai l'intention de* + infinitive.
> Give a good deal of information for each sub-division, as suggested in brackets. See Exam technique S12.

4 If you have a stressful lifestyle
- Say whether you work too hard. Mention school work, homework and your part-time job.
- Say whether you sleep well. Mention the reasons for that.
- Say what makes you feel stressed, and what you do to avoid being stressed.
- Say what you think are the best ways of relieving stress.

Suggested words for your plan: *travail, dormir, éviter – stress*. Add a maximum of two words to this list.
To say what makes you feel stressed, starting with *Ce que je trouve stressant, c'est …*
Use *Pour me relaxer, je …* to introduce the last sub-division.

5 If you smoke
- Say whether you have tried smoking and what you think of it.
- Say whether your friends / members of your family smoke and whether it is a problem.
- Say why you think young people start smoking. Explain why many continue to smoke later on.
- Explain the consequences of smoking in terms of health.

Suggested words for your plan: *essayer, opinion, famille*. Add a maximum of three words to this list.
Use *commencer à, continuer à, s'arrêter de* when 'start', 'continue' and 'stop' are followed by a verb: *ils commencent à fumer …*
To explain the consequences of smoking, use *le cancer du poumon / de la gorge*.

6 If you drink alcohol
- Say how often you drink alcohol and what you think of it.
- Say whether you think alcohol should be more expensive than it is.
- Say what you think the minimum legal age for drinking alcohol should be and say why.
- Explain what problems arise from people abusing alcohol.

Suggested words for your list: *opinion, prix*. Add a maximum of four words to this list.
Use *devrait être* for 'should be', but with age use *avoir*: *on devrait avoir seize ans …*
Use *Quand les gens boivent trop d'alcool …* to introduce the final sub-division.

7 ! At this point you may be asked …
- if you take drugs.
- what you have done recently to improve your fitness.
- how you intend to change your lifestyle in order to improve your health.
- about the importance of peer group pressure in trying to have a healthy lifestyle.

See Exam technique S3.
Choose the **two** options that you think are the most likely. In your plan, write **three** words for each of the two options you have chosen. For the first option here you might choose: *opinion, prix, conséquences*. Prepare for the two options you have chosen using your reminder words.
Remember to check the total number of words you have used. It should be 40 or fewer.

 Lien

Foundation sample assessment tasks for this Context can be found in the Foundation Book.

Higher – Writing

Les rapports avec les autres

You are writing to your French friend about relationships with family and friends and also about your choices for the future. You could include:

1. how you get on with your family
2. details of the person you get on with best
3. what you like to do with that person
4. what happened last time you went out as a family
5. details about your friends
6. where you intend to live in the future
7. what you plan to do when you leave home.

info

Important information:
This sample task is for practice purposes only and should not be used as an actual assessment task. Study it to find out how to plan your Controlled Assessment efficiently to gain maximum marks and / or work through it as a mock exam task before the actual Controlled Assessment.

1 How you get on with your family

- Introduce the members of your family and say something different about each person.
- Mention the people you get on well with and say why.
- Mention who you have arguments with and say why.
- Give a short account of an argument.

Stratégie

Start your plan. Here are some suggested words for bullet point 1 of this sample task: *famille, membres, s'entendre, disputes, exemple.*

Use *je ne m'entends pas bien avec* … to say that you don't get on with someone.

Use *se disputer for* 'to have an argument': *je me suis disputé(e) avec* … (I had an argument with …).

2 Details of the person you get on with best.

- Mention how he / she is related to you. Give his / her name, age and a physical description.
- Describe his / her personality and say which features of his / her personality you like.
- Say what you have in common and how you are different.
- Say how he / she gets on with the rest of the family.

Stratégie

Suggested words for your plan: *informations personnelles, personnalité, ressemblances, différences, famille.*

'Best' is a difficult word. *Le meilleur* is used with a noun, *le mieux* is used with a verb. In this case, use *le mieux,* e.g. *la personne avec qui je m'entends le mieux, c'est* … (the person I get on with best is …).

Use *pourtant, cependant, par contre, d'une part* … *d'autre part* … to introduce something that contrasts with what you have just said.

3 What you like to do with that person.

- Write about the activities that you do together and what you think of them.
- Mention your favourite activity (what, when, where, frequency).
- Write about what you like but he / she doesn't like and vice versa. Mention his / her favourite activity.
- Mention how often you go out together and if you would like to go out more frequently.

Stratégie

Suggested words for your plan: *activités, ma / sa sortie préférée (informations), fréquence.*

Use a variety of verbs to describe activities: *faire, jouer, aller, écouter, regarder,* etc.

Remember that when one verb follows another, the second one should be in the infinitive: *j'aime jouer, il n'aime pas faire.*

Remember that you can only write verbs as the infinitive or the past participle in your plan.

4 What happened last time you went out as a family.
- Mention when you went out, how you travelled and how long it took to get there.
- Mention where you went and why that particular place was chosen.
- Describe what you and other members of the family did together and / or separately.
- Include what was good about the day and what wasn't so good.

Suggested words for your plan: *informations, activités ensemble / séparément.* Add a maximum of two words to this list.

Use expressions such as *d'abord, après, ensuite, finalement* to sequence the events you are describing in the perfect tense.

Use the imperfect tense to give your opinion and say what things were like: *c'était … , il y avait …* See Exam technique W5.

5 Details about your friends
- Introduce them. who they are and why you are friends with them.
- Include what you like doing with them and when and where it takes place.
- Give details about your best friend and say how long you have been best friends for.
- Give details of an outing with your best friend and say what you thought of it.

Suggested words for your plan: *qui, activités, meilleur.* Add a maximum of three words to this list.

Use object pronouns *(le, la, l', les)* in order to avoid repetition of friends' names. Remember that the place of these pronouns is before the verb in French: *je l'aime bien.*

Use present tense + *depuis* to say how long you have been friends: *nous sommes copains depuis …*

Including the name of a place in your plan might be enough to account for a whole sub-division within a bullet point, e.g. for the last sub-division of bullet point 5, 'Bournemouth' might remind you of where you went for your outing, what you did there, when you went, how you got there, what the weather was like and whether you had a good time. See Exam technique W2.

6 Where you intend to live in the future
- Write about when you intend to leave home and why.
- Write about where you intend to live and why that particular place.
- Mention how you will keep in touch with your family and how frequently.
- Mention how often you will visit them and why.

Suggested words for your plan: *quand, raison.* Add a maximum of four words to this list.

Use various ways of referring to a future event, e.g. the future tense, *aller* + infinitive, *j'aimerais, je voudrais, j'espère, j'ai l'intention de …*
See Exam technique W8.

Use *garder le contact avec* for 'to keep in touch with'.

7 What you plan to do when you leave home.
- Mention whether you would like to take a gap year and what you would do.
- Include whether you intend to get married and when.
- Include whether you would like to have children and why (not).
- Conclude by saying how important family and friends are to you and why.

Add a maximum of six words to your plan.

Use *une année sabbatique* for 'a gap year' and use the conditional to say what you would do during it: *j'irais …*

Use *se marier* for 'to get married'. As you will use *je*, make sure you also use *me*.

Remember to check the total number of words you have used in your plan. It must be 40 or fewer.

Lien

Foundation sample assessment tasks for this Context can be found in the Foundation Book.

Exam technique – Speaking

S1 Responding to the bullet points

In a Speaking task, there are likely to be between three and seven bullet points on the task you are given to prepare. One of the bullet points will be the unpredictable element and will appear as an exclamation mark. The teacher will ask you questions based on these bullet points. You could break down the bullet points into sub-divisions, as in this course book, to help you find interesting details to talk about, if your teacher has not already done it for you. It is important that you respond to every question / bullet point in the exam to gain as many marks as possible.

S2 The Speaking plan

You are allowed to write a maximum of 40 words in your plan. Those words can be in French or English. Choose them carefully so that your plan works well as a reminder of what you want to say. Try to use a maximum of six words per bullet point. Remember that you are not allowed to use conjugated verbs (i.e. verbs with an ending other than the infinitive or the past participle) in your plan. Visuals, codes, letters or initialled words, e.g. *j … s … a …* for *je suis allé*, are not allowed.

S3 Preparing for the !

The exclamation mark (often the last bullet point) is there to test you on something that you have not prepared. As you cannot predict exactly what you are going to be asked, it is often referred to as 'the unpredictable element'. However, the unpredictable is often predictable! Ask yourself: what question would logically follow the questions I have already answered? Practise guessing what the unpredictable bullet point might be about. You are likely to come up with two or three possibilities. Prepare answers to cover those possibilities. Practise your possible responses. When you are asked the question, focus on the meaning of the question itself to make sure you understand it and then give your full answer.

Exam technique – Writing

W1 Help available

Your teacher is allowed to discuss each task with you in English, including the kind of language you may need and how to use your preparatory work. You can have access to a dictionary, your French books, Kerboodle and internet resources. This is the stage when you will prepare your plan using the Task Planning Form.

When you actually perform the task, you can have access to a dictionary. You will also have the task itself, your plan and your teacher's feedback on your plan, i.e. the Task Planning Form. You cannot use your exercise book, course book or any drafts you may have written to help you practise.

W2 The Writing plan

In your Writing plan you can write a maximum of 40 words. Visuals, conjugated verbs or codes are not allowed.

Use your plan to remind yourself of what you should be writing next. Although it is more helpful to you to write French words in your plan, you can also use English words. Try to divide the 40 words equally between the six to eight bullet points of the task. Don't go over your allowance of 40 words.

W3 AQA administration

For the writing part of your exam, you have to do two different tasks (at two different times). When your teacher has taught you the necessary language for you to complete a task, you will be given the task to prepare. You may be asked to prepare a plan using the Task Planning Form. You will get some feedback on your plan from your teacher at that point. You will then prepare your final version, under the direct supervision of your teacher.

You will have 60 minutes to complete each task. You will work in exam conditions and will not be allowed to communicate with others.

Grade booster

To reach grade B, you need to …

■ Have a good variety of vocabulary and structures, e.g. in your answer for bullet point 4 of the sample Controlled Assessment on page 53, you will inevitably use the perfect and the imperfect tenses. Show that you know how to use both tenses correctly: for the perfect tense, use *j'ai, je suis, je me suis* (+ past participle) as appropriate. Don't forget to add the agreements wherever necessary. Use varied vocabulary and check it against the rest of the task to ensure that you don't repeat words unnecessarily.

■ Convey a lot of information clearly, e.g. as the language needed for bullet point 2 is fairly simple, try to write 40 to 50 words for this bullet point. Check your accuracy carefully.

To reach grade A, you need to …

■ Express and explain ideas and points of view with clarity, e.g. for bullet point 7, explain your ideas about gap years, getting married and having children. Give a reason for your opinion each time.

■ Develop the majority of the points you make, paying attention to accuracy, particularly with verb and tense formation. Think of sub-divisions of the main bullet points, e.g. for bullet point 3: what / when / where / who with / how often / opinion. Write about each bullet point with those sub-divisions in mind. However, try to avoid repetition.

To reach grade A*, you need to …

■ Give a fully relevant and detailed response to the task which is largely accurate, e.g. for bullet point 1, give a lot of information about several family members, such as name, age and personality features. In your account of an argument, include reasons and how the matter was resolved.

■ Handle complex sentences with confidence, making very few errors in the process, e.g. for bullet point 5, include sentences using the present tense + *depuis*, object pronouns and past tenses in your answer, paying particular attention to accuracy.

3.1 F   Qu'est-ce que tu as fait?

Objectifs

Talking about activities you have carried out

The perfect tense with *avoir* and *être* (singular)

Using the present and perfect tenses together

1 **V** Sort these activities into three groups: music, sport, or cinema.

J'ai vu un dessin animé.	J'ai chanté dans une chorale.
J'ai fait de la planche à voile.	J'ai joué du violon.
Je suis arrivé au ciné en bus.	Je suis tombé cinq fois à la patinoire.
J'ai écouté de la musique sur mon lecteur mp3.	J'ai aimé les acteurs.
J'ai acheté les billets.	Je suis rentré du concert à minuit.
J'ai fait du patinage.	Je suis allé au stade.

LES VACANCES DE FÉVRIER

Qu'est-ce que les jeunes de 16 ans ont fait pendant les vacances de février? Nous avons interviewé cinq filles et garçons, qui nous ont donné des réponses très variées.

Alexandre chante dans une chorale, et il a chanté presque tous les jours. Le soir, il est rentré chez lui et il a joué du violon.

Amina est allée quatre fois, à la piscine olympique. À chaque fois, elle a nagé pendant deux heures.

Julie est allée six fois au centre-ville, et elle a vu deux films de guerre, un film romantique et trois films policiers pendant la semaine. Et le soir, elle a regardé des films d'horreur en DVD.

Maxine a fait du cheval en Espagne avec sa sœur. Elle avait peur parce que l'année dernière elle est tombée, mais cette fois il n'y a pas eu de problèmes.

Guillaume a récemment fêté son anniversaire, et il a reçu beaucoup d'argent. Il est allé au centre commercial avec ses copains et il a acheté une nouvelle tablette tactile.

2a 📖 🎧 Read the text and write the name of the person who is interested in each of these activities.

1 le cinéma
2 l'informatique
3 l'équitation
4 la musique
5 la natation

2b 📖 🎧 Note whether each of these statements is true (**T**), false (**F**) or not mentioned (**?**) in the article.

1 Alexandre played the trumpet every evening.
2 Julie enjoyed the romantic film.
3 Guillaume has recently celebrated his birthday.
4 Amina spent four hours in the water.
5 Maxine went abroad.

3a **G** With a partner, copy the sentences and fill in each gap with the correct part of *avoir* or *être*.

1 Je ____ arrivé à midi.
2 Tu ____ travaillé dans le jardin?
3 Nadine ____ allée au cinéma.
4 Marc ____ fini ses devoirs.

> est   a   suis   as

3b **G** Copy the sentences and fill in each gap with the correct past participle.

1 J'ai ____ aux cartes.
2 Est-ce que tu as ____ la télé?
3 Ta sœur est ____ à la patinoire?
4 Il a ____ son anniversaire.

> est regardé   tombée   joué   fêté

4a 🎧 Listen to Section A. Marc is talking about last weekend and next weekend. Choose the correct sentence endings.

1 Marc went to the **shopping centre / beach / swimming pool**.
2 He was accompanied by his **parents / friends / grandparents**.
3 Before swimming they watched **football / played sports / sunbathed**.
4 Marc's favourite rugby team **is Toulouse / plays in Toulouse / drew with Toulouse**.
5 Next weekend he's going **to the beach / to see his parents / to Bordeaux**.

4b 🎧 Now listen to Sections A and B. Copy and complete the grid with the activities each speaker mentions. Give as many details as you can.

	last Saturday	last Sunday	next weekend
Marc			
Nadia			

5 ✏ Write an account of an exciting weekend, including:
- where you went
- who went with you
- at least four activities
- your opinions on how much you enjoyed them.

Samedi dernier	je suis parti(e)	avec mon copain / ma copine / ma famille.
	je suis allé(e)	au concert / à la piscine / à la patinoire.
J'ai trouvé ça		marrant / fantastique / amusant / relaxant.

Grammaire pages 183–184

The perfect tense with *avoir* and *être* (singular)

You use the perfect tense to describe actions or events that took place in the past. To form the perfect tense, use the present tense of *avoir* and the past participle. With -er verbs, the past participle ends in -é, with -ir verbs it ends in -i.

j'ai joué	I played
tu as fini	you finished
il / elle a fait	he / she did

être verbs

The perfect tense of some verbs (especially verbs of movement) is formed with the present tense of *être* instead of *avoir*. The past participle then agrees with the subject of the sentence, e.g. e*lle est arrivée* (she arrived / she has arrived).

être	past participle
je suis	*allé(e), arrivé(e), monté(e)*
tu es	*rentré(e), resté(e), tombé(e)*
il / elle est	*parti(e), sorti(e)*

Also revise negatives with the perfect tense.
See page 68 ➡

Stratégie 5

Using the present and perfect tenses together

Use more than one tense in your writing to add interest and gain credit. Contrast what you normally do (present tense) with something different you did in the past (**perfect tense**):

*Normalement / D'habitude le week-end, je reste à la maison ou je vais en ville, mais samedi dernier **je suis parti(e)** à la plage avec mon copain.*

Lien
3.1 Groundwork is available in the Foundation book.

3.1 H   Mon week-end

Objectifs

Discussing weekend activities

The perfect tense with *avoir* and *être* (singular and plural)

Using three time frames: past, present and future

Trois jeunes nous parlent de leur week-end

Charlotte

Samedi, j'ai fait la grasse matinée – je me suis réveillée à 9h30, mais je suis restée au lit jusqu'à 10h30! Puis je suis descendue dans la cuisine pour prendre mon petit déjeuner préféré: un chocolat chaud avec un bon croissant frais. Ensuite, j'ai rangé ma chambre et j'ai fait la lessive. Dans l'après-midi, j'ai fait du jardinage avec mes parents. Samedi soir, on a joué aux cartes et j'ai perdu toutes les parties. Tant pis, c'était marrant! Dimanche, j'ai fini mes devoirs de maths, quelle barbe! Puis j'ai regardé mon feuilleton favori et j'ai lu les actualités en ligne. Enfin, ma meilleure copine et moi, nous avons bavardé au portable pendant une heure.

Alexis

Samedi dernier, je ne suis pas sorti avec mes copains, ils sont allés en ville sans moi. Mon père m'a dit que je n'avais pas le droit de sortir à cause de mes mauvaises notes au lycée. J'ai dû rester à la maison pour travailler. En réalité, ma sœur et moi, nous sommes montés dans ma chambre, où nous avons surfé sur le net. On a chatté aussi avec des copains, puis nous avons écouté de la musique. Enfin, je me suis couché à minuit.

Marine

D'abord, je suis allée chercher le pain dans la boulangerie en face de chez nous. Ensuite, ma mère et moi, nous avons promené le chien, comme d'habitude. En fin de matinée, je suis montée dans ma chambre et j'ai joué de la clarinette. Plus tard, j'ai aidé mes parents et nous avons préparé le dîner ensemble. La télé ne me dit rien, c'est idiot, alors le soir, j'ai lu mes magazines et quelques bandes dessinées. Dimanche, j'ai aidé ma sœur à faire ses devoirs d'anglais parce qu'elle ne comprend pas très bien les langues étrangères. Je l'aide beaucoup en ce moment.

1a 📖 Find in the text the French for these expressions. Write the infinitive for each one.

1	to walk the dog	7	to chat online
2	to do some gardening	8	to tidy the bedroom
3	to play the clarinet	9	to fetch the bread
4	to read magazines	10	to do the washing
5	to play cards	11	to read the news online
6	to do one's homework	12	to prepare dinner

1b 📖 🎧 Read the text and answer these questions in English.

1 What does Charlotte mention doing first on Saturday?
2 Name two things she did after watching TV on Sunday.
3 Why was Alexis not allowed out?
4 What was he supposed to do and what did he really do?
5 Why did Marine prefer reading on Saturday evening?
6 How do you think she gets on with her sister? Give a reason for your answer.

Using three time frames: past, present and future

Stratégie 1b

Show your knowledge of different time frames by using up to three in your writing and speaking. In the example below, the first part (your usual routine) is in the present, the exception to your routine (last Saturday) is in the past, rounding off possibly with what you intend doing in the future:

D'habitude le samedi, je promène le chien, mais samedi dernier, j'ai fait la grasse matinée et samedi prochain, je vais sortir avec mes copains.

2 **G** Transform these sentences into the perfect tense

Exemple: Je regarde la télé. → <u>J'ai regardé</u> la télé.

1   Je finis mes devoirs.
2   Est-ce que tu fais du jardinage?
3   Elle sort le week-end.
4   Nous jouons aux cartes.
5   Vous lisez les actualités en ligne?
6   Ils vont en ville.
7   Tu restes au lit samedi matin, Flora?
8   Il part à quelle heure?

3a 🎧 Listen to five people talking about what they did last weekend and what they intend to do next weekend. Match each person with the correct activity.

1   Olivier
2   Richard
3   Danielle
4   Jasmine
5   Julie

a   le cinéma
b   le cyclisme
c   la musique
d   le théâtre
e   le foot

3b 🎧 Listen again and answer the questions in English.

1   Why does Olivier have to stay at home next weekend?
2   Do you think Richard enjoyed going to the match? Why?
3   What was Danielle's problem last weekend?
4   What was the drawback of the meal for Jasmine?
5   What did Julie watch last weekend and why?

4 🗨 Prepare and present (to your partner or your class) an account of a boring weekend you have had, then of an exciting one you have planned. Say:

- where you went
- who with
- what you did
- why you found it boring
- what you intend doing next weekend
- how you think it will turn out.

Samedi après-midi / soir, Dimanche,	je suis allé(e) je suis sorti(e)	au cinéma / au stade / à la piscine / en ville. avec mes ami(e)s.
Je n'irai plus au stade Je (ne) veux (pas) y retourner	parce que	c'était trop cher. j'ai trouvé le match ennuyeux.
J'ai trouvé le week-end	fatigant / ennuyeux / stressant.	
Le week-end prochain	je vais aller … / j'irai …	avec …
Ce sera	marrant / amusant / relaxant / tellement passionnant.	

Grammaire   *page 183–184*

The perfect tense with *avoir* and *être* (singular and plural)

You've already met the singular forms – now put them together with the plural forms:

avoir	past participle
j'ai	cherché
tu as	fait
il / elle / on a	fini
nous avons	attendu
vous avez	lu
ils / elles ont	bu
être	**past participle**
je suis	arrivé(e)
tu es	parti(e)
il / elle / on est	venu(e)(s)
nous sommes	allé(e)(s)
vous êtes	resté(e)(s)
ils / elles sont	parti(e)(s)

Remember, the past participle of *être* verbs always agrees with the subject in number and gender: *ils sont partis mais ma sœur est restée à la maison.*

Also learn about the perfect tense with negatives and reflexives.   *See page 69* ➡

Objectifs

Talking about shopping

The perfect tense with *avoir*: irregular verbs

Using emphatic language

3.2 F Au centre commercial tout est possible!

1 **V** Sort these words into three groups: shopping centre facilities, things to buy or adjectives.

| des jouets | cinquante magasins | des vêtements | gratuit |

| des équipements de sport | un bowling | des machines à laver |

| pratique | un cinéma | nouveau | le parking | énorme |

Un nouveau centre commercial

Venez au nouveau centre commercial Clair-Soleil. Il est moderne, il est pratique, le choix est énorme et les prix sont bas!

Il y a cinq restaurants, un bowling, un cinéma et environ cinquante magasins extrêmement différents: on peut y acheter des équipements de sport, des vêtements, des frigos, des télés, des machines à laver ...

Nos clients disent ...

Il y a quelque chose pour toute la famille. Il y a même des jouets pour les enfants.

Carole Machin

Tout le monde parle du centre Clair-Soleil! Samedi, je vais y aller avec mon cousin. Je vais acheter un cadeau pour son anniversaire.

N'oubliez pas, pour les automobilistes, le parking est gratuit!

Thomas Deniau

Samedi dernier, je suis allé au nouveau centre commercial Clair-Soleil. C'est fantastique! J'ai pris le bus pour y aller, c'est pratique.

Nadine Lescaut

Je suis allée à Clair-Soleil samedi dernier et j'ai beaucoup aimé le choix de magasins. C'est vraiment super et donc je vais y retourner le week-end prochain.

2a 📖 🎧 Read the information on the poster. Decide whether these statements are true (**T**), false (**F**) or not mentioned in the text (**?**).

1 The prices are high.

2 There are about fifty shops.

3 The centre has a free car park.

4 Thomas went there by car.

5 Nadine liked the choice of restaurants.

6 She wants to go back to the centre.

2b 📖 🎧 Read the poster again. Copy the sentences and fill in each gap with the correct word.

offrir	recevoir
cinémas	magasins
ouvert	raisonnables
hauts	est
a	payant

1 Les prix ne sont pas _____.
2 Il y a un grand choix de _____.
3 Thomas _____ arrivé en bus.
4 Le parking n'est pas _____.
5 Carole va _____ un cadeau à son cousin.

3a 🎧 Six interviewees are talking about money and shopping. Listen to Section A and choose the correct word to complete each sentence.

1 Simon likes buying **books / DVDs / computer games**.
2 Next weekend he wants to buy presents for his **family / friends / girlfriend**.
3 David likes **big department stores / small shops / the market**.
4 He thinks the prices in small shops are **more expensive than / cheaper than / about the same as** bigger shops.
5 Nicolas likes the shopping centre because **there is plenty to do / he never tires of shopping / there are fewer people there**.

3b 🎧 Now listen to Section B and correct the mistakes in these sentences.

1 Laurie receives 20 euros a week pocket money.
2 She buys clothes, make-up and has many pairs of socks.
3 Nathan earns money by washing the windows.
4 He wants to buy himself a new bike.
5 Maude bought a new violin recently.

4 🄶 Copy the sentences and fill in each gap with the correct irregular past participle, choosing from the grammar box.

1 Il a _____ un Coca au McDo du centre commercial.
2 Tu as _____ du shopping au centre-ville?
3 J'ai _____ un bon film au cinéma.
4 J'ai _____ une publicité pour un nouveau magasin de jouets.
5 Elles ont _____ le bus pour aller au marché.
6 J'ai _____ mes nouveaux vêtements.

5 ✏️ Write a paragraph for your Facebook page about your pocket money and / or earnings last week and what you spent it on.

- Say when you earned or received the money.
- Mention who gave you pocket money and how much.
- Give your opinion on the money you received.
- Say what clothes or other items you bought, where and why.

Exemple: La semaine dernière, j'ai reçu 25 euros d'argent de poche plus 15 euros de mes grands-parents – super! Alors, j'ai acheté des vêtements neufs au centre commercial: un grand sweat rouge et …

Grammaire — page 183

The perfect tense with *avoir*: irregular verbs

Many verbs have irregular past participles. Copy and learn the table below, making an extra column with English translations.

avoir	past participle
j'ai	eu (avoir)
tu as	lu (lire)
il a	vu (voir)
elle a	mis (mettre)
on a	bu (boire)
nous avons	pris (prendre)
vous avez	reçu (recevoir)
ils / elles ont	fait (faire)

Also learn about irregular *être* verbs in the perfect tense.

See page 68 ➡

Stratégie 5

Using emphatic language

Add weight to your opinions by using short, punchy expressions with exclamation marks to show how strongly you feel:

C'est super / fantastique / bien / moche, ça!

Je n'aime pas ça, moi!

Ça, c'est bien!

Lien

3.2 Groundwork is available in the Foundation book.

3.2 H — La mode: bonheur ou horreur?

La taille zéro et ses effets

A On entend souvent parler de la taille zéro américaine. C'est à la mode en ce moment et on voit des mannequins et des vedettes très très minces. Selon plusieurs experts, c'est la mode qui est à l'origine du problème de l'image de la fille et de l'anorexie. La presse pour adolescentes est pleine de photos de top models, d'articles sur les régimes, les produits de beauté et les maisons de couture.

B Beaucoup de jeunes lectrices veulent imiter ces mannequins et les magazines leur donnent l'impression que c'est en perdant des kilos qu'elles vont devenir belles. Les jeunes filles deviennent anorexiques ou boulimiques car elles voudraient être comme les top models.

C Une étude publiée dans la revue française *Forum Santé* en janvier révèle que les adolescentes qui lisent des articles sur les régimes ont deux fois plus de chances d'avoir des troubles alimentaires cinq ans plus tard.

D La réalité de l'anorexie est affreuse. Dans son livre *Ce matin, j'ai décidé d'arrêter de manger,* Justine raconte comment, à 14 ans, elle a commencé un régime «pour être belle» et a fini par perdre 36 kilos.

E Pour vendre les vêtements des couturiers, on idéalise les personnes qui les portent, mais certaines villes ont décidé de combattre ce problème. Les mannequins trop minces ou trop jeunes ne sont plus admis aux défilés. Quand notre reporter a cherché l'avis du ministre de la Santé, il lui a répondu: «L'image de la femme idéale dans les magazines de mode n'existe pas. On aime toutes les filles, grosses ou maigres, grandes ou petites.»

1a 📖 🎧 Read the article and choose a title for each paragraph.

1 Ban on models who are too thin
2 Images of very thin celebrities
3 A personal account of the effects of anorexia
4 Results of a recent study
5 Starting a diet to look better

1b 📖 🎧 Answer the following questions in English.

1 According to experts, what is to blame for anorexia?
2 How do models and fashion magazines influence young girls?
3 What is the finding of the study in *Forum Santé*?
4 What effect did anorexia have on Justine?
5 What is the view of the Minister of Health?

> **Working out meanings from the context**
>
> When you come across a word you do not recognise, you need to use the context and the surrounding words you do know to work out the meaning. In a sentence such as *l'homme porte un gilet chic*, you can reasonably assume that *gilet* is an item of clothing because a man is **wearing** it and it is described as **smart**.

Stratégie 1a

2a 🎧 Listen to all four speakers and find two expressions for each one.

1	Julien	**a**	black clothes
2	Émy	**b**	clothes that are too big
3	Annabelle	**c**	stylish clothes
4	Hugo	**d**	retro style clothes

e head covered
f bright colours
g good quality
h piercings

2b 🎧 Listen again and decide whether these statements are true (**T**), false (**F**) or not mentioned in the audio (**?**).

1 Julien thinks sweatshirts and jeans look too casual.
2 He dressed smartly for a recent funeral.
3 Émy wears make-up most weekends.
4 She already has a pierced nose and tongue.
5 Annabelle follows sixties fashion.
6 She criticises her mother's dress sense.
7 Hugo always wears a hoodie.
8 He's going to put on a black tracksuit and white trainers this evening.

3 Ⓖ Rewrite the sentences, replacing the highlighted words with a pronoun: *le, la, l'* or *les*.

1 On aime toutes les filles .
2 Il porte son chapeau noir le week-end.
3 Elle déteste la mode .
4 Tu as acheté le short au marché?
5 Vous appréciez la taille zéro ?
6 Nous préférons les piercings .

> ### Direct object pronouns
>
> *Grammaire page 179*
>
> Direct object pronouns replace the noun and the article. In English we use the words 'him', 'her', 'it' and 'them'. The French for 'it' can be *le, la* or *l'* and for 'them' is *les*. The direct object pronoun in French is placed before the verb.
>
> *Je vends le vélo.* ▸ *Je le vends.*
>
> *Il achète les chaussures.* ▸ *Il les achète.*
>
> *Elle aime la boutique.* ▸ *Elle l'aime.*
>
> *Il a critiqué le style – Il l'a critiqué.*
>
> Also learn about indirect object pronouns.   *See page 69* ➡

4 💬 Work with a group to prepare statements about 'Why I (don't) spend all of my money on clothes and fashion'. Choose one of the speech bubbles to start. Discuss:

- ■ what you think of fashion and why
- ■ what else you spend your money on
- ■ what you think of the effects of fashion on young girls.

> Je vais vous expliquer pourquoi je dépense tout mon argent pour m'habiller à la mode.

> Je vais vous expliquer pourquoi je ne dépense pas tout mon argent pour m'habiller à la mode.

Pour moi, le look est	très important / essentiel / fantastique.	
J'adore / Je préfère	les vêtements / les pantalons	en cuir / en coton / en laine / en jean.
	les robes / les jupes	long(ue)(s) / court(e)(s) / large(s) / étroit(e)(s).
	les baskets / les chaussures	uni(e)(s) / à rayures / à carreaux.
Parce que c'est	confortable / plus chic / pratique / plus chaud en hiver.	
Je ne suis pas du type mode. Je déteste les vêtements chics.		
J'ai horreur de l'image de la fille mince / taille zéro. C'est affreux, l'anorexie.		

3.3 F On peut communiquer plus facilement

Objectifs

Talking about new communication technology

Comparative adjectives

Justifying opinions

1 Ⓥ Sort these words into three groups: *cinéma*, *TV* or *Internet / en ligne*.
Then give your opinion using *j'adore les* … (love),
je déteste les … (hate), or *les …, ça m'est égal* (indifference).

un feuilleton	un forum	un film policier	un podcast
un tweet	un film de science-fiction	un documentaire	un jeu télévisé
une page Web	une émission sportive	un film d'horreur	un film de guerre

Technomec
Je garde le contact avec mes copains et ma famille au portable et sur Internet. C'est plus rapide au portable d'envoyer des textos en train, en bus, en ville, partout. Franchement, je trouve Facebook plus intéressant pour communiquer – on peut publier des photos, des clips et des documents sans problème. Je sais qu'il y a certains dangers, mais je fais bien attention: je ne révèle pas trop de données personnelles sur mon profil Facebook.

Logicielle
Je suis d'accord avec toi, Technomec. Les textos par portable sont plus rapides (et moins chers qu'un appel!), mais j'ai horreur des réseaux sociaux comme Facebook. Franchement, je trouve que tout le monde révèle des données personnelles trop facilement. C'est dangereux pour les victimes éventuelles, par exemple les jeunes filles innocentes. Il faut faire attention quand on utilise la technologie!

Supertweeter
Je te comprends, Logicielle. Un de mes copains a dit une bêtise sur son compte Twitter – il a exprimé ses opinions politiques un peu extrêmes. On l'a accusé d'inciter au terrorisme et au racisme. Quel idiot! Mais, comme toi, Technomec, même si la confidentialité est menacée, je trouve que Facebook est plus pratique pour contacter et informer ses copains et ses parents.

2 📖 🎧 Read the three forum texts. Which four sentences below are true?

1 Technomec thinks texting is more interesting than communicating on Facebook.
2 He limits the personal information he discloses on Facebook.
3 Logicielle agrees totally with Technomec.
4 She worries about internet stalkers preying on young people.
5 She doesn't mind giving her personal details on Facebook.
6 Supertweeter finds Logicielle's views a bit on the extreme side.
7 He is not very sympathetic towards his friend, who was accused of inciting racism.
8 He still prefers to use social networks, despite the dangers.

3a 🎧 Listen to the four statements and match them with the illustrations.

3b 🎧 Listen again and decide whether the statements are positive (**P**), negative (**N**) or positive and negative (**P + N**).

4 **G** With a partner, make these sentences comparative by completing them with a word that matches your opinion: *plus*, *moins* or *aussi*. Say if you agree or disagree with your partner's opinion (*c'est vrai / je ne suis pas d'accord*).

Exemple: La radio est <u>plus</u> amusante que le cinéma.

1 Les télés connectées sont _____ pratiques que les ordinateurs.
2 La lecture est _____ amusante que la musique.
3 Les textos sont _____ faciles que les e-mails.
4 Les tablettes sont _____ utiles que les portables.
5 Les films romantiques sont _____ intéressants que les films d'horreur.
6 La musique est _____ relaxante que le sport.

5 ✏️ With a partner, prepare statements for an online debate about the advantages and disadvantages of communication technology. One of you loves new technology, the other dislikes it.

■ Pourquoi tu utilises un portable / Internet / les réseaux sociaux comme Facebook?
■ Quels sont les avantages?
■ Quels sont les inconvénients?

On peut	garder le contact avec les copains / la famille. envoyer des textos. publier des photos / clips / vidéos / documents.
C'est plus intéressant pour communiquer / informer.	
On révèle des données personnelles trop facilement.	
C'est l'ennemi de la vie privée / des victimes potentielles.	
On peut dire des bêtises.	
Il faut faire attention à la technologie.	

Comparative adjectives

Grammaire page 176

Use the words *plus*, *moins* or *aussi* (as), followed by an adjective, then *que* and the thing you are comparing.

La télé est moins utile qu'Internet. – TV is less useful than the internet.

C'est plus pratique. – It's more practical.

Two exceptions are: *meilleur* (better) and *pire* (worse).

Les films téléchargés sont meilleurs que les DVD. – Downloaded films are better than DVDs.

Les émissions de télé sont pires que la publicité. – TV programmes are worse than the adverts.

Also learn about using *on* to say 'we' or 'people'. See page 68 ➡

Justifying opinions

Stratégie 5

When you have given your opinion, it is a good idea to give a reason why you hold that view. Useful phrases for adding a reason are *parce que / car / pour cette raison / à cause de cela*. So if you say something like *les réseaux sociaux sont dangereux*, you could add *parce que la confidentialité est menacée*.

⊂⊂⊃ **Lien**

3.3 Groundwork is available in the Foundation book.

3.3 H Communication facilitée ou coupée?

1 **V** Match each verb with a phrase you could use it with.

1	envoyer	4	jouer	a	en ligne	d	des textos
2	télécharger	5	regarder	b	un tweet	e	des films
3	aller	6	faire	c	plusieurs chaînes	f	sur un site Internet

Je cherche l'avis des autres. Moi, je ne peux pas vivre sans mon smartphone. Je fais des tweets et j'envoie des textos et des e-mails à toutes mes amies et le smartphone est indispensable pour appeler mes parents si je suis en retard. Avec mon nouveau smartphone, je peux télécharger des films, des morceaux de musique et des documents. Je peux aussi aller sur les meilleurs sites Internet pour faire des achats, réserver des billets et participer aux réseaux sociaux comme Facebook. Je peux même consulter mon compte bancaire! C'était le meilleur modèle dans le magasin. J'utilise tout le temps mon smartphone quand je sors avec mes copines. Que pensez-vous des nouvelles technologies? **Maudit**

Je trouve Internet très utile pour chercher des renseignements quand je fais mes devoirs, alors j'utilise tout le temps mon ordi portable. En plus, je suis bloggeur et j'ai reçu plus de 10 000 visites sur mon site. Je participe à des forums et je me suis fait de nouveaux amis grâce à Internet. C'est aussi la forme de communication la plus rapide et le meilleur moyen de rester en contact avec les autres. Je ne peux pas vivre non plus sans ma console de jeux. Je passe des heures à jouer à des jeux vidéo. Je joue en ligne aussi, bien sûr. **Jacquesadit**

Pour mon anniversaire, mes parents m'ont offert la tablette que je leur avais demandée. Je l'ai choisie parce qu'elle a un écran tactile et la plus grande mémoire possible. En plus, elle est plus légère qu'un ordinateur portable et facile à porter. Je l'utilise souvent au lycée, mais pas pendant les examens – on n'a pas le droit à cause des tricheurs!
À la maison, on a aussi une télé connectée. Je peux regarder plus de cent émissions différentes et être connecté sur Internet immédiatement. J'en ai de la chance! **Praline2**

2a 📖 🎧 Match the pieces of equipment (A–E) with the bloggers.

2b 📖 🎧 Who says the following?

1 I love blogging.

2 There are a lot of programmes to choose from.

3 I can check my bank balance online.

4 I'm lucky.

5 Thanks to new technology I've made new friends.

6 I've set up my own website.

7 My parents feel reassured.

3 **G** Write sentences using the comparative and the superlative, following the example given.

Exemple: La radio est <u>plus amusante que</u> le cinéma, mais la télé est <u>la plus amusante</u>.

1 les portables … les lecteurs mp3 … les blogs
2 la lecture … la musique … le sport
3 le portable … Internet … la télé
4 les journaux … les magazines … les romans
5 les films d'amour … les films d'horreur … les comédies

| dangereux | meilleur | pratique | intéressant |
| relaxant | marrant | utile | pire | amusant |

Grammaire *page 176*

Superlative adjectives

To say something is 'the most', add *le / la / les + plus* before the adjective:

C'est la chaîne la plus intéressante. – It's the most interesting channel.

Two exceptions are *le meilleur / la meilleure* (best) and *le / la pire* (worst):

C'est le meilleur modèle. – It's the best model.

Also learn about verbs of liking and disliking + infinitive.

See page 69 ➡

4a 🎧 Match the letters of the items you hear (a–h) with the concerns (1–6). You can use the same letter more than once.

1 health issues	3 irritating noise	5 lack of variety
2 crime	4 false identity issues	6 expense

4b 🎧 Listen to the eight speakers again (a–h) and answer these questions in English.

a What spoilt this person's visit to a restaurant?
b How, allegedly, are mobiles responsible for violence?
c Whose health do mobile phones possibly threaten most?
d What might happen to lots of young people chatting online?
e What sort of scam mentioned here may result in online fraud?
f What harmful effects can too much time in front of a computer screen cause?
g Name the advantage and disadvantage of new technologies mentioned by this speaker.
h According to this person, what is wrong with TV and what is the effect of TV on young people?

Stratégie 5

Using language to draw conclusions

In any discussion, argument or debate, aim to be balanced and present facts or pros and cons with equal weight. However, conclude with your own standpoint, using expressions such as *pour ma part, d'après moi, à mon avis, je trouve que, je suis pour / contre* and, finally: *pour conclure …*

5 🗨 Work with a partner to prepare a balanced argument: *les avantages et les inconvénients des nouvelles technologies.*

	Avantages	Inconvénients
(téléphone) portable / smartphone	On peut envoyer des textos / contacter ses parents / ses amis facilement / faire des achats en ligne / consulter son compte bancaire / participer aux réseaux sociaux / télécharger des films / faire des tweets.	C'est trop cher / facile à voler / perdre. Quand ça sonne, ça m'énerve.
Internet / ordinateur portable	On peut l'utiliser pour faire du shopping / ses devoirs. L'ordinateur portable est plus rapide et pratique / moins lourd qu'un PC.	On peut passer trop de temps devant l'ordinateur. C'est mauvais pour la santé.
télé par satellite / télé connectée	Il y a plus de choix / beaucoup d'émissions. On est connecté aussi, alors …	Il y a beaucoup de mauvaises / vieilles émissions, par exemple …
tablette	C'est rapide / pratique / moins lourd qu'un ordinateur portable / facile à porter. … avec la plus grande mémoire possible / un écran tactile.	

(G) Free time and the media

1 Rewrite these jumbled sentences with the words in the correct order.

1 Je / sortie /ne / pas / suis / hier soir
2 n' / pas / a / fait / Elle / les courses
3 n' / pas / Il / a / trouvé / ça amusant
4 n' / Tu / es / pas / tombé / sur la glace
5 à la maison / es / Tu / n' / resté / pas
6 n' / au tennis / joué / pas / ai / Je

2a Copy sentences 1–4 and fill in each gap with the correct part of *être*.

1 Je _____ revenu au centre commercial à pied.
2 Il _____ mort à l'âge de quatre-vingt-cinq ans.
3 Ils _____ nés samedi dernier.
4 Tu _____ venue toute seule, Alice?

2b Now copy sentences 5–8 and fill in each gap with the correct past participle from the grammar box.

5 Elle est _____ en avril. Son anniversaire est le vingt-cinq, je crois. (**naître**)
6 Il est _____ célèbre grâce à la mode. (**devenir**)
7 Elles sont _____ au centre en bus. (**venir**)
8 Vous êtes _____ à quelle heure, Marc et Ben? (**revenir**)

3 Replace each infinitive with the correct form of the verb. In each case, note whether *on* means 'we' or the impersonal 'you' / 'people'.

1 Qu'est-ce qu'on faire ce soir?
2 On regarder un film ensemble, si tu veux.
3 Est-ce qu'on pouvoir se faire des amis sur Internet?
4 On dire que les téléphones portables sont dangereux, mais on ne savoir pas vraiment.
5 Si on rester trop longtemps devant son ordinateur, on avoir mal aux yeux.
6 On sortir ? On aller où?

Negatives with the perfect tense

To make a negative statement in the perfect tense, *ne / n'* comes before the form of *avoir / être* and *pas* comes straight after.

Il a regardé la télé.	He watched TV.
Il n'a pas regardé la télé.	He didn't watch TV.
Je suis sorti.	I went out.
Je ne suis pas sorti.	I didn't go out.

Grammaire page 188

The perfect tense with *être*: irregular verbs

Some of the *être* verbs have irregular past participles:

English	infinitive	past participle
to come	*venir*	*venu*
to become	*devenir*	*devenu*
to come back	*revenir*	*revenu*
to be born	*naître*	*né*
to die	*mourir*	*mort*

Remember, with all *être* verbs the past participle ending agrees with the subject (*je, tu*, etc.) in gender (masculine or feminine) and number (singular or plural):

– *Tu es née où, Amina?*
– *Je suis née à Paris, mais mes parents sont nés au Maroc.*

Grammaire page 183

Using *on* to say 'we' or 'people'

Most French people use *on* to mean 'we' in casual speech:

On sort ce soir. – We are going out tonight.

On can also be the equivalent of 'people' or 'they' or the impersonal 'you':

On dit que c'est bien. – People say it is good.

Comment dit-on 'computer' en français? – How do you say 'computer' in French?

On peut communiquer plus facilement. – You can communicate more easily.

On is followed by the same verb ending as *il / elle*. Check the verb tables on pages 193–197 if you are unsure of the endings.

Grammaire page 178

4 Translate these sentences into French, using the correct form of the verbs in brackets. Pay particular attention to the word order.

1 She woke up. (**se réveiller**)
2 We went for a walk. (**se promener**)
3 They met at the swimming pool. (**se rencontrer / masculine**)
4 You didn't buy a present. (**acheter / tu**)
5 My sister never got bored. (**s'ennuyer**)
6 I didn't try any more. (**essayer**)

Grammaire pages 183–184

The perfect tense with negatives and reflexives

All reflexive verbs take *être* in the perfect tense, but also include **reflexive pronouns**:

(je) **me**, *(tu)* **te**, *(il / elle)* **se**, *(nous)* **nous**, *(vous)* **vous**, *(ils / elles)* **se**

*Je **me** suis réveillé tard.*   I woke up late.

*Elle **s'**est habillée en noir.*   She dressed (herself) in black.

Remember the word order for negatives in the perfect tense:

Elle a crié. (She screamed.) → *Elle n'a pas crié.* (She didn't scream.)

The same applies to other negatives: *Ils n'ont jamais deviné.* (They never guessed.)

With reflexive verbs, the *ne* goes before the reflexive pronoun.

Je me suis ennuyée. (I got bored.) → *Je ne me suis pas ennuyée.* (I didn't get bored.)

Nous nous sommes levés. (We got up.) → *Nous ne nous sommes pas levés.* (We didn't get up.)

5a Copy the sentences and fill in each gap with *lui* or *leur*.

1 Je n'aime pas ses amis. Je ne _____ parle jamais.
2 C'est l'anniversaire de ma sœur. Je _____ offre des fleurs.
3 Tu réponds à Alice? Oui, je _____ réponds tout de suite.

5b Translate these sentences containing indirect object pronouns into French.

1 He's showing her the clothes.
2 I tell them the time (*l'heure*).
3 You buy them an ice cream.

Grammaire page 179

Indirect object pronouns

These pronouns replace the indirect object, in English '(to) him', '(to her)' and '(to) them'. In French *lui* is used for *him* and *her*, it is never shortened and goes before the verb:

Je parle à Pierre.   I'm talking to Pierre.

→ *Je **lui** parle.*   I'm talking to him.

Tu offres un cadeau à Amina? – Are you giving Amina a present?

*Qu'est-ce que tu **lui** offres?* – What are you giving (to) her?

To say '(to) them', use *leur*, which also goes before the verb:

*Je **leur** montre mes cadeaux d'anniversaire.* – I'm showing them my birthday presents.

6 Copy the captions for each set of pictures and fill in each gap with the correct infinitive.

1 Je déteste _____, je préfère _____.

2 J'aime _____, mais je préfère _____.

3 Je n'aime pas _____, je préfère _____.

4 Je déteste _____, je préfère _____.

Grammaire page 181

Verbs of liking and disliking + infinitive

When *j'aime*, *je déteste* or *je préfère* is followed by a verb, the second verb is in the infinitive.

Note how the infinitive in French translates as '-ing' in English:

J'aime porter une robe. – I like wearing a dress.

Je déteste faire les magasins. – I hate going shopping.

Je préfère aller à la patinoire. – I prefer going ice skating.

Free time and the media

Topic 3.1 Free time activities (at home and away)

3.1 F Qu'est-ce que tu as fait? ➡ *pages 56–57*

	à chaque fois	each time
	apprécier	to appreciate
	avoir peur	to be afraid
	barbant(e)	tedious, boring
la	*chorale*	choir
le	*dessin animé*	cartoon
l'	*écran (m)*	screen, monitor
	ennuyeux(-euse)	boring
	faire du cheval	to go horseriding
	fatigant(e)	tiring
	fêter	to celebrate
les	*films de guerre (m)*	war films
les	*films policiers (m)*	thrillers
les	*films romantiques (m)*	romantic films
l'	*informatique (f)*	ICT, computer studies
	intitulé(e)	entitled
	marrant(e)	funny
le	*patinage*	ice skating
la	*patinoire*	ice skating rink
	pendant deux heures	for two hours
la	*piscine*	swimming pool
la	*planche à voile*	windsurfing
	recevoir	to receive, to get
	rester	to stay
le	*violon*	violin

3.1 H Mon week-end ➡ *pages 58–59*

s'	*amuser*	to enjoy oneself, to have a good time
se	*coucher*	to go to bed
les	*actualités (f)*	news
	avoir le droit de	to have the right to, to be allowed to
la	*bande dessinée*	comic strip
	bavarder	to chat

	aller chercher	to fetch
	comprendre	to understand
	ensemble	together
	faire la grasse matinée	to have a lie-in
	frais (fraîche)	fresh
	jusqu'à	until
la	*langue étrangère*	foreign language
les	*mauvaises notes (f)*	bad marks (at school)
la	*partie (de cartes)*	game (of cards)
	quelle barbe!	boring!
	stressant(e)	stressful
la	*télé ne me dit rien*	TV doesn't interest me at all
	tellement passionnant	so exciting

Topic 3.2 Shopping, money, fashion, trends

3.2 F Au centre commercial tout est possible! ➡ *pages 60–61*

l'	*automobiliste (m)*	motorist
	c'est payant	you have to pay
le	*choix*	choice
le	*client*	customer
	devenir	to become
	donc	so, therefore
	énorme	huge, enormous
l'	*équipement de sport (m)*	sports equipment
	extrêmement	extremely
	gratuit(e)	free
le	*jouet*	toy
la	*machine à laver*	washing machine
le	*magasin*	shop
	moche	rubbish, no good
	mourir	to die
	naître	to be born
	nouveau (nouvelle)	new
	offrir un cadeau	to give a present / gift
le	*parking*	car park

	pratique	practical, convenient
les	prix bas (m)	low prices
	prochain(e)	next
	tout le monde	everybody
	y	there

3.2 H La mode: bonheur ou horreur?
➡ *pages 62–63*

	affreux(-euse)	awful, terrible
l'	anorexie (f)	anorexia
	boulimique	bulimic
	combattre	to fight
la	couleur vive	bold colour
le	couturier	fashion designer
	deux fois plus	twice as much
	elles voudraient être	they would like to be
	en perdant	by losing
l'	étude (f)	study
	j'ai horreur de	I can't stand the thought of
le	lecteur / la lectrice	reader
	maigre	thin
la	maison de couture	fashion house
le	mannequin	model
la	mode	fashion
	raconter	to tell
le	régime	diet
	selon	according to
la	taille zéro	size zero
les	troubles alimentaires (m)	eating disorders
la	vedette	star, famous person

Topic 3.3 Advantages and disadvantages of new technology

3.3 F On peut communiquer plus facilement
➡ *pages 64–65*

la	bêtise	something stupid
	communiquer	to communicate
la	confidentialité menacée	confidentiality threatened
le	documentaire	(TV) documentary
les	données personnelles (f)	personal details

l'	émission sportive (f)	(TV) sports programme
l'	ennemi (m)	enemy
	exprimer	to express
le	feuilleton	TV soap (opera)
les	films d'horreur (m)	horror films
les	films de science-fiction (m)	science-fiction films
	franchement	frankly
	garder le contact	to keep in touch
	il faut faire attention	you need to be careful
	inciter	to stir up, to incite
le	podcast	podcast
le	jeu télévisé	TV game show
	naïf(-ve)	naive, unsuspecting
	partout	everywhere
le	réseau social	social network
	révéler	to reveal, to disclose
	sinon	if not, otherwise
les	textos (m)	text messages
la	victime éventuelle	potential victim

3.3 H Communication facilitée ou coupée?
➡ *pages 66–67*

la	chaîne	(TV) channel
le	compte bancaire	bank account
la	fraude	fraud
des	inconnus (m)	strangers
l'	inconvénient (m)	disadvantage
	indispensable	essential
les	jeunes délinquants (m)	juvenile delinquants
	léger(-ère)	light
	on risque de …	you might end up …
la	santé	health
	sonner	to ring
	télécharger	to download
	tout le temps	all the time
le	tricheur	cheat
	vérifier le montant	to check the balance (of an account)
	voler	to steal

4.1 F Vive les vacances!

1 **V** Choose the odd one out in each set.

1 le ski nautique la voile la natation la promenade en bateau le cyclisme

2 la Chine la France le Portugal la Russie la Belgique

3 la montagne la plage le ski les sports d'hiver la neige

4 le pique-nique le camping l'hôtel le logement la villa

5 la cuisine les glaces le pique-nique le restaurant le bord de la mer

Sondage: les vacances que je préfère ...

77% des Français aiment passer leurs vacances au bord de la mer, comme Valérie ...

«Je pars en vacances avec ma famille. Tous les ans, on va au bord de la mer, pas loin de Bordeaux. J'adore bronzer sur la plage et nager dans la mer. L'année dernière, il faisait trop chaud.»

35% aiment passer des vacances à la campagne, comme Églantine ...

«Moi, j'aime les vacances à la campagne parce que j'adore le calme et l'air est pur. Ma famille a passé des vacances en France. Mon père veut aller au Portugal mais il fait trop chaud, je crois. J'aime faire des promenades en forêt avec mes parents; j'aime aussi faire des pique-niques dans la nature. Je n'aime pas aller au bord de la mer en été car je trouve qu'il y a trop de monde sur les plages et on dit que bronzer est mauvais pour la santé.»

23% aiment partir à l'étranger, comme Guillaume ...

«J'aime partir à l'étranger parce que je veux connaître des cultures différentes. La plage, ça va, mais j'aime surtout rester dans une grande ville parce que j'adore visiter les musées et les monuments historiques. L'année dernière, je suis allé en Angleterre et j'ai visité Londres. Il y avait beaucoup de choses à faire et c'était vraiment intéressant mais malheureusement il a fait mauvais presque tous les jours.»

57% aiment les sports d'hiver, comme Safina ...

«Je n'aime pas partir au mois d'août, pendant les grandes vacances, parce qu'il fait souvent trop chaud. Je préfère partir à la montagne pour faire du ski. Quand je suis en vacances, j'aime me relaxer. J'aime partir avec mes amies parce que j'ai plus de liberté. Je ne m'entends pas bien avec mes parents. L'année prochaine, je voudrais aller aux États-Unis, à New York.»

2a Read the report and choose the photo that best fits each speaker's preferred holiday.

2b Read the report again. Who says the following?

1 I love peace and quiet.
2 I like sunbathing.
3 I'm interested in foreign culture.
4 Sunbathing is bad for you.
5 I think it is important to relax on holiday.

Coping with longer reading passages

Don't be put off if there are a number of words that you don't know in longer texts. Read the questions first so you can scan for the words you need. Then you can focus on these in order to complete the activity.

Stratégie 2b

3a 🎧 Listen to five people describing the holidays they like and their last holiday. Choose the correct accommodation (a–f) for each speaker (1–5). There is an extra option that you will not need.

a   a hotel by the sea
b   a cottage in the country
c   a cottage by a lake

d   a chalet in the mountains
e   a youth hostel in city
f   camping in the mountains

3b 🎧 Listen again. Which three sentences are true?

1   Chloë went water skiing in Portugal.
2   Martin went sailing on a lake in the mountains.
3   Thérèse hired a boat in the Loire Valley.

4   Thierry went skiing with his brother.
5   Fabienne went to Brussels with her sister.
6   She likes to go sightseeing and shopping.

4 ***G*** Copy the sentences and fill in each gap with *en*, *au*, *aux* or *à*.

1   Je veux aller _____ États-Unis.
2   Mes grands-parents habitent _____ Canada.
3   Je vais faire du shopping _____ New York.
4   Cette année, je vais _____ Rome _____ Italie.
5   En juillet, je suis allé _____ pays de Galles.
6   Je voudrais aller _____ Caraïbes.

> ## How to say 'to' or 'in' a country
> *Grammaire*   *page 190*
>
> If you want to say 'to' or 'in' a country in French, you need to know the gender of the country. Feminine countries (*la France, l'Angleterre, l'Espagne*) take *en*.
>
> Masculine countries (*le Portugal, le Canada*) take *au*. If the country is plural (*les États-Unis*) use *aux*. Cities take *à*.
>
> *Je vais à Londres.*   I am going to London.
>
> Also learn how to recognise some useful verbs in the imperfect tense.
>
> *See page 84* ➡

5 🗨 Work with a partner. Prepare answers to the following questions, then take turns to ask and answer. Give reasons for your answers.

▪ Où est-ce que tu aimes partir en vacances? Pourquoi?
▪ Quelle sorte de logement préfères-tu?
▪ Qu'est-ce que tu aimes faire en vacances?
▪ Tu aimes mieux partir en vacances en famille ou avec des amis? Pourquoi?
▪ Où es-tu parti(e) l'année dernière?
▪ Comment sont tes vacances idéales? Pourquoi?

> ## Using language that you know
> *Stratégie 5*
>
> When speaking French in the exam, avoid guessing at words you do not know. Use what you are sure is correct. If you are talking about holidays, for example, and you stayed in a campsite but you forget the French for 'campsite', it is better to say *j'ai logé dans un hôtel* (I stayed in a hotel) rather than making up a word that may be incorrect.

J'aime partir en Espagne	parce qu'il y fait chaud.
J'aime aller en vacances avec ma famille	parce que je m'entends bien avec mes frères.
Je préfère loger dans un hôtel.	
En vacances, j'aime aller à la plage pour bronzer et nager.	
Pour mes vacances idéales, je voudrais partir en Chine.	
L'année dernière, je suis allé(e) dans le nord de l'Espagne.	C'était vraiment intéressant.

⊖⊖⊖ *Lien*

4.1 Groundwork is available in the Foundation book.

Où est-ce que tu aimes partir en vacances? Pourquoi?

J'aime partir en Espagne parce qu'il fait chaud. Et toi?

4.1 H Tu as passé de bonnes vacances?

Les vacances des Français

Les Français ont la réputation de ne pas aimer le travail, de ne penser qu'aux loisirs. Ces jugements sont certainement un peu inexacts, mais il est vrai de dire que la plupart des Français sont très attachés à leurs vacances.

La destination la plus populaire en hiver est la montagne: pendant les vacances de février, une semaine dans une station de ski est le rêve de beaucoup de Français. Mais en août, plus de 35 millions de Français partent en vacances et reviennent au bord de la mer, dans les stations balnéaires des côtes de la Méditerranée ou de l'Atlantique, à la recherche du soleil.

Pour ceux qui aiment le calme, il reste la campagne. On peut y faire des promenades, aller à la pêche dans les rivières, nager dans les lacs, redécouvrir l'histoire d'une région, admirer les paysages. On a remarqué que ce «tourisme vert» est devenu plus populaire récemment. Encore plus de touristes vont retourner à la campagne à l'avenir car le milieu rural est à la mode.

En général, les Français n'aiment pas traverser les frontières et préfèrent rester dans leur pays. Seulement 15% des Français ont visité un pays étranger pendant leurs vacances et ce nombre va diminuer en raison de l'impact négatif de l'aviation sur l'environnement. La plupart de ces séjours se passent dans un pays voisin, surtout l'Espagne. Les Français aiment revoir les belles plages espagnoles.

1a 📖 Find in the article the French for these phrases.

1 the most popular	5 green tourism
2 seaside resorts	6 fashionable
3 in search of sun	7 a foreign country
4 to admire the scenery	8 a neighbouring country

1b 📖 🎧 Read the article. Decide whether these statements are true (**T**), false (**F**) or not mentioned in the text (**?**).

1 French people enjoy winter sports.
2 The Mediterranean coast is more popular than the Atlantic coast.
3 There is nothing to do in the countryside.
4 In general, French people prefer to go abroad for their holidays.
5 25% of French people do not go away on holiday.
6 French people will travel less by plane in the future.

Recognising prefixes

Many adjectives beginning with *in-* (such as *inexact*) are the equivalent of the English 'un-' or '-less', e.g. *inconfortable* (uncomfortable), *inutile* (useless). Look out for these when reading or listening to French. Verbs beginning with *re-* (such as *retourner*) often mean to do something again, e.g. *revenir* (to come back), *revoir* (to see again). How many can you find in the article?

Stratégie 1b

2a 🎧 Listen to Section A of Océane talking about her holiday preferences and complete these sentences in English.

1 Océane likes to go to the _____ for her holidays.
2 The sound of the waves helps her to _____ .
3 She thinks that swimming in the sea is _____ .
4 She prefers to stay in a hotel with a _____ .
5 She prefers to stay in France for her holidays because she doesn't like _____ .

2b 🎧 Listen to Section B. Which two sentences are true?

1 Océane doesn't want to spend time doing household tasks when she is on holiday.
2 It was very sunny when she went camping.
3 She doesn't get on very well with her parents.
4 She has to save up to go away with her friends.
5 She would like to travel around the world.

3 **ⓖ** Match the beginnings and endings of the sentences. Then copy a–e and fill in the correct imperfect tense endings.

1 Je suis resté à la maison
2 Maintenant, j'aime aller à la plage, mais
3 J'ai bronzé à la plage et
4 Je n'ai pas nagé parce que
5 Ils sont tombés plusieurs fois
6 Nous avons bu une limonade

a l'eau ét_____ trop froide.
b quand ils fais_____ du ski.
c parce qu'il pleuv_____ .
d parce que nous av_____ soif.
e c'ét_____ relaxant au soleil.
f avant j'aim_____ mieux la campagne.

The imperfect tense
This tense is used to describe what was happening, what used to happen or what something was like:

Il pleuvait si souvent que le camping était inondé. – It was raining so often that the campsite was flooded.

Remove the *-ons* from the present tense *nous* form of the verb and add the following endings:

-*ais*	-*ions*
-*ais*	-*iez*
-*ait*	-*aient*

jouons → jou + ais → *je jouais*
Être is irregular: *j'étais*.

Also learn about using *quand* + imperfect tense. *See page 85* ➡

Grammaire page 184

4 🖊 Write about a recent holiday, real or imaginary. Include information about:

- where you went and who with
- what the weather was like
- where you stayed and what it was like
- what there was to do / see in the area and your opinion of your visit.

L'année dernière / l'été dernier, je suis allé(e)	en France / à Londres / … avec ma famille / des amis / …
Il faisait	beau / chaud / froid / mauvais. du soleil.
Il y avait	du vent.
Il pleuvait / neigeait.	
On a logé dans un hôtel / un gîte / une chambre d'hôte / une caravane On a fait du camping	au bord de la mer / à la campagne / à la montagne / en ville.
Dans la région / ville il y avait … C'était super / intéressant / fatigant.	

Setting the scene
When you are starting a written or spoken activity, try to use an imperfect tense to set the scene before using the perfect: *Samedi dernier, **il faisait** mauvais, donc **j'ai décidé** de faire les magasins.*

Il y avait ('there was' or 'there were') is a very useful imperfect form.

Stratégie 4

4 Holidays

4.2 F   Que faire en vacances?

Objectifs

Past and future holiday activities

Perfect, present and immediate future tenses

Past and future time expressions

1 🅥 Sort these words into three groups: seaside activities, places to stay or sporting facilities.

se baigner   un centre d'escalade   une colonie de vacances   des pistes cyclables
une patinoire   un dortoir   un gîte   faire de la voile   bronzer

A

L'été dernier, j'ai passé une semaine avec mes amis dans une auberge de jeunesse, près des gorges du Verdon dans le sud de la France. Nous avons fait de l'escalade et du canoë-kayak, et le vendredi nous avons fait une randonnée de 20 kilomètres! Le soir, on a mangé dans le village ou à l'auberge. Nous avons partagé un dortoir avec des garçons d'Allemagne et de Belgique. C'était super mais fatigant!

B

L'année prochaine, je pars en vacances en octobre. Je vais aller dans les montagnes du Maroc où il fait beau en automne, mais très chaud en été. Je vais faire une longue randonnée guidée avec mes amis. Des poneys vont porter nos bagages et nous allons faire du camping dans de petits villages. Nous devons acheter des provisions en route et préparer les repas. Je n'aime pas faire la cuisine!

Marcel, 17 ans

C

L'année dernière, je suis allée à Biarritz avec ma famille. Nous avons logé dans un petit hôtel près de la plage. J'ai fait du surf avec mon frère, et nous avons joué au volley-ball sur la plage. Ma mère aime se baigner et mon père fait de la voile. Des vacances idéales pour toute la famille!

Patricia, 14 ans

D

L'été prochain, je vais en colonie de vacances avec mes amis. La colonie est située à la campagne, près d'une rivière. Nous allons faire des promenades à vélo dans la forêt où il y a beaucoup de pistes cyclables. Le jeudi, nous allons visiter un parc d'attractions dans la région. Nous allons loger dans de petits chalets pour quatre personnes. Les repas sont servis dans un restaurant près des chalets. J'espère qu'il va faire beau!

2a 📖 🎧 Choose a suitable heading for paragraphs A, B, C and D from the list (1–6).

1 Hiking in North Africa
2 A holiday camp in the countryside
3 A holiday at home
4 Adventure activities in the south of France
5 Sightseeing in the city
6 A family holiday by the sea

2b 📖 🎧 Complete these sentences in English.

1 Marcel went _____ and canoeing in the *gorges du Verdon*.
2 He shared a dormitory with people from _____ and Belgium.
3 He will go to Morocco in the month of _____.
4 Patricia's father likes _____.
5 Next summer she will go _____ in the forest.
6 She will also visit a _____.

Past and future time expressions

Spot the difference … When reading or listening about the things that happened at different times, be careful not to get confused between *dernier* (last), followed by past tense verbs, and *prochain* (next) followed by verbs in the future tense.

Stratégie 2a–2b

76 *soixante-seize*

3 **G** Copy the sentences and fill in each gap with the correct form of the verb in brackets. Look carefully at the clues at the beginning, which will help you to decide.

1 Tous les ans, je _____ en vacances en Normandie. (**aller**)
2 Il y a deux ans, nous _____ la Bretagne. (**visiter**)
3 L'année prochaine, je _____ une chambre familiale avec demi-pension. (**réserver**)
4 Hier, les enfants _____ une promenade à vélo. (**faire**)
5 La semaine dernière, nous _____ dans une grande villa. (**loger**)
6 Dans deux ans, je _____ aux États-Unis. (**voyager**)

4a 🎧 Listen to Section A. Lucas is describing his plans for a visit to Bordeaux. In what order does he mention the activities shown?

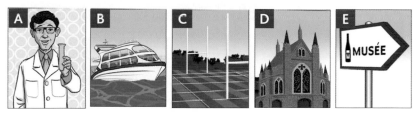

4b 🎧 Listen to Isabelle in Section B. Which three sentences are true?

1 Isabelle went away in the summer.
2 She loves winter sports.
3 Her parents went with her to stay with her uncle.
4 Her uncle lives in a small village in the mountains.
5 He owns a chalet.
6 She went skiing with her cousin.
7 One day she went ice skating.

5 🖉 Write an account of last year's holiday and your plans for this year (real or imaginary). Include information about the destination, accommodation and activities. Give your opinion.

PAST		FUTURE	
L'année dernière, L'été dernier,	je suis allé(e) ... avec ... j'ai logé dans ...	Cette année, L'été prochain,	je vais aller / loger ...
D'abord, / Puis, / Le lendemain,	j'ai fait / joué / visité / mangé ...	Au début, / Ensuite, / Après ça,	je voudrais faire / jouer / visiter ...
C'étaient les vacances les plus amusantes / relaxantes / ennuyeuses de ma vie.		J'espère passer des vacances sportives / intéressantes / relaxantes.	

Grammaire pages 182–185

Perfect, present and immediate future tenses

Learn how to use verbs in the perfect, present and future tenses.

J'ai visité l'Italie. – I visited Italy.

Je visite l'Italie. – I am visiting / I visit Italy.

Je vais visiter l'Italie. – I am going to visit Italy.

Faire and aller

j'ai fait > je fais > je vais faire

je suis allé > je vais > je vais aller

Also learn about using *faire* and *jouer* for past and future activities.   *See page 84* ➡

Stratégie 5

Expressions of sequence

When you are writing in the past or future tenses, use adverbs to structure what you want to say.

D'abord and *au début* both mean 'first' or 'at the beginning'. *Ensuite* and *après* mean 'next' or 'afterwards'.

You can also use times of day (*le matin, l'après-midi, le soir*), days of the week or *le lendemain*, 'the next day'. Don't forget *hier* and *demain*: 'yesterday' and 'tomorrow'.

🔗 **Lien**

4.2 Groundwork is available in the Foundation book.

4.2 H Mes vacances idéales

Qu'est-ce que vous voudriez faire en vacances?

A Vous avez toujours un guide à la main, vous cherchez donc les sites, les musées et les lieux des grands événements historiques (les champs de bataille, les cavernes et les grottes).

B Vous voulez vous sentir mieux. Au début de votre séjour, essayez un traitement dans notre station thermale. Plus tard dans la semaine, vous pouvez vous baigner en eau salée, ou avant votre départ, pourquoi ne pas essayer un massage?

C Louez un de nos bateaux bien équipés et naviguez doucement sur le canal. Vous pourrez vous relaxer en regardant les jolis paysages ou vous pourrez faire les magasins dans les grandes villes qui se trouvent au bord du canal.

D Tu as moins de quatorze ans? Tu t'ennuies avec tes parents? Viens dans notre centre de vacances. Alpinisme, escalade, motoneige, parapente: essaie une nouvelle activité chaque jour. Ne bronze pas idiot! C'est interdit.

E Venez voir les grands artisans de la région travailler le bois. Ils font souvent le même travail de père en fils. Si vous préférez, dégustez les plats traditionnels de la région.

1a 📖 Match the French words with their English translations.

1	les champs	a	the scenery
2	les grottes	b	the stay
3	se sentir mieux	c	fields
4	salé	d	wood
5	les paysages	e	to taste
6	le bois	f	caves
7	déguster	g	to feel better
8	le séjour	h	salty

1b 📖 🎧 Answer the questions by choosing the letter of the appropriate holiday in the article (A–E).

1 Which holiday will you choose if you want a lazy day indoors?
2 Which holiday will you avoid if you are not interested in the past?
3 Which holiday is suitable for a twelve year old on his / her own?
4 Where can you experience local cooking?
5 For which holiday will you be hiring your own transport?
6 On which holiday will you spend time in the countryside and in town?

2 **G** Copy the sentences and fill in each gap with a verb in the conditional. Choose from the infinitives below.

1 S'il faisait froid, je _____ à la maison.
2 S'il avait assez d'argent, il _____ du ski.
3 Si on me donnait le choix, je _____ à la plage.
4 Si mes parents gagnaient à la loterie, nous _____ aux États-Unis.
5 Si c'était possible, elle _____ en Inde.
6 Pendant nos vacances idéales, nous _____ des plats traditionnels.

| manger | partir | bronzer | rester | aller | faire |

3a Listen and match each picture with the correct speaker. Write **R** (Rosalie), **A** (Alex) or **M** (Morgane).

 1 2 3 4

3b Listen again and note what the speaker who refers to them thinks of the following. Is their attitude positive (**P**), negative (**N**) or positive and negative (**P + N**)?

1 water sports
2 walking in the woods
3 fishing
4 school work
5 theme parks
6 barge holidays

4 Work with a partner. Prepare a description of your ideal holiday: *Mes vacances idéales.* Include the following:

■ Describe the sort of holiday you would like to go on if you had a lot of money.
■ Say where you would go, who with and where you would stay.
■ Mention at least three activities you would do or places you would visit.

Listen to each other's descriptions. Note down the details in French under the headings: *destination, avec qui, logement, activités / visites.* Then check with each other that your notes are correct.

Si j'avais beaucoup d'argent,	j'irais aux États-Unis / en Australie / ...	avec ...
	je logerais dans ...	
Lundi / mardi,	je ferais ...	
Le lendemain matin / après-midi / soir,	je visiterais ...	
Plus tard,	je jouerais ...	

Grammaire *page 185*

The conditional

When you want to say what you **would** do, you use the conditional. To form the conditional, you use the same stem as the future tense, but with the imperfect tense endings.

For most verbs the stem is the infinitive, e.g. *jouer* → *je jouerais*.

But remember the irregular forms, e.g. *avoir* → *j'aurais*,

J'irais à la pêche au bord d'un lac tranquille. – I would go fishing by a peaceful lake.

Also learn about using *quand* and future tense.   *See page 85* ➡

Stratégie 3a–3b

Using clues in questions

When attempting a listening activity, remember to use the clues in the questions to help you focus on key phrases in the script. Think about the words you might hear before you listen.

Stratégie 4

Structuring a sequence

Add interest to what you say by adding a sequence to your answers. You can use days of the week (*lundi, je nagerai dans la mer, mardi, je ferai une excursion...*). Expressions such as *plus tard, deux jours plus tard, le lendemain matin / après-midi / soir* are also useful.

4.3 F   Les excursions

1 ⓥ Sort these words into four groups: air travel, road travel, train travel or travel by sea. (Some words fit in more than one category.)

le vol   la salle d'attente   les feux rouges   un horaire

un sens interdit   l'autoroute   stationner   le quai

composter   le bateau   le port   la gare routière

la gare SNCF   l'aéroport   l'hôtesse de l'air   le trottoir

Une visite à Québec

L'été dernier, nous avons passé des vacances chez ma tante au Canada. Un jour, nous sommes allés à la ville de Québec en train. Nous sommes partis de la maison à neuf heures et le voyage a duré environ quarante minutes. C'est une des villes les plus historiques du Canada, et il y a beaucoup de choses à faire.

Le matin, nous avons visité le Vieux-Québec. Mes parents aiment l'histoire et les arts, et ils sont allés au musée des Beaux-Arts, mais mon frère et moi, nous avons fait du shopping dans les petits magasins. C'était la fête musicale d'été et il y avait beaucoup de musiciens dans les rues. C'était très pittoresque. Après une pause-café, nous avons visité la cathédrale de Notre-Dame et la Citadelle de Québec avec nos parents. C'est le monument le plus célèbre de la ville et il y a de belles vues du sommet.

L'après-midi, nous avons fait une promenade en bateau sur la rivière. C'était très intéressant. Puis mon père et mon frère sont allés en métro au stade municipal pour regarder un match de base-ball. Ma mère et moi, on a décidé d'aller au parc aquarium de Québec. Nous y sommes allées en bus. Il y avait beaucoup de poissons et d'animaux des océans. Pour moi, c'était la meilleure visite du jour. Enfin, nous avons pris un taxi pour la gare. Mon père et mon frère sont arrivés du stade en taxi aussi, cinq minutes avant le départ du train, pour rentrer chez ma tante.

Lola, 14 ans

2a 📖 🎧 Read the text and match the pictures to the family members.

1 Lola and her brother
2 Lola and her mum
3 her brother and her dad
4 the whole family

2b 📖 🎧 Which three sentences are true?

1 They arrived in Quebec at 9.00 in the morning.
2 The musicians were taking part in the spring music festival.
3 There are good views from the Citadelle.
4 The boat trip in the morning was interesting.
5 Lola thought the visit to the aquarium was the best part of the day.
6 They all went to the railway station by taxi.

3 **ⓖ** Copy the sentences and fill in each gap with the correct French phrase, as indicated in brackets

1 Les TGV sont les trains _____. (**fastest**)
2 La plage de La Baule est _____ d'Europe. (**longest**)
3 Le Concorde était l'avion _____ du monde. (**fastest**)
4 Nous avons mangé dans _____ restaurant de la ville. (**best**)
5 Je passé mes vacances dans _____ maison de la région. (**prettiest**)
6 Est-ce que la tour Eiffel est le monument _____ de Paris? (**most visited**)

| la plus longue | le plus rapide | le meilleur |
| les plus rapides | le plus visité | la plus jolie |

Grammaire page 176

Superlative adjectives

To say 'the most', use *le / la / les plus* + adjective:

C'est la plus belle chambre. – It is the most beautiful room.

To say 'the best', use *meilleur / meilleure / meilleurs / meilleures*:

C'est le meilleur camping. – It is the best campsite.

Also learn about the *tu* form of the imperative.

See page 84 ➡

4a 🎧 Listen to the advice given in Section A and complete these sentences in English.

1 You can get a taxi from the _____ to go to the _____.
2 Bus number _____ will take you to the _____.
3 You can visit the main sights on _____ with a guide from the _____.
4 A journey of _____ minutes by _____ will take you to the beach.
5 The metro station to go to the _____ is 100 metres from the _____.

4b 🎧 Listen to Section B and match the English answers (a–e) with the French questions that you hear (1–5).

a The nearest underground station is opposite the post office.
b Ten euros for adults and six euros for children.
c You can get a bus from outside the hotel.
d To book tickets for the helicopter trip.
e About two hours.

5 ✏ Describe a day out while on holiday (real or imaginary) Write about how you travelled, what the journey was like, the activities you did and things you saw. Give reasons and opinions.

Using intensifiers

Use intensifiers to add variety to your written language, e.g. *très* (very), *trop* (too), *assez* (quite), *vraiment* (really).

Le voyage était assez confortable, mais trop long. – The journey was quite comfortable but too long.

Stratégie 5

Un jour, je suis allé(e)	à un parc d'attractions / à une forêt /... au centre-ville / au bord de la mer / ...		
J'ai voyagé	en voiture / en bus / en train / ...	parce que	c'est pratique / rapide / pas trop cher.
Le voyage a duré On est partis à / on est arrivés à	(environ) ... heures.		
On a	fait une excursion en car. fait une promenade en bateau. fait du cheval. loué des vélos.	C'était (vraiment) amusant / fatigant / casse-pieds.	
On a visité un château / des monuments / une ferme / le théâtre / ...	Je l'ai trouvé intéressant / ennuyeux / agréable.		

 **Lien**

4.3 Groundwork is available in the Foundation book.

4.3 H Visitez la région!

On vous propose …

A Bienvenue à bord de notre bateau au design contemporain avec climatisation, pour une heure quarante-cinq minutes de croisière. Vous allez découvrir un Paris majestueux à travers la verrière panoramique. Amusez-vous pendant notre nouvelle soirée musicale! Dîner servi entre 19h00 et 20h30 (50 euros en sus). Départ du pont de l'Alma, accessible en métro (à cinq minutes du pont).

1

B Visitez la maison et le jardin de l'artiste impressionniste Claude Monet. Départ de votre hôtel en car grand tourisme. Déjeuner au restaurant à Giverny. Continuation vers Rouen et visite guidée de la ville. Vous y serez logé dans un hôtel 2**. Dîner et logement compris.

2

3

C Nous vous proposons un vol à bord d'un hélicoptère privé, d'une durée de 15 minutes, 30 minutes ou 45 minutes. Un vol en hélicoptère inoubliable. Une fois dans les airs, vous allez découvrir les monuments de Paris: la tour Eiffel, la Défense, etc.! Pour deux personnes (les enfants ne sont pas admis à bord).

1a 📖 🎧 Match each photo (1–3) with the correct advert (A–C). Then find the French equivalents of these English words / phrases in the adverts. Identify the correct advert for each word or phrase.

| air-conditioning | a flight | accommodation | unforgettable |

| musical evening | included |

1b 📖 🎧 Read the adverts and decide whether the sentences are true (**T**), false (**F**) or not mentioned (**?**).

1 The boat trip on the Seine is in a vintage boat.
2 The meal on the boat is not included in the price.
3 The visit to Monet's house lasts one hour.
4 The night is spent in Rouen.
5 The helicopter leaves from near the Eiffel Tower.
6 Children are not allowed in the helicopter.

2 **G** Rewrite these sentences, replacing the highlighted words with the pronoun *y*.

1 Je suis allé au centre-ville en bus .

2 Nous sommes arrivés au camping deux heures plus tard.

3 J'ai bronzé à la plage toute la journée.

4 Il a mangé au restaurant presque tous les soirs.

5 Nous sommes montés dans le train avec tous nos bagages.

6 Il a décidé d'aller à la gare en taxi.

3a 🎧 Listen to the journey descriptions (**1–5**). Which is the means of transport mentioned in each?

car	train	boat	plane	bus

3b 🎧 There were problems with all of these journeys. Give two reasons why in each case.

4 🗣 Prepare a guide's introduction to an excursion in your area. Welcome the visitors and explain the main highlights of the trip: places to be visited, meals, timings. Practise with a partner, then, if possible, record your speech for your teacher to hear.

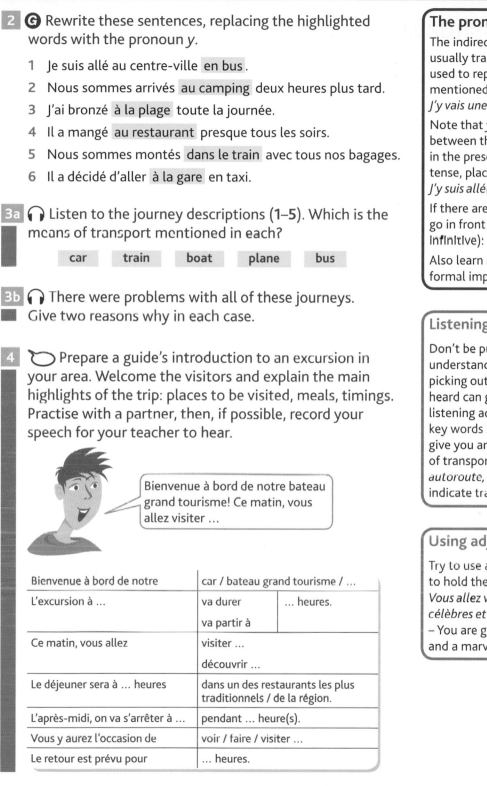

Bienvenue à bord de notre bateau grand tourisme! Ce matin, vous allez visiter …

Bienvenue à bord de notre	car / bateau grand tourisme / …	
L'excursion à …	va durer	… heures.
	va partir à	
Ce matin, vous allez	visiter …	
	découvrir …	
Le déjeuner sera à … heures	dans un des restaurants les plus traditionnels / de la région.	
L'après-midi, on va s'arrêter à …	pendant … heure(s).	
Vous y aurez l'occasion de	voir / faire / visiter …	
Le retour est prévu pour	… heures.	

Grammaire page 179

The pronoun *y*

The indirect object pronoun *y*, usually translated as 'there', is used to replace a place already mentioned: *J'adore nager à la piscine. J'y vais une fois par semaine.*

Note that *y* is always placed between the subject and the verb in the present tense. In the perfect tense, place it before *avoir* or *être*: *J'y suis allé(e).*

If there are two verbs together, *y* will go in front of the second verb (the infinitive): *Il a refusé d'y aller.*

Also learn about informal and formal imperatives. *See page 85* ➡

Stratégie 3a-3b

Listening for gist

Don't be put off if you do not understand everything you hear, as picking out the gist of what you've heard can gain you marks. In the listening activity, there are several key words in each description to give you an idea of the means of transport that was used, e.g. *autoroute, essence* and *parking* all indicate travel by road.

Stratégie 4

Using adjectives

Try to use adjectives in your speaking to hold the listener's interest. e.g *Vous allez visiter les monuments célèbres et un château merveilleux.* – You are going to visit famous sites and a marvellous castle.

(G) Holidays

1 Copy the sentences and fill in each gap with the correct verb in the imperfect.

1 Il y _____ du soleil à Marseille.
2 J'ai dormi sous la tente. C'_____ amusant!
3 Hier, il _____, alors je suis allée au musée d'art moderne.
4 Je ne suis pas sortie parce qu'il _____ trop froid.
5 Je ne suis pas allé à la plage, car il _____ mauvais temps.
6 Il _____ quand je suis arrivée dans les Alpes. C'_____ beau!

avait	était	était	faisait
neigeait	pleuvait	faisait	

The imperfect tense

Use the imperfect tense to describe what something was like in the past.

C'était super!	It was great!
Il faisait froid.	It was cold.
Il y avait du soleil.	It was sunny.
Il pleuvait.	It was raining.
Il neigeait.	It was snowing.

Grammaire page 184

2 Copy the sentences and fill in each gap with the correct form of *jouer* or *faire*.

1 Demain, je _____ du vélo, mais samedi prochain je _____ au tennis.
2 Samedi dernier, j'_____ au basket et j'_____ de la natation.
3 Pendant les vacances, l'été dernier, mes parents _____ de la voile, et mon frère et moi, nous _____ au volley-ball.
4 En colonie de vacances, l'année prochaine, nous _____ de l'escalade, et les petits enfants _____ au foot.

vont jouer	ai fait	avons joué	vais faire
ai joué	vais jouer	allons faire	ont fait

Faire and *jouer* for past and future activities

When describing activities that you have done or plan to do, don't forget to use *jouer* with games that you play, and *faire* with other sports and activities. Remember that *faire* is an irregular verb. Check it in the verb tables on page 195.

Use the perfect tense to talk about past activities:

*Hier, **il a joué** au rugby.*

Use the immediate future (present tense of *aller* + *jouer / faire*) to talk about future activities:

*Demain, **il va faire** du cheval.*

Grammaire page 187

3 Underline the imperative (command) in the following sentences, then translate each one into English.

Exemple: Achète les billets!   *Buy the tickets!*

1 Visite le port!
2 Loue un vélo!
3 Va au guichet!
4 Prends un bus!
5 Mange le fromage de la ferme!
6 N'oublie pas le pourboire pour le guide!

The imperative (*tu* form)

Use an imperative (command) when giving orders or instructions.

Use the *tu* form when speaking to someone your own age or someone you know very well. This is usually the *tu* form of the present tense. However, with -*er* verbs, remove the *s* at the end.

Tu vas à la piscine.   You go to the swimming pool.
→ *Va à la piscine!*   Go to the swimming pool!

Grammaire page 185

4 Match the beginnings and endings of the sentences. Then copy sentences 1–6 and fill in each gap with the correct verb.

1 Quand j'_____ petite,
2 Quand ils _____ un but,
3 Quand ma sœur s'_____,
4 Quand on _____ en Irlande,
5 Quand tu _____ en vacances,
6 Quand il _____ à la poissonnerie,

a il se levait à cinq heures.
b j'allais souvent à Paris.
c elle jouait aux cartes.
d tu voyageais en train.
e il faisait toujours beau!
f tout le monde criait.

| allait | ennuyait | étais | marquaient |
| partais | travaillait |

> ### Grammaire — page 191
> ### *Quand* + imperfect tense
> Use the imperfect tense after *quand* to describe what was happening, what used to happen or what something was like:
> *Quand il habitait en Grande-Bretagne, il allait souvent à Londres.* – When he lived in Great Britain, he often went to London.

5 Decide whether the verbs in brackets need to be in the future tense or the present. Copy the sentences and fill in each gap with the correct form of the verb.

1 Quand ils _____ la ville, ils iront au musée d'art moderne. (**visiter**)
2 Quand on _____ au Maroc, je t'enverrai une carte postale. (**aller**)
3 Quand je _____ en Suisse, c'est pour voir mes parents. (**aller**)
4 Il _____ les photos quand vous rentrerez d'Écosse. (**voir**)
5 Quand tu _____ là-bas, tu pourras admirer la mer. (**être**)
6 Quand j'_____ de l'argent, je pars en vacances! (**avoir**)
7 Je _____ en vacances quand je serai plus riche. (**partir**)
8 Quand tu _____ à la gare, il sera huit heures. (**arriver**)

> ### Grammaire — page 191
> ### *Quand* + future tense
> Use the future tense after *quand* to express something that is due to happen in the future:
> *Quand j'irai en Espagne, je voyagerai en train.* – When I go to Spain, I will travel by train.
> However, use the present tense to express a general statement:
> *Quand je vais en Espagne, je voyage toujours en train.* – When I go to Spain, I always travel by train.

6 Rewrite the following sentences, replacing each infinitive with the correct form of the imperative, as shown in brackets.

Exemple: Prendre un vélo! (**tu**) → <u>Prends</u> un vélo!

1 Tourner à droite! (**tu**)
2 Voyager en bateau! (**vous**)
3 Réserver une chambre confortable! (**tu**)
4 Ne stationner pas devant la gare! (**vous**)
5 Ne quitter pas l'hôtel! (**vous**)
6 N'oublier pas ta valise! (**tu**)

> ### Grammaire — page 185
> ### Informal and formal imperatives
> Use the imperative when giving orders or instructions: the *tu* form when speaking to someone of your age or that you know well, but the *vous* form to someone you don't know well, or more than one person.
> *Va à la piscine!* – Go to the swimming pool!
> *Allez au camping!* – Go to the campsite!

V   # Holidays

Topic 4.1 Holiday possibilities and preferences

4.1 F Vive les vacances! ➡ *pages 72–73*

l'	*alpinisme (m)*	mountaineering
l'	*auberge de jeunesse (f)*	youth hostel
le	*bord de la mer*	seaside
	bronzer	to sunbathe
la	*campagne*	countryside
le	*Canada*	Canada
les	*Caraïbes*	Caribbean
la	*Chine*	China
l'	*Espagne (f)*	Spain
les	*États-Unis (m)*	United States
à	*l'étranger*	abroad
la	*forêt*	forest
le	*gîte*	holiday cottage
le	*logement*	housing, accommodation
	louer	to hire
la	*montagne*	mountain
les	*monuments historiques (m)*	historic monuments / sights
le	*pays de Galles*	Wales
la	*plage*	beach
la	*voile*	sailing

4.1 H Tu as passé de bonnes vacances?
➡ *pages 74–75*

l'	*Atlantique (m)*	the Atlantic
l'	*avenir (m)*	future
la	*chambre d'hôte*	bed and breakfast
la	*côte*	coast
	étranger(-ère)	foreign
	inondé(e)	flooded
	loger	to live, to stay

la	*méduse*	jelly fish
la	*Méditerranée*	the Mediterranean
le	*paysage*	scenery
la	*plupart*	most
le	*rêve*	dream
le	*sable*	sand
le	*séjour*	stay
la	*station balnéaire*	seaside resort
la	*station de ski*	ski resort
la	*vague*	wave
	voisin(e)	neighbouring

Topic 4.2 Where you've been and where you're going

4.2 F Que faire en vacances? ➡ *pages 76–77*

	à l'heure	on time
	au début	at the beginning
les	*bagages*	luggage
se	*baigner*	to bathe, to swim
le	*client*	customer
le	*canoë-kayak*	canoeing
la	*colonie de vacances*	holiday camp
	d'abord	first of all
la	*demi-pension*	half board
le	*dortoir*	dormitory
	ensuite	next
l'	*escalade (f)*	rock-climbing
le	*lendemain*	the next day
l'	*oncle (m)*	uncle
le	*parc d'attractions*	theme park
	partager	to share
la	*piste cyclable*	cycle track
le / la	*propriétaire*	owner
la	*randonnée*	walk, hike

4.2 H Mes vacances idéales ➡ *pages 78–79*

	au bord de	by the edge of
la	bataille	battle
	chaque	each
	doucement	gently
s'	ennuyer	to be bored
l'	événement	event
l'	excursion (f)	excursion
l'	horaire (m)	timetable
s'	inquiéter	to worry
	interdit(e)	forbidden
le	lieu	place
	même	same
le	parachutisme	parachuting
le	parapente	hang-gliding
la	pêche	fishing
la	station thermale	spa resort
	sauf	except
le	travail scolaire	school work

Topic 4.3 What to see on holiday and getting around

4.3 F Les excursions ➡ *pages 80–81*

	autoroute (f)	motorway
l'	autoroute (f)	motorway
	avant	before
	célèbre	famous
	composter	to punch (a ticket)
	coûter	to cost
le	départ	departure
	devant	in front of
	durer	to last (a period of time)
	enfin	finally
	environ	about
la	fête	festival
le	guichet	ticket office
	pittoresque	picturesque
le	pourboire	tip
	pratique	practical

le	quai	platform
la	salle d'attente	waiting room
le	sens interdit	no entry
la	station de métro	underground station
	stationner	to park
le	trottoir	pavement
le	vol	flight
la	vue	view

4.3 H Visitez la région! ➡ *pages 82–83*

	admis(e)	admitted
	avoir l'occasion de	to have the chance to
	bienvenue	welcome
à	bord	on board
la	correspondance	change (train)
la	croisière	cruise
	décoller	to take off
	découvrir	to discover
l'	essence (f)	petrol
	pénible	annoying, a nuisance
	plein(e)	full
	privé(e)	private
la	traversée	crossing
	vers	towards

Higher – Exam practice

A

Vannes, le 26 février

Monsieur,

Je viens de rentrer de mon séjour de deux semaines en Martinique et je voudrais vous faire les réflexions suivantes:

Il n'y avait pas de représentant de votre organisation à l'aéroport et nous avons dû attendre deux heures dans le car à l'aéroport avant de partir pour l'hôtel.

Nous avions réservé une chambre à deux lits avec salle de bains. En arrivant, nous avons trouvé une chambre à un grand lit sans salle de bains.

Selon la brochure, l'hôtel est très près de la mer. En réalité, elle était au moins à vingt minutes à pied.

La plage était sale à cause de la pollution du port juste à côté.

La brochure indiquait qu'il y avait des distractions tous les soirs. Le samedi, il y a eu une soirée disco, mais c'est tout.

Les excursions étaient mal organisées et souvent, elles ont été annulées sans explication.

À cause de tout ceci, je trouve que vous devriez nous rembourser une partie de la somme que nous avons payée avant de partir.

Je vous prie de recevoir, Monsieur, l'expression de mes salutations distinguées,

J Crougneau

J. Crougneau

B

Nantes, le 3 mars

Monsieur,

Nous sommes désolés d'apprendre que vos vacances en Martinique ne vous ont pas plu.

En effet, notre représentant était malade à ce moment-là, et c'est à cause de cela que vous avez eu des problèmes. D'habitude, il est bien organisé, mais cette fois-ci:

Le chauffeur du car n'avait pas la liste des hôtels de ses clients et a dû téléphoner au bureau.

La nouvelle réceptionniste de l'hôtel n'a pas trouvé votre réservation avec votre demande de chambre.

On a demandé au patron de l'hôtel d'organiser les excursions, mais lui aussi était malade.

Nous nous en excusons et vous prions d'accepter un chèque de 200 euros que vous trouverez avec cette lettre.

Nous vous prions, Monsieur, de recevoir l'expression de nos sentiments les meilleurs,

R Guyot

R. Guyot

Coping with more formal language

At GCSE, you will not have to produce this type of formal letter, and you do not need to fully understand all the language used. For example, the last sentence is just an elaborate way of concluding, and is not vital to understanding. Focus on the main body of the letters to find the information you need.

Stratégie 1a–1b

Martinique – destination idéale pour toute la famille!

1a 📖 Read letter A and decide whether the following statements are true (**T**), false (**F**) or not mentioned (**?**).

1 The journey from the airport to the hotel took two hours.
2 They were expecting a room with a bath.
3 The beach was very close to the hotel.
4 The beach was polluted.
5 The hotel had an indoor swimming pool.
6 There was entertainment on Saturday evening.
7 They went on excursions every day.
8 They expect a complete refund of the price of their holiday.

Total = 8 marks

1b 📖 Read letter B, the response from the travel company. Choose the correct endings for the sentences.

1 The holiday representative did not meet the family because …
   a he was on holiday.
   b he was ill.
   c he was late.
2 The coach driver was delayed leaving the airport because …
   a the coach had broken down.
   b he had to wait for another plane to arrive
   c he did not know exactly where he had to go.

3 There were problems with the hotel room because …
   a the new receptionist could not find the family's booking.
   b the new receptionist did not know what the rooms were like.
   c some of the rooms were not available.
4 The excursions should have been organised by …
   a the holiday representative.
   b the receptionist.
   c the hotel owner.

5 The cheque for 200 euros …
   a is included with the letter.
   b will be sent later.
   c was sent earlier.
6 In general, Monsieur Guyot …
   a is apologising for the problems.
   b is not willing to take responsibility for the problems.
   c is trying to argue that there was nothing really wrong.

Total = 6 marks

2a 🎧 Mr Crougneau's daughter Maëlle is telling her friend Rosanne about how she spent her birthday while in Martinique. Listen to Section A and choose the four pictures that match her experience (1–4).

Total = 4 marks

2b 🎧 Listen to Section B and answer the questions in English.

1 How high does sugar cane grow?
2 Why do the birds perch on the sugar cane?
3 What was Maëlle's opinion of the visit to see rum being made? Give two reasons.
4 Why did her father buy some rum?
5 Where did she see bananas growing?
6 What surprised her about the coffee beans?
7 What suggests that she prefers chocolate to coffee?

Total = 8 marks

Total for Reading and Listening = 26 marks

Understanding cognates in listening passages

Stratégie 2b

It is sometimes difficult to understand cognates or near-cognates (words that are the same as or similar to the English) in listening passages because of their different pronunciation. Think about the context of an unfamiliar word. It may help you to recognise it. For example, listen to the words *rhum*, *canne*, *exotique*, *insectes*, *alcool*. What do they mean in English?

Higher – Speaking

En vacances

You are on holiday in France. You have agreed to take part in a survey about holidays. Your teacher will play the part of the person carrying out the survey and will ask you the following:

1 personal details

2 details about your accommodation

3 why you chose the area

4 what you did yesterday

5 what you have planned for today

6 where you intend to spend your next holiday

7 !

> **info**
>
> **Important information:**
> This sample task is for practice purposes only and should not be used as an actual assessment task. Study it to find out how to plan your Controlled Assessment efficiently to gain maximum marks and / or work through it as a mock exam task before the actual Controlled Assessment.

! Remember, you will have to respond to something that you have not yet prepared.

---

1 Personal details

- Say your name and spell it. Say when and where you were born.
- Say how you travelled, how long it took and what you did during the journey.
- Say how long you are staying for and ask what's on in the area during your stay.
- Give details about your family and their areas of special interest.

> **Stratégie**
>
> Start your plan. Write a maximum of six words. Here are some suggested words for bullet point 1: *nom, anniversaire, voyage, séjour, famille, loisirs.* Remember that you must not write more than 40 words in total.
> Use *prendre* or *durer* to say how long the journey took.
> Start your question about what's on in the area with *Qu'est-ce qu'il y a …?*

---

2 Details about your accommodation

- Say where your hotel is located and give a short description of it.
- Describe the hotel facilities – inside and outside.
- Describe your room and compare it to your room at home.
- Say what you think of the accommodation: the standard and value for money.

> **Stratégie**
>
> Suggested words for your plan: *où, description, équipement, chambre, comparaison, opinion.*
> Use *à l'intérieur / à l'extérieur* for 'inside' / 'outside'.
> Use *plus / moins / aussi … que* when comparing rooms.
> You can give your opinion for each of the sub-divisions suggested for bullet point 2. Use different ways of doing so: *je pense / je trouve que c'est … / j'aime (bien / assez) … / je n'aime pas (beaucoup / du tout) …*

---

3 Why you chose the area

- Give two reasons why you chose the area.
- Say what you did last year for your summer holiday.
- Compare it to your own area at home and to your last holiday destination.
- Say which area you prefer and give reasons.

> **Stratégie**
>
> Suggested words for your plan: *mer, soleil, Torquay, comparaisons* (home town), *préférence.*
> Show that you can use complex grammatical structures such as *choisir de* + verb, *j'ai aimé / je n'ai pas aimé* + verb. Link up opinions and reasons using *car, parce que* and *par contre.*
> Show initiative by comparing the area to last year's holiday destination and to your own area.
> Use words that suggest something to you on your plan. It could be a holiday destination.

4 What you did yesterday

- Say where you went yesterday morning and what you did.
- Say what you thought of it and give reasons for your opinion.
- Say what you did for the rest of the day and compare it to what you normally do at home.
- Say what other members of your family did and what they thought of it.

Suggested words for your plan: *matin, après-midi, comparaison (d'habitude)*. Add two more words to this list.

To give your opinion, use the perfect tense, e.g. *j'ai pensé que …, j'ai trouvé que …*, followed by the imperfect (usually *c'était*).

Normalement and *d'habitude* are followed by a verb in the present tense.

Express points of view using complex language. See Exam technique S11.

Stratégie

5 What you have planned for today

- Say what your own plans for today are (morning, afternoon and evening).
- Say why you chose those activities.
- Say what you will do if it rains or if you are prevented from doing what you have planned.
- Say what others in your family want to do today and mention alternatives in case that proves impossible.

Suggested words for your plan: *activités, raisons, pluie*. Add a maximum of three words to this list.

Take care! The title of bullet point 5 is in the past tense (what you have planned for today) but most of what you will say is likely to be in the future tense, e.g. *j'irai …*, or using a construction that suggests the future, e.g. *je vais +* infinitive / *je voudrais* / *j'espère* / *j'ai l'intention de …*

You can show initiative by relating your chosen activities for the day to your usual areas of interest, e.g. *D'habitude, chez moi, je …* See Exam technique S10.

Stratégie

6 Where you intend to spend your next holiday

- Say where you intend to spend your next holiday, mentioning the type of holiday and accommodation.
- Give one or two reasons for your choice.
- Say how long you would like to go for and why that particular length of time.
- Say what you would like to do or visit there and why.

Suggested words for your plan: *où, pourquoi*. Add a maximum of four words to this list.

Show that you can use a variety of tenses within the same answer, e.g. the future for the first sub-division in bullet point 6 (where you intend to spend your next holiday), present and past for the second one, and the conditional for the last two. See Exam technique S12.

Stratégie

7 ! The conclusion to the survey might be…

- how the resort could be made more appealing to various groups of people.
- what you think the area has to offer compared to other areas.
- the impact of tourism on the local environment.
- what you think of a new housing development project targeted at tourists.

Choose the **two** options that you think are the most likely. In your plan, write **three** words for each of the two options you have chosen, e.g. for the first option (how the resort could be made more appealing to various groups) you might choose *adultes, jeunes, familles*. Prepare for the two options you have chosen using your reminder words.

Remember to check the total number of words you have used. It should be 40 or fewer.

Stratégie

Lien

Foundation sample assessment tasks for this Context can be found in the Foundation Book.

Higher – Writing

Mes loisirs

You are writing an email to your French friend Sabine, who has asked you:

1 what you do with your free time when you stay in
2 what you do when you go out
3 how much money you receive and from whom
4 how you like spending your money
5 if you have a mobile phone
6 if you are interested in fashion
7 if you are sporty.

> **info**
>
> **Important information:**
> This sample task is for practice purposes only and should not be used as an actual assessment task. Study it to find out how to plan your Controlled Assessment efficiently to gain maximum marks and / or work through it as a mock exam task before the actual Controlled Assessment.

1 What you do with your free time when you stay in
- Write about music that you listen to and play.
- Write about how much TV you watch, your favourite programmes and what you watched last night.
- Mention what you like and don't like doing on the computer.
- Mention what happened last time you had a friend round.

Stratégie

Start your plan. Some suggested words for bullet point 1: *musique, télé (hier), ordinateur (activités), inviter*.

Don't use many names (groups, singers) or titles of TV programmes in English. Explain what they are instead, e.g. *J'aime beaucoup les émissions de sport …*

Show your knowledge of the perfect tense by using a combination of verbs that take *avoir* and *être*, including reflexive verbs, e.g. *j'ai regardé …, nous sommes monté(e)s …, nous nous sommes couché(e)s …*

2 What you do when you go out
- Include where you go and what you do.
- Mention when you go and who with.
- Describe what happened last time you went out.
- Explain the potential problems linked with young people staying out late at night.

Stratégie

Suggested words for your plan: *Cirencester, week-end, copains, dernier, tard – problèmes*.

Rather than just naming the person / people you go out with, explain what they are like and how you get on with them, e.g. *Je m'entends bien avec … parce que …*

You could introduce the last sub-division for bullet point 2 with *Quand les jeunes sortent tard le soir, …*

3 How much money you receive and from whom
- Say how much money you receive per week or per month, and whether it is pocket money or money that you earn.
- Say whether you think it is enough, and why or why not.
- Compare the pocket money you get with what your brothers / sisters / friends get.
- Say how much you would like to get ideally and say why.

Stratégie

Suggested words for your plan: *combien, provenance, assez, comparaison – autres, idéalement*.

Think of various ways of expressing your opinion, e.g. *je pense que … / à mon avis, … / je trouve que c'est …*

Use the conditional to account for the last sub-division for bullet point 3, e.g. *je voudrais / j'aimerais*. If the next word is a verb, use it in the infinitive.

Make your writing complex using irregular verbs (*je reçois, je dois*), different tenses (*j'aimerais avoir …, on me donne …*), comparisons (*plus / moins … que …*) but not so complex that it contains many errors. See Exam technique W8.

4 How you like spending your money
- Include how much you regularly save, what for and when that happens.
- Mention what you like buying with your money and who it is for.
- Give details of how you spent your money last month and what you thought of what you bought.
- Describe what you would do if you won the lottery.

Stratégie

Suggested words for your plan: *économiser, raison, acheter, loterie*. Add a maximum of two words to this list.

Use *j'aime m'acheter …* to say what you like buying for yourself.

Start the last sub-division for bullet point 4 with *Si je gagnais la loterie, je …* and follow it with a verb in the conditional. Don't use *je voudrais / j'aimerais*. You have already used them in bullet point 3.

5 If you have a mobile phone
- Say that you have a mobile phone and how you got it.
- Describe what it can do and what you like doing with it.
- Include how much you spend on it monthly and who pays for it.
- Give your opinion of your mobile and how it compares to your previous mobile.

Stratégie

Suggested words for your plan: *portable, Internet, dépenser*. Add a maximum of three words to this list.

If you were given your mobile, start your sentence with (*mon père*) *m'a donné …*

Use *mon ancien portable* to refer to your previous mobile. If your new mobile has more features, you might want to say *avec mon nouveau portable, je peux aussi …*

Remember that the word for 'better' is *meilleur*, and 'worse' is *pire*.

6 If you are interested in fashion
- Say what clothes you like wearing and describe them.
- Say whether fashion is important to you and why.
- Describe a fashionable item you bought recently and say how much it cost.
- Explain why it is difficult to keep up with fashion.

Stratégie

Suggested words for your plan: *vêtements, importance*. Add a maximum of four words to this list.

Use colours and materials to describe clothes, e.g. *vert / verts / verte / vertes* (make sure you choose the correct version), *en coton / en cuir*, etc.

Use *suivre la mode* for 'to keep up with fashion'.

In your plan, you may want to use grammatical markers to help you remember what tense you should use at that point, e.g. *récemment*. See Exam technique W2.

7 If you are sporty
- Mention which sports you like and dislike and say why.
- Include how far and how frequently you walk and / or cycle in order to keep fit.
- Say whether your diet helps your fitness and what you should avoid eating.
- Say whether it is important to play sport and be fit and say why.

Stratégie

Add a maximum of six words to your plan.

Combine the sports you play (use *jouer*) and the sports you do (use *faire*) in the same sentence and say which you prefer and why. See Exam technique W11.

Introduce the idea of what you do to keep fit with *pour garder la forme, je …*

 Lien

Foundation sample assessment tasks for this Context can be found in the Foundation Book.

Exam technique – Speaking

S4 Help available

Your teacher is allowed to discuss each task with you in English, including the kind of language you may need and how to use your preparatory work. You can have access to a dictionary, your French books, Kerboodle and internet resources. This is the stage when you will prepare your plan using the Task Planning Form.

You will then give this to your teacher, who will give you feedback on how you have met the requirements of the task.

When you actually perform the task, you will only have access to your plan and your teacher's comments (i.e. the Task Planning Form).

S5 AQA administration

For the Speaking part of your exam, you have to do two different tasks (at two different times). One of the tasks will be recorded and sent to a moderator. Each task will last between four and six minutes.

When your teacher thinks that you have been taught the language you need and feels that you are ready, you will be given the task to prepare. It could be a task designed by the AQA Examination Board or a task designed by French teachers in your school.

S6 Marking of the tasks

Your teacher will mark your work. A moderator (i.e. an examiner) will sample the work of your school and check that it has been marked correctly. A senior examiner will check the work of the moderator. This complicated but secure system ensures that candidates are given the correct mark.

The Speaking part of your exam counts for 30% of the French GCSE. Each task is marked out of 30 marks. As there are two Speaking tasks, the total number of marks available for Speaking is 60.

For each task, the marks are divided in the following way, with the maximum number of marks available shown in each case: 10 marks for Communication, 10 marks for Range of language and Accuracy, 5 marks for Pronunciation and Intonation, 5 marks for Interaction and Fluency.

Grade booster

To reach grade B, you need to ...

■ Develop most of your answers well, using some complex sentences, e.g. for bullet point 3 of the sample Controlled Assessment on page 90, link up your opinions and reasons.

■ Answer without hesitation, using a good range of vocabulary, e.g. for bullet point 4, make sure that you say all members of the family did different activities. Use different verbs each time, e.g. *aller, faire, jouer, visiter, ...*

To reach grade A, you need to ...

■ Attempt a variety of verb tenses, e.g. for bullet point 6, include sentences in the present, past, future and conditional.

■ Express ideas and points of view using complex sentences and a very good range of vocabulary, e.g. for bullet point 2, give opinions combined with comparisons.

To reach grade A*, you need to ...

■ Have a wide range of vocabulary and use a number of more complex structures, e.g. for bullet point 5, show off your vocabulary by using a variety of activities for different people.

■ Respond readily and show initiative on several occasions, e.g. for bullet point 1, you can show initiative in different ways, e.g. by asking a question.

Exam technique – Writing

W4 Responding to the bullet points

In a Writing task, there are typically between six and eight bullet points. All bullet points are written in English. Although you have to write a response to the title of the task, it is recommended that you deal with every bullet point that is given below it so that you don't miss out any important information.

W5 Using different tenses

If you are aiming at grade A, as well as a knowledge of the present, past and immediate future, you should also show that you know the future tense, the pluperfect and the conditional.

W6 How much to write

If you are aiming at grades C–A*, you should produce 400–600 words across the two tasks (i.e. 200–300 words per task). Although there is flexibility, aim to write approximately 40 words per bullet point.

You may produce a draft, but this is for your use only. Your teacher cannot comment on it and you cannot have access to any draft when you write the final version.

Grade booster

To reach grade B, you need to ...

- Be able to explain ideas, using appropriate vocabulary and complex sentences, e.g. for bullet point 2 of the sample Controlled Assessment on page 92, write about young people staying out late at night, problems, your own safety, alcohol and drugs.

- Write with some accuracy. There may be errors in your attempt at more complex sentences but verb and tense formations should be usually correct, e.g. for bullet point 4, you can potentially use the present, past and conditional. Take care with the accuracy of verb endings.

To reach grade A, you need to ...

- Write 40 to 50 words per bullet point, conveying a lot of relevant information clearly, e.g. for bullet point 1, you could give a lot of details. Limit yourself to 40–50 words and focus on quality of communication.

- Be generally accurate in your attempts at complex sentences and verb tenses.

To reach grade A*, you need to ...

- Use a wide variety of vocabulary and structures with accuracy, e.g. for bullet point 5, use vocabulary that describes the various functions of your mobile: taking photos, internet access, downloading music, etc. Use complex structures that you know are correct: *Je peux télécharger tout ce que je veux.*

- Use more complex sentences and verb tenses successfully, e.g. for bullet point 6, combine complex structures and verb tenses: *Le pull que j'ai acheté récemment n'était pas trop cher et il était très joli.*

5.1 F Ma maison

1 **V** Choose the correct word to match each definition (1–7).

1 On y dort.

2 On y prépare le repas.

3 On y va pour faire du ski.

4 On le prend pour monter au sixième étage par exemple.

5 On s'y lave.

6 C'est une machine qui fait la vaisselle.

7 La salle à manger, la chambre et la cuisine en sont.

la salle de bains	des pièces	la cuisine
la chambre	l'ascenseur
un lave-vaisselle	à la montagne

LOCATIONS VACANCES

A **Le Barroux:** Maison récente avec vue sur la campagne – pour six personnes – chambres (il y en a trois) – piscine privée – à huit cents mètres du village. Grand jardin, cuisine, séjour, salle de bains, WC. Confort, machine à laver, lave-vaisselle, four à micro-ondes, frigo, congélateur, télévision, lecteur DVD. 750 euros par semaine.

B **Nice:** Appartement au rez-de-chaussée – trois pièces pour quatre personnes. Deux chambres, une salle de bains, WC, salon, cuisine. Les habitants actuels y habitent depuis six ans. Commerces 4 km. Plage 500 m. 600 euros par semaine.

C **Chamonix:** Chalet de montagne. Vue extraordinaire du Mont Blanc. Cinq pièces pour six personnes. Trois étages, quatre chambres, deux salles de bains. Très récent. Assez grande terrasse, balcon, sous-sol.

Équipement: frigo, four, cuisinière, lave-vaisselle, micro-ondes, aspirateur, télévision. 800 euros la semaine.

D **Immeuble de luxe:** Interphone, ascenseur. Cinquième étage. Tout confort. Petite cuisine, séjour, chambre. En plein centre, à cinq minutes de l'Arc de Triomphe et à dix minutes de la Tour Eiffel. 1100 euros par semaine.

2a 📖 🎧 Read the adverts and decide which would be most suitable for each of these situations.

1 Your father would like a sea view.

2 Your brother would like a swimming pool.

3 Your mother wants to be in the countryside.

4 Your sister wants to see Paris.

5 You would prefer a holiday in the mountains.

2b 📖 🎧 Read the adverts again and note which places satisfy these situations. In some cases there are two possibilities, so write them both down.

1 There are five people in your family.
2 You want a garden.
3 There has to be a lift.
4 You want to be on the ground floor.
5 You want a dishwasher and a microwave oven.

━━ *Lien*
5.1 Groundwork is available in the Foundation book.

3a 🎧 Listen to the recording of a French TV programme similar to 'Location, location, location' (Sections A–D). Copy and complete the grid with one advantage and one disadvantage of each property shown to Nicolas and Marine.

	advantages	disadvantages
A		
B		
C		
D		

3b 🎧 Listen again and decide which of the four properties is Nicolas' favourite and why, and which is Marine's favourite and why.

4 Ⓖ Copy the sentences and fill in each gap as indicated in brackets. Then translate the sentences into English.

1 J'habite ici _____. (**for three years**)
2 Greg habite cette maison _____. (**for six months**)
3 J'habite mon appartement _____. (**for a year**)
4 Nous sommes dans la salle à manger _____. (**for an hour**)
5 Elle regarde la télé dans la salle de séjour _____. (**for two hours**)
6 J'habite en France _____. (**since I was born**)

5 💬 Work with a partner. Prepare answers to the following questions, then take turns to ask and answer.

- Où habites-tu?
- Tu y habites depuis quand?
- Il y a combien de chambres?
- Quelles autres pièces y a-t-il dans la maison?
- Qu'est-ce qu'il y a dans ta chambre?
- Tu habitais où avant?
- Tu aimes ta maison?

Grammaire (page 190)

Using *depuis*

Sometimes *depuis* is translated by 'for' and sometimes by 'since'. In English we use the past tense before both these words, but in French you use the present tense before *depuis*:

J'habite ici depuis ma naissance. – I have been living here since I was born.

J'habite ici depuis six ans. – I have been living here for six years.

Also learn about *en* meaning 'of it', 'of them'. *See page 108* ➡

Stratégie 5

Qualifiers and intensifiers

When using adjectives in your conversation, remember to add qualifiers and intensifiers such as *très* (very), *un peu* (a bit), *assez* (quite), *trop* (too) and *vraiment* (really). Example: *J'habite dans une assez grande maison.*

J'habite (dans) Nous habitons dans	une (assez) grande maison (au centre-ville). un (très) petit appartement (dans un village).	
J'y habite	depuis (trois) ans / depuis ma naissance.	
Avant, j'habitais	dans le centre-ville / dans un appartement.	
Au rez-de-chaussée, Dans la salle de séjour,	nous avons / il y a	une cuisine / une salle de bains. une table / des chaises.
La maison / l'appartement	se trouve / est situé(e)	près de … / dans le centre de …
J'aime bien / Je n'aime pas	ma maison	parce qu'elle est …

Où habites-tu?

J'habite une assez grande maison au centre-ville, avec ma famille.

5.1 H Le logement

La nouvelle maison de Mani!

Le rappeur Mani Mustafa nous présente sa maison

«Salut! J'habite depuis six mois dans une maison très spacieuse qui est située dans le centre de Marseille. C'est une grande ville industrielle qui se trouve au bord de la mer, dans le sud de la France, et il fait toujours beau en été. Ma maison a été construite dans les années quatre-vingt-dix, donc elle est assez moderne, avec huit chambres, deux salles de séjour, trois salles de bains, une grande piscine et une petite salle de musculation. Je suis né au Sénégal, où j'ai habité pendant plusieurs années. Je suis parti quand j'avais seize ans et j'habite en France depuis huit ans.»

La maison de Jazmine

Nous allons maintenant visiter le village d'origine de Mani, qui se trouve près de Dakar, la capitale du Sénégal. On rencontre la famille de Jazmine, qui nous invite chez elle. On a donc la possibilité de vous montrer une maison comme celle où Mani habitait dans sa jeunesse. La différence est étonnante! Il n'y a que deux chambres, et pour aller aux WC il faut aller derrière la maison. Il n'y a pas de robinet non plus, il faut aller à la pompe au bout de la rue. Jazmine est allée au café du village avec ses copines hier soir, où elles ont regardé une émission au sujet de son héros Mani, et aujourd'hui elle rêve d'avoir une maison comme la sienne.

1a 📖 Read the text and find phrases similar in meaning to the ones below.

1 avec beaucoup d'espace
2 a été faite
3 pour quelques années
4 dans sa maison
5 quand il était jeune
6 surprenante
7 elle aimerait beaucoup avoir

1b 📖 🎧 Read about Mani's and Jazmine's houses. Which four sentences are true?

1 In Marseille, the weather is usually nice in July and August.
2 Mani has lived in his present house for the last six years.
3 There are several bathrooms in his house.
4 He left Senegal when he was eight years old.
5 Jazmine's home is less comfortable than Mani's.
6 The cold water tap is just outside her house.
7 Jazmine watched Mani on TV last night.
8 Jazmine does not like Mani's house much.

Stratégie 2a-2b

2a 🎧 There are controversial plans to build up to 10,000 houses on the outskirts of Marseille. Listen to this radio debate about it and answer the questions in English.

Section A

1 Why has it become necessary to build so many houses in Marseille?

Section B

2 On what ground does Madame Cartier object to the building of new homes on the outskirts of town?

Section C

3 How does Monsieur Estève explain the number of new homes needed?

2b 🎧 Listen again and select the correct word for each sentence.

Section A

1 There are **homeless / unemployed / poor** people in Marseille.

2 Marseille is a **tourist / industrial / small** town.

Section B

3 In some parts of the town, there are **expensive houses / blocks of flats / derelict houses**.

4 Madame Cartier thinks that new homes are **necessary / unnecessary / not a long-term solution**.

Section C

5 Monsieur Estève and Madame Cartier would agree where the new homes need to be built if the number needed were **small / large / enormous**.

6 According to Monsieur Estève, building new homes outside town will **solve / reduce / not affect** homelessness.

3 Ⓖ Copy the sentences and fill in each gap as indicated in English. Then translate the sentences into English.

1 J'ai habité à Marseille _____. (**for three years**)

2 Ils sont là _____. (**for six months**)

3 Elle y habite _____. (**for a year**)

4 Nous y avons habité _____. (**for five years**)

5 Elle a regardé la télé _____. (**for two hours**)

6 Elle est en Suisse _____. (**since last year**)

4 ✏️ You are a member of a pressure group for the preservation of green sites. Write a letter to the local Planning Committee that highlights the problems associated with building on green sites.

Monsieur / Madame le / la Ministre, J'habite à … depuis …		
Récemment, on a construit … à l'extérieur de la ville.		
Il faut arrêter la construction	en banlieue / sur les espaces verts	parce que …
À la place, il faut …		
Le problème du logement est causé par … / Pour le résoudre, on doit …		

Focused listening

Before you listen to a recording, study the questions you are going to have to answer about it. If you are asked one question only about a particular section of the recording, anticipate what the answer might be and focus on listening for it specifically. You do not need to understand every word on the recording to get the information you need.

Be aware that in general, the order of the questions follows the order of the text you are listening to.

Depuis and *pendant*

Depuis can mean 'for' or 'since'. In English we use the past tense, but in French we use the present tense:

Jazmine habite dans son village depuis sa naissance. – Jazmine has been living in her village since she was born.

Mani habite sa maison depuis six mois. – Mani has been living in his house for six months.

For a completed activity in the past, use the perfect tense and *pendant*:

J'ai habité là-bas pendant cinq ans. – I lived there for five years.

Also learn about using *se trouver* and *être situé(e)* to say where something is. *See page 109* ➡

Ⓖrammaire page 190

5.2 F   Ma région

1 **V** Match the activities (1–8) with where they usually take place (a–h).

1 On peut voir un film.
2 On peut faire de la gymnastique.
3 On peut faire de la voile.
4 On peut prendre un café.
5 On peut faire les courses.
6 On peut danser.
7 On peut jouer au foot.
8 On peut faire du ski.

a au stade
b au café
c à la plage
d au centre de sports
e au cinéma
f au centre commercial
g en boîte de nuit
h à la montagne

A Clément habite une maison à la campagne près d'Orange qui est une petite ville touristique dans le sud-est. Il y habite depuis sa naissance. Il aime bien là où il est parce que c'est tranquille. Cependant, le jeudi, la ville est assez animée parce que c'est jour de marché. En été, il y a les Chorégies qui sont des spectacles de danse, de théâtre et de musique. Il y a alors de l'animation en ville parce que beaucoup de gens viennent voir ces spectacles.

B Émilie est étudiante à Montpellier qui est une grande ville universitaire située dans le sud. Elle a un petit studio à Palavas, un joli petit village au bord de la mer. Ce qui lui plaît à Palavas, c'est la plage, bien sûr. Quand elle a du temps libre, elle fait de la voile. Quelquefois, elle passe la nuit chez ses copines qui partagent un appartement au centre de Montpellier. Elle aime sortir avec elles au cinéma ou en boîte de nuit.

C Benjamin a dix-huit ans. Il travaille dans une usine dans la banlieue de Calais qui est un port dans le nord. Il habite chez ses parents dans une maison individuelle près du centre. Qu'est-ce qu'il y a à faire à Calais? Comme c'est au bord de la mer, on peut faire tous les sports nautiques, bien sûr, mais ce n'est pas une région chaude et la plage est souvent déserte. En ville, on peut faire du shopping et pour les jeunes, il y a des cafés, des centres de sports et le cinéma.

D Élodie habite à Jausiers qui est un petit village de montagne dans les Alpes. Pour ceux qui aiment le ski, c'est parfait. En hiver, il y a toujours beaucoup de neige et il fait froid. Élodie est monitrice de ski l'hiver et l'été, elle fait faire des randonnées aux touristes. Elle aime beaucoup sa vie à la montagne car elle est très sportive. Elle adore faire du VTT et de l'alpinisme.

2a 📖 🎧 Read the four paragraphs and name the town or village where these activities are possible.

1 going to a concert
2 mountain biking
3 sailing
4 going to a nightclub
5 indoor sports
6 hiking

2b 📖 🎧 Read the text again and decide whether these statements are true (**T**), false (**F**) or not mentioned in the text (**?**).

1 Clément has always lived in Orange.
2 Orange is a quiet town, particularly on Thursdays.
3 Émilie lives in Montpellier and goes to the Palavas university.
4 She has friends she goes out with in Palavas.
5 Benjamin lives with his parents in the suburbs of Calais.
6 He often goes swimming in the sea.
7 Élodie lives in a small mountain village in the Alps.
8 In the summer, she takes tourists hiking.

3a 🎧 🎥 Arnaud has just moved from Avignon to Vitrolles. Cécile and Julien are his new school friends. Watch the video and / or listen to the audio track. Which towns do these adjectives refer to: Avignon (**A**) or Vitrolles (**V**)?

> polluée   sale   animée   touristique
> industrielle   grande

3b 🎧 🎥 Watch or listen again. According to the conversation, which four statements refer to Avignon (**A**) and which refer to Vitrolles (**V**)?

1 It is quite a big town.
2 There are a lot of shops there.
3 There is a lot for tourists to see.
4 There is too much traffic in town.
5 There is a lot of pollution.
6 You can watch a film there.
7 There are a lot of cafés there.
8 You can go ice skating there.

Stratégie 3a–3b

Listening to a recording twice

Before listening to a recording for the first time, read the questions you have to answer about it. Then listen and answer as many questions as you can.

Before listening for the second time, focus on the questions you have not yet answered and anticipate where on the recording those answers should be. Make sure you know what type of answer is required, e.g. a number, a time, a place, a reason.

4 Ⓖ 🗣 Work with a partner. Partner A asks if you can go to one of the places shown and Partner B answers. Then swap parts.

Exemple: A Est-ce qu'on peut aller au cinéma?
            B Non, on ne peut pas aller au cinéma.

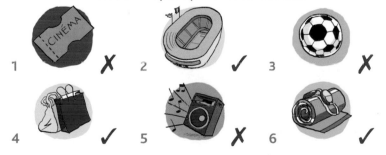

1 ✗   2 ✓   3 ✗   4 ✓   5 ✗   6 ✓

Grammaire   page 187

Saying what you can and can't do

In English, we use 'you can' or 'you can't' to mean 'people can / can't'. In the same way, the French use *on peut* and *on ne peut pas* followed by the infinitive.

On peut aller au cinéma. – You can go to the cinema.

On ne peut pas manger ici. – You can't eat here.

Also learn more about the adjectives *vieux, nouveau, beau*. See page 108 ➡

5 ✏ Write the text for a French website, giving information about your home town or village (real or imaginary).

Exemple: *Southampton est une grande ville au bord de la mer. Elle se trouve dans le sud de l'Angleterre.*

Lien

5.2 Groundwork is available in the Foundation book.

5.2 H Des mondes différents

Ma ville

A Je m'appelle André et j'habite à Genève, une grande ville suisse. Cette ville est tout près de la frontière française, et on y parle français. C'est une ville très historique qui a été fondée pendant l'époque romaine, mais qui est maintenant un des plus grands centres financiers du monde. C'est une ville verte, située au bord d'un très grand lac, avec beaucoup de jardins publics. J'habite dans une maisonnette au centre-ville, pas loin du lac.

Qu'est-ce qu'on peut faire à Genève? Les montagnes ne sont pas loin, donc en hiver, on peut faire du ski. Je suis content d'habiter ici parce que j'adore skier, mais ce week-end, il n'y a pas assez de neige, alors ce que je vais faire, c'est du VTT à la campagne. Quand je ne fais pas de sport, j'aime jouer du saxophone. Au mois de juillet, il y aura un festival de jazz qui est organisé par la ville de Montreux, près de Genève, et je vais y participer avec d'autres jeunes musiciens.

B Je suis Maha. J'habite dans un petit appartement au cinquième étage d'un HLM aux Buttes-Chaumont, dans le 19ème arrondissement de Paris. C'est un quartier de Paris qui était assez riche à une époque mais qui est maintenant un peu démodé. Je trouve que c'est un immeuble avec plein de problèmes.

L'appartement est déjà trop petit pour moi et mes frères, et bientôt il y aura un nouveau bébé! C'est vrai que c'est plus animé ici qu'à la campagne, mais c'est aussi plus bruyant. Il y a beaucoup de difficultés aussi, par exemple on voit des graffitis qui ont été faits par des ados partout dans le quartier. Ça, c'est quelque chose que je ne ferais jamais, et mes frères non plus. Le problème principal, c'est qu'il n'y a pas assez de choses à faire pour les jeunes. Pour améliorer la situation, on devrait construire un centre culturel ou sportif où on pourrait aller s'amuser le soir.

1a Read the text and find phrases similar in meaning to the ones below.

1 une très vieille ville
2 une petite maison
3 je vais en faire partie
4 un immeuble

5 n'est plus à la mode
6 beaucoup de problèmes
7 il y a plus de bruit
8 des activités

9 il faudrait faire la construction
10 il serait possible

1b Read the text again and decide who the statements are about. Complete each sentence with the name André or Maha.

1 _____ n'habite pas en France.
2 Ce n'est pas tellement joli là où _____ habite.
3 Là où _____ habite, c'est plus calme qu'à Paris.
4 _____ aime la campagne et aussi la musique.
5 La famille de _____ sera bientôt plus grande.
6 Quelques jeunes posent des problèmes près de chez _____ .

2a 🎧 Listen to Section A. Which three of these statements are true?

1 Henri lives on the island of La Réunion in the Indian Ocean.
2 The weather is cool in July there.
3 The weather is very hot in January.
4 Half the population are of local origin.
5 Henri doesn't want to live there in the future.

2b 🎧 Listen to Section B. Which three of these statements are true?

1 Caroline lives in a village in western Canada.
2 The climate there is very cold in winter, with wet, warm summers.
3 The air is clear and unpolluted.
4 They have snow for six months of the year.
5 Her village has a good feeling of community.

3 Ⓖ Work with a partner. Partner A reads out a sentence, and Partner B says a sentence that means the same, but using *on* instead of the passive. Then swap parts.

1 Des appartements ont été construits.
2 J'ai été invité à manger.
3 La vaisselle a été faite.
4 Les touristes sont accueillis.
5 Les motoneiges sont utilisées quand la route est fermée.

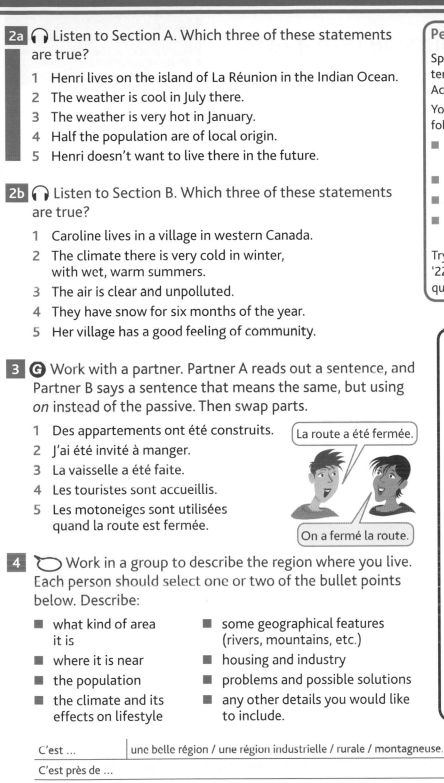

La route a été fermée.

On a fermé la route.

4 🗨 Work in a group to describe the region where you live. Each person should select one or two of the bullet points below. Describe:

- what kind of area it is
- where it is near
- the population
- the climate and its effects on lifestyle
- some geographical features (rivers, mountains, etc.)
- housing and industry
- problems and possible solutions
- any other details you would like to include.

Percentages and fractions

Spot three fractions and one temperature when you listen to Activity 2.

You need to be able to recognise the following uses of numbers:

- fractions: *un quart* (a quarter), *un tiers* (a third), *la moitié* (half)
- temperature: *trente degrés*
- percentages: *cinquante pour cent*
- decimals: *2,3 – deux virgule trois* (2.3 – two point three).

Try to say in French: 'half of the time'; '22 degrees'; '20 per cent'; 'three quarters of the population', '4.5'.

The passive voice and *on*

The passive is used to say what is being done to someone or something. Use the appropriate tense of *être* plus the past participle:

J'ai été invité(e). – I was invited.

La maison sera vendue. – The house will be sold.

Genève a été fondée pendant l'époque romaine. – Geneva was founded in Roman times.

It is much more common to convey the same meaning by using *on*:

On fait les lits. – The beds are made.

On parle français. – French is spoken.

Also revise prepositions of place, e.g. *au bord de, pas loin de*.

See page 109 ➡

C'est …	une belle région / une région industrielle / rurale / montagneuse.
C'est près de …	
La population est …	
En hiver / été, le climat est	chaud / froid / sec / pluvieux.
Il y a	une rivière / des montagnes / des châteaux.
	beaucoup de grandes maisons / petits appartements / HLM.
L'industrie principale est	l'agriculture / le tourisme.
Les problèmes sont	le climat / la pauvreté / les tensions raciales.

5.3 F   Les jours de fête à la maison

1 **V** Match the special occasions (1–7) with their definitions (a–g).

1 Le réveillon
2 Le jour de Noël
3 Un anniversaire
4 Le jour de l'An
5 La fête des Mères
6 Le jour de Pâques
7 La fête de l'Aïd

a C'est une fête musulmane, à la fin du Ramadan.
b C'est le jour où on se dit: «Bonne année».
c C'est une fête qu'on fait le trente et un décembre.
d On fait la fête pour célébrer le jour où on est né.
e C'est une fête chrétienne, au printemps.
f C'est le vingt-cinq décembre.
g C'est le jour où on dit: «Bonne fête, maman».

La tradition de l'Aïd el-Fitre

Le mois de Ramadan est fini. C'est enfin la fête de l'Aïd el-Fitre. Pendant le Ramadan, on n'a pas le droit de manger pendant la journée, seulement le soir et tôt le matin.

Pour la fête de l'Aïd el-Fitre, traditionnellement, les hommes portent leurs plus beaux vêtements et les femmes préparent des plats cuisinés pour l'occasion.

Hommes et femmes rendent visite à leurs amis et à leur famille. Certaines familles préfèrent sortir ou se promener plutôt que de rendre visite aux oncles et aux cousins.

Les enfants savent bien que c'est aussi leur fête et reçoivent des cadeaux de toutes sortes.

C'est un jour où on va à la mosquée parce que c'est une fête religieuse.

La plus grande partie de la journée, cependant, se passe en famille autour de la table. On mange, on boit (mais on ne boit pas d'alcool) et on s'amuse. C'est une occasion joyeuse que tout le monde apprécie.

2a 📖 🎧 Read the text and decide whether these statements are true (**T**), false (**F**) or not mentioned in the text (**?**).

1 Eid is celebrated just before the period of Ramadan.
2 During Ramadan, eating is not allowed during the daytime.
3 For Eid, people visit their friends and their relatives.
4 Some families prefer staying at home, however.
5 Children give presents to their parents.
6 As Eid is a religious day, people go to the mosque.
7 Little time is spent around the table.

2b 📖 🎧 Read the text again and answer these questions in English.

1 What do men traditionally wear for Eid?
2 How do women contribute to the day?
3 Why do children in particular like Eid?
4 What do the family actually do for most of the day?

3a 🎧 Listen to Antoine and Thomas exchanging information about their birthdays and identify the person who …

1 could not be there for Thomas's birthday.
2 paid for Thomas to have download vouchers.
3 was ill on his birthday.
4 gave Antoine a television for his birthday.

3b 🎧 Listen again and correct the mistakes in these statements.

1 Thomas did not go to school on his birthday and his friends came to his house later to play games.
2 Thomas's friends gave him a mobile phone.
3 Antoine's birthday (15th January) was a cold day with some snow.
4 Antoine spent his birthday watching television.

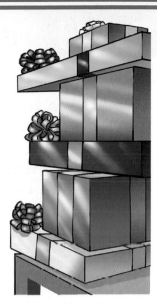

4 🄶 Transform these sentences so they state what things were like last year. Use the imperfect tense.

Exemple: Il fait beau pour mon anniversaire. ▸
             <u>L'année dernière, il faisait</u> beau pour mon anniversaire.

1 J'ai quatorze ans.
2 La cuisine de ma tante, c'est délicieux!
3 Je suis à la maison à Noël.
4 Il y a du monde au réveillon.
5 C'est dommage. Il est malade le jour de son anniversaire.

5 🖋 Write a social networking site message to your friends, telling them about your birthday. Mention:

- when your birthday is and how old you are
- how you normally spend your birthday (where, what you do)
- what you did for your last birthday (using the perfect tense)
- what you thought of it (using *faire, avoir* and *être* in the imperfect tense)
- what your favourite festival is (and why)
- what you do / did for that festival.

Mon anniversaire, c'est le …	
Normalement, pour mon anniversaire, je …	
À mon dernier anniversaire,	j'ai reçu … / j'ai mangé … / je suis allé(e) …
C'était	génial / barbant.
Il faisait	froid / beau.
Ma fête préférée, c'est	Noël / Pâques / l'Aïd / la Saint-Valentin.
Je préfère … parce que	je reçois … / on mange … / on va …

Grammaire *page 184*

Common imperfect expressions

You sometimes need to use the imperfect tense to describe what something was like, how someone was feeling or where something / somebody was. You need to learn these five by heart: *j'avais* (I had), *j'étais* (I was), *il y avait* (there was / there were), *c'était* (it was) and *il faisait chaud / froid* (it was hot / cold).

Find out more about the imperfect tense. *See page 108* ➡

Stratégie 5

Including negatives

When writing, include what you don't do as well as what you do. As well as *ne … pas*, include expressions such as *ne … jamais* (never) and *ne … plus* (no more, no longer). Include three things you don't do, never do or no longer do on your birthday.

∞∞∞ **Lien**

5.3 Groundwork is available in the Foundation book.

5.3 H   On fait la fête

Noël et le jour de l'An

Tu aimes Noël, Marc?

Bien sûr. J'ai un petit frère de cinq ans et une petite sœur de sept ans, et eux, ils croient toujours au père Noël. Moi, je pense que je n'y croyais plus à leur âge. Le matin du vingt-cinq, ils réveillent tout le monde entre quatre et cinq heures! On descend tous pour admirer ce que le père Noël a apporté et les petits commencent à ouvrir leurs cadeaux tout de suite. Moi, maintenant, je fais partie des adultes, et pour ne pas rompre le charme de l'occasion, je joue le jeu de quelqu'un qui croit encore au père Noël. Plus tard, comme chaque année, ma mère prépare le repas traditionnel de Noël. Je l'aide un peu parce qu'il y a beaucoup de choses à faire. En général, on n'est jamais seuls à table. Mes deux cousins arrivent en fin de matinée avec leurs parents et on passe le reste de la journée à faire la fête.

Tu réveillonnes?

Pour la Saint-Sylvestre, c'est-à-dire la veille du jour de l'An, oui. L'année dernière, comme j'avais seize ans, mes parents m'ont permis de sortir et de réveillonner chez un de mes copains. Je n'avais jamais réveillonné avec des copains avant. C'était génial! On s'est retrouvés en début de soirée chez Luc. Ses parents l'avaient laissé réarranger le garage pour pouvoir y faire la fête. On était à peu près une vingtaine et on a dansé, chanté et mangé jusqu'au lever du jour. Au moment où on se disait «bonne année» à minuit, les parents de Luc sont venus voir si tout se passait bien. C'est là que j'ai rencontré Marine qui est toujours ma petite amie maintenant. Les réveillons, à mon avis, c'est extra.

1a 📖 Read the text and find phrases similar in meaning to the ones below.

1 évidemment
2 immédiatement
3 je fais comme si
4 le 31 décembre

5 donné la permission
6 faire la fête le soir du 31 décembre
7 approximativement
8 jusqu'au matin

1b 📖🎧 Read the text again and decide whether these statements are true (**T**), false (**F**) or not mentioned (**?**).

A 1 Marc's brother and sister still believe in Father Christmas.
2 Marc also believed in Father Christmas when he was their age.
3 Now he pretends to believe, in order not to break the magic for his brother and sister.
4 His father helps with preparing the Christmas meal.
5 His aunt and uncle's family arrive just after lunch.
B 6 Marc went to a party on December 31st last year.
7 Luc's parents had prepared the garage for the party.
8 Luc's parents had their own party with their friends.
9 Marc met his girlfriend at Luc's party.

Dealing with 'not mentioned in the text'

Stratégie 1b

Assume that each statement is true and look for confirmation of this in the text. If you can't find evidence that it is true (or indeed false), the likelihood is that it is not mentioned in the text.

2a 🎧 Listen to Section A and answer the questions in English.

1   Why was this birthday celebration different from usual?
2   What does Rachid think about Moroccan cuisine?
3   Explain two of the three problems that arose.

2b 🎧 Listen to Section B and choose the correct ending for each sentence.

1   Quand on ne mange pas pendant la journée,
2   Quand on fait la fête pendant trois jours,
3   Avant, Rachid allait chez
4   L'oncle et la tante de Rachid n'ont pas dormi
5   Rachid et ses cousins ont couché
6   La tante de Rachid a passé son temps

a   c'est la fête de l'Aïd.
b   dans la cuisine.
c   c'est le Ramadan.
d   dans la même chambre.
e   dans une chambre.
f   ses grands-parents.

3 🄖 Complete the sentences by replacing the infinitives with the correct form of the imperfect and perfect tenses.

1   Pendant que je `manger` au restaurant, on m' `voler` mon porte-monnaie.
2   Quand elle `dormir` , sa mère `téléphoner` pour lui dire «bon anniversaire».
3   Comme il `faire` mauvais à Noël, nous `rester` à la maison.
4   Je `arriver` au moment où mon père `préparer` un repas pour la fin du Ramadan.
5   Nous `visiter` le Louvre à Pâques quand nous `être` à Paris.

4 🗨 Work with a partner. Exchange information about what you do for a festival of your choice. Mention:

■   the preparations
■   what happens normally on the day (what you do, what you like)
■   what happened last year (use the perfect and imperfect tenses)
■   what you thought of it (use the imperfect tense)
■   what you intend to do this year (use *je voudrais* or *je vais* followed by an infinitive).

> **Combining perfect and imperfect tenses**
>
> The imperfect tense endings are: *-ais, -ais, -ait, -ions, -iez, -aient* (see page 75).
>
> The imperfect verb stem is taken from the *nous* form of the present tense (without its *-ons* ending).
>
> You can use the imperfect and perfect tenses in the same sentence, saying what was happening (imperfect) and what happened (perfect). Use words like *quand* (when), *pendant* (during) and *comme, car, parce que* (because) to link them:
>
> *Pendant que nous mangions, un groupe a joué de la musique.* – While we were eating, a group played music.
>
> Also learn about the indefinite adjectives *chaque* and *quelque*.
>
> *See page 109* ➡
>
> **Grammaire** *pages 183–184*

Quel est ton jour de fête préféré?	C'est Noël / Aïd / ...
Pour Noël / Aïd / ..., d'habitude mes parents ...	
Pour les aider, je ...	
Le jour de Noël / de l'Aïd / ...,	je reçois ... / on mange ... / on va ...
J'aime bien ...	
L'année dernière, on a ...	
On était ...	
C'était / J'ai pensé que c'était ...	
Cette année, je voudrais ... / je vais ...	

Quel est ton jour de fête préféré?

Moi, je préfère la Saint-Sylvestre. L'année dernière, j'ai réveillonné jusqu'à trois heures du matin. C'était super! Et toi?

(G) Home and local area

1 Match the questions and the answers using the English in brackets to help you.

1 Il y a combien de pièces dans ta maison? (*There are eight of them.*)
2 Vous avez combien de chambres? (*We have three of them.*)
3 Il y a combien de salles de bains? (*There are two of them.*)
4 Comment est le garage? (*There is none.*)
5 Vous avez un jardin? (*Yes, we have one.*)
6 Vous mettez des fleurs aux fenêtres. (*Yes, we do.*)

a Oui, on en met!
b Il y en a huit.
c Il y en a deux.
d Oui, on en a un.
e Il n'y en a pas.
f On en a trois.

Grammaire page 179

En meaning 'of it', 'of them'
En is used to avoid repeating a noun introduced with a number or *du / de la / de l' / des*. It goes before the verb.
*Vous avez deux salles de bains? Non, on **en** a trois!*
Do you have two bathrooms? No, we have three (of them)!

2 Complete the captions with the correct adjective taken from the word snake.

1 un _____ jardin

2 une _____ rivière

3 une _____ église

4 un _____ château

5 un _____ hôtel

6 un _____ escalier

vieillevieuxbelnouvelbellebeau

Grammaire page 175

Three adjectives: *vieux*, *nouveau*, *beau*
These three common adjectives come before the noun:
*un **vieux** musée* – an old museum
*un **nouveau** centre commercial* – a new shopping centre
*un **beau** tableau* – a beautiful painting
Their feminine forms are *vieille*, *nouvelle* and *belle*:
*une **nouvelle** piscine* – a new swimming pool
They have a special form used before a vowel or a silent *h*:
*un **vieil** homme* – an old man
*un **nouvel** aéroport* – a new airport
*un **bel** endroit* – a beautiful place

3 Choose the correct translation for each sentence.

1 *Je dormais quand tu as appelé.*
   a I was asleep when you called.
   b I will be asleep when you call.
2 *Avant, je ne regardais jamais la télévision.*
   a I have never watched television.
   b I never used to watch television.
3 *Elle visitait le musée quand je suis arrivée.*
   a She wanted to visit the museum when I arrived.
   b She was visiting the museum when I arrived.
4 *Il lavait la voiture tous les dimanches.*
   a He used to wash the car every Sunday.
   b He washes the car every Sunday.

Grammaire page 184

The imperfect tense
The imperfect tense is used to describe what something was like in the past, or what someone used to do regularly in the past. In the singular, it usually ends in *-ais* or *-ait*. You don't pronounce the final *s* or *t*.

habiter	to live
j'habitais	I used to live; I lived
tu habitais	you used to live; you lived
il / elle habitait	he / she used to live; he / she lived

4 Replace all the highlighted verbs with a suitable form of *être situé* or *se trouver*. Don't forget to make the verbs and past participles agree with the subject.

L'hôtel Villa Caroline **1** `est` dans un environnement de rêve car il **2** `est` en face d'une plage extraordinaire. La piscine **3** `est` sur une magnifique pelouse. Nos chambres **4** `sont` au cinquième étage, elles sont calmes et confortables. On peut prendre l'ascenseur pour descendre au sous-sol où **5** `il y a` un parking. Le soir, on peut prendre un bateau pour aller s'amuser dans les bars et les boîtes de nuit qui **6** `sont` sur une petite île.

> **_Se trouver_ and _être situé_**
>
> *Grammaire page 187*
>
> For variety, you can often replace *être* with verbs such as *se trouver* (to be found) or *être situé* (to be situated). The two are practically interchangeable, but use a mixture for variety.
>
> *Le parking se trouve au sous-sol.* – The car park can be found in the basement.
>
> Don't forget to make *situé* agree with the subject:
>
> *Les églises sont souvent situées sur une colline.* – The churches are often situated on a hill.

5 Look at the picture. Copy the sentences and fill in each gap using the appropriate preposition from the grammar box.

1 Mon immeuble se trouve _____ église.
2 Mon appartement est situé _____ pharmacie.
3 Le parking se trouve _____ pharmacie.
4 La pharmacie est _____ jardin public.
5 Il y a de belles fleurs _____ pelouse.
6 Le jardin public est _____ terrain de sport.

> **Prepositions of place**
>
> *Grammaire page 193*
>
> When using the following prepositions make sure you use the correct form of *du, de la, de l'* or *des* depending on the noun that follows.
>
> | | |
> |---|---|
> | *à côté de* | next to |
> | *près de* | near |
> | *en dessous de* | under |
> | *au-dessus de* | above |
> | *en face de* | opposite |
> | *au milieu de* | in the middle of |
>
> For example:
>
> *près de l'église* – near the church
>
> *en face des toilettes* – opposite the toilets

6 Copy the sentences and fill in each gap with *quelque(s)* or *chaque*.

1 Il fait son lit _____ matin.
2 Il y a _____ usines dans ma région.
3 Elle a gardé une clé pour _____ porte.
4 J'ai oublié _____ chose dans le bureau.
5 Il a visité _____ immeubles horribles.
6 Il y a un ordinateur dans _____ chambre.
7 J'ai _____ beaux meubles dans le salon.
8 Elle a mis _____ fleurs dans la pièce.

> **Indefinite adjectives: _chaque_ and _quelque_**
>
> *Grammaire page 176*
>
> The adjective *chaque* means 'each' or 'every'. It is always singular:
>
> | | |
> |---|---|
> | *chaque jour* | every day |
> | *chaque pièce* | each room |
>
> The adjective *quelque(s)* means 'some'. You are more likely to use it in the plural:
>
> *quelques fleurs* some flowers
>
> It is, however, useful to know the phrase *quelque chose* (something).

Home and local area

Topic 5.1 Home

5.1 F Ma maison ➡ pages 96–97

l'	appartement (m)	apartment, flat
l'	ascenseur (m)	lift
l'	aspirateur (m)	vacuum cleaner
le	balcon	balcony
le	chalet	chalet
la	campagne	countryside
le	congélateur	freezer
c'est	dommage	it is a pity
	dormir	to sleep
le	four à micro-ondes	microwave oven
le	frigo	fridge
l'	immeuble (m)	block of flats
	isolé(e)	isolated
le	jardin	garden
	joli(e)	pretty
le	lave-vaisselle	dishwasher
	loin	far
la	montagne	mountain
la	pièce	room
de la	place	some space
le	repas	meal
	sauf	except
le	sous-sol	the basement
la	terrasse	patio
	vieux / vieille	old
la	vue	view

5.1 H Le logement ➡ pages 98–99

	à l'extérieur	outside
	autant que possible	as much as possible
	autour de	around
la	banlieue	suburbs, outskirts
la	construction	construction
	croire	to believe

	étonnant(e)	surprising
les	espaces verts (m)	parks, green spaces
la	jeunesse	youth
le	lieu de travail	workplace
	ne … plus	no more, no longer
l'	ouvrier / ouvrière (m / f)	worker
	plaire	to please
	rêver de	to dream of
le	robinet	tap
les	sans-abri (m)	homeless people
	sans doute	without doubt
se	séparer	to separate
	spacieux(-ieuse)	spacious

Topic 5.2 My local area

5.2 F Ma région ➡ pages 100–101

	à demain	see you tomorrow
l'	alpinisme (m)	mountaineering
l'	animation (f)	liveliness
	animé(e)	lively
	attendre	to wait for
	beau / belle	beautiful
à la	campagne	in the country
la	circulation	traffic
	connaître	to know
	danser	to dance
	génial(e)	great
la	maison individuelle	detached house
la	monitrice	female instructor
la	naissance	birth
	nouveau / nouvelle	new
	partager	to share
	partout	everywhere
	propre	clean
la	randonnée	hike
le	spectacle	show

les	sports nautiques (m)	water sports
	tranquille	quiet
l'	usine (f)	factory
la	voile	sailing
le	VTT	mountain bike

5.2 H Des mondes différents ➡ *pages 102–103*

	à une époque	at one time
	ailleurs	elsewhere
	améliorer	to improve
l'	arrondissement (m)	administrative district (of Paris)
	au dessus de	above
	bruyant(e)	noisy
	construire	to build
se	déplacer	to move around
	en dessous de	below, beneath
la	forêt	forest
la	frontière	border
le	HLM	block of high rise council flats
la	moitié	half
la	motoneige	snowmobile
la	pauvreté	poverty
	pluvieux(-ieuse)	rainy
le	quart	quarter
	respirer	to breathe
le	tiers	third

Topic 5.3 Routine and celebrations

5.3 F Les jours de fête à la maison
➡ *pages 104–105*

l'	Aïd (m)	Eid
l'	anniversaire(m)	birthday
le	cadeau	present
	célébrer	to celebrate
	chrétien(ne)	Christian
	dommage	pity
	faire la fête	to have a party / celebration
	fêter	to celebrate
la	fête des Mères	Mothers' day

le	jour de l'An	New Year's day
la	journée	day
	musulman(e)	Muslim
	Noël	Christmas
l'	occasion (f)	occasion, opportunity
	offrir	to offer
	Pâques	Easter
le	portable	mobile phone
le	printemps	spring
	recevoir	to receive
	religieux(-ieuse)	religious
	render visite à	to visit (someone)
le	réveillon	Christmas Eve / New Year's Eve party
	télécharger	to download

5.3 H On fait la fête ➡ *pages 106–107*

	à mon avis	in my opinion
	apporter	to bring
	entouré(e) de	surrounded by
les	festivités (f)	festivities
le	grenier	attic
	incroyable	incredible
	laisser	to leave (something behind), to let (someone do something)
le	lever du jour	daybreak
les	lits superposés (m)	bunk beds
	permettre	to allow
se	retrouver	to meet again
	réveillonner	to party overnight (for Christmas or New Year's Eve)
	rigoler	to have a laugh
la	veille	the evening / day before
la	vingtaine	about 20
	voler	to steal

6.1 F Les problèmes de l'environnement

1 ⓥ Match the English and French phrases. Most of the French words are very similar to the English words.

1 save gas and electricity
2 floods
3 organic products
4 tornadoes and storms
5 plastic bags (or 'sacks')
6 the protection of the environment
7 recycling bottles
8 to protect the planet

a protéger la planète
b les tornades et les tempêtes
c les inondations
d la protection de l'environnement
e économiser le gaz et l'électricité
f le recyclage des bouteilles
g les sacs en plastique
h les produits bio

Notre Terre en danger

A **Tout le monde utilise trop de plastique mais il est très difficile à recycler.** Dans certains pays, il y a des montagnes de déchets. Avant, il y avait des sacs en plastique gratuits dans tous les supermarchés. Maintenant, personne ne les utilise. À la place, on prend des sacs en coton et on les réutilise.

B **Chaque année il y a de nouveaux records de températures.** Il y a de plus en plus de tempêtes et de tornades. Avant, il y avait une grosse tornade par an, maintenant il y en a plusieurs! Dans certains pays, il fait de plus en plus chaud. Les glaciers vont fondre, le niveau de l'eau va monter. Les villes et les villages près de la mer sont en danger.

C **Beaucoup d'espèces d'animaux sont en danger d'extinction.** Les usines où sont fabriqués tous les produits dont on a besoin sont responsables de la pollution de nos rivières. Elles y mettent tous leurs déchets. Les eaux polluées arrivent dans les mers et causent la mort de milliers de poissons. Notre industrie et notre agriculture causent la destruction de l'habitat des animaux, des oiseaux et des insectes.

2a 📖 🎧 Read the article and choose an English title for each paragraph (A–C).

1 Destruction of habitats   2 Recycling   3 Global warming

2b 📖 🎧 Below are five solutions. Decide which of the three problems outlined above (A–C) each one is aimed at resolving.

Vous pouvez sauver la planète …

1 en achetant des produits qui ne polluent pas les rivières.
2 en recyclant les déchets.
3 en voyageant en train, pas en avion.
4 en utilisant des sacs en coton.
5 en protégeant le monde animal.

3a 📖 🎧 Listen to Section A. Put these environmental issues into the order in which they are mentioned in the discussion.

climate change   river pollution
traffic fumes   pollution of the seas
destruction of the rain forest   extinction of wildlife

3b 🎧 Listen to Section B and answer the questions in English.

1 What does Sandrine think is the most serious environmental problem?
2 What is causing it, according to her?
3 Éric has a different cause to blame. Which one?
4 What problem does Adrien mention?
5 What do Sandrine and Adrien agree is the most serious problem?

4 **G** Copy the sentences and fill in each gap with the correct present participle. Choose from the verbs below.

1 Mon père pollue en _____ une grosse voiture.
2 En _____ mes courses à pied, je ne pollue pas.
3 Je protège l'environnement en _____ des pommes françaises.
4 Je protège l'environnement en _____ les produits emballés dans du plastique.
5 Sascha protège l'environnement en _____ des sacs en coton.
6 Et moi, je protège l'environnement en _____ mes déchets.

faire   refuser   conduire   utiliser
acheter   recycler

5 🗩 Work in a small group. Discuss the various environmental problems mentioned on these two pages and agree on an order of importance. Then present the agreed order to the class: *le problème le plus grave, c'est …, puis c'est …, ensuite, c'est …,* etc. For each problem, suggest a way to improve the situation.

Le problème le plus grave, c'est	le changement climatique.
	la pollution des rivières et de la mer (des mers).
	la pollution de l'air.
	la destruction de l'habitat des animaux.
On peut protéger l'environnement en	faisant des pistes cyclables / recyclant les déchets.
	faisant des économies d'eau / de gaz / d'électricité.
	se déplaçant à vélo / à pied.
	n'utilisant pas de sacs en plastique.
On ne doit pas	polluer la mer / les rivières.

Stratégie 3b

Pronunciation of similar words

While listening, you will notice that although many French and English words are similar to look at, they are often pronounced quite differently. As you carry out the listening task, check the pronunciation of *-tion* (in *pollution, extinction, destruction, circulation*), *i* (in *plastique*), *é* (in *pollué*) and *è* (in *problème*).

Grammaire *page 186*

Present participles

The present participle in French ends in *-ant*, and it is used if you want to say 'by doing something':

Je protège l'environnement en recyclant mes bouteilles en plastique. – I protect the environment by recycling my plastic bottles.

To form the present participle in French, take the *nous* form of the present tense, remove the *-ons*, and replace it with *-ant*.

Also learn about indefinite pronouns: *tout le monde* and *personne*.   *See page 120* ➡

🔗 *Lien*

6.1 Groundwork is available in the Foundation book.

6.1 H — Planète en danger

La destruction de la planète

A La destruction de la planète est un problème mondial. En Terre Adélie (la partie française de l'Antarctique), la glace est en train de fondre. Nos émissions de dioxyde de carbone contribuent à l'effet de serre. Le résultat de cet effet est le réchauffement de la planète.

B Le niveau de la mer monte et les vagues menacent les Maldives. Les îles sont seulement à un mètre au-dessus de la mer, et on pense que le niveau de la mer va monter de deux mètres avant la fin du siècle.

C Chaque année, il y a de nouveaux records de températures. Partout dans le monde, il y a de plus en

plus d'inondations, de tempêtes et de tornades. Beaucoup de scientifiques pensent que la pollution mondiale provoque un effet de serre et entraîne le réchauffement de la planète, et donc le changement climatique.

D En 1998, le protocole de Kyoto réunit beaucoup de pays qui décident collectivement un plan d'action. Les objectifs sont de réduire les émissions de dioxyde de carbone entre 2008 et 2012. Bien que plus de cent cinquante

pays signent cet accord à ce moment-là, les États-Unis, la Chine et l'Inde, tous des gros pollueurs, refusent de signer.

E L'association Les Amis de la Terre nous donne à tous les conseils suivants:

- Bien que ce soit gênant, essayez de ne pas utiliser votre voiture.
- À condition qu'il ne fasse pas trop froid, réduisez votre consommation de gaz et d'électricité.
- Bien que ce ne soit pas la solution de facilité, évitez de voyager en avion.

Allons-nous arriver à sauvegarder notre planète pour les générations futures? Il est important de faire quelque chose avant qu'il ne soit trop tard.

1a 📖 Find in the article the French for these words and phrases. Use the anagrams to help you.

1	greenhouse effect	**le chantfeufémer de la natèple**
2	global warming	**l'fefte de reser**
3	scientist	**le siquitnefcie**
4	climate change	**le gemchentan quetlaimic**
5	to reduce	**rudeiré**
6	inconvenient	**agêntn**
7	flood	**l'ointannodi**

1b 📖🎧 Read the article and match the five paragraphs (A–E) with the headings (1–5).

1 How scientists explain climate change
2 The melting of ice fields
3 What individuals can do
4 Rising seas
5 A partly successful solution

1c 📖 🎧 Read the article again and answer the questions in English.

1 According to the text, what causes global warming?
2 What is the threat to the Maldives?
3 What other examples of climate change are there in the text?
4 What is the importance of the Kyoto protocol?
5 What do Friends of the Earth ask individuals to do to help with the problem?

2a 🎧 Listen to a class discussion, in four sections, one for each student's viewpoint. Copy the grid below and write the name of the student in the correct box: Alexis, Marie, Sébastien or Claire. (*la fracturation hydraulique* = fracking, a method for extracting shale gas)

	Fracking	Nuclear energy	Renewable energy
in support of			
against			

2b 🎧 Listen again and decide whether these statements are true (**T**), false (**F**) or not mentioned (**?**).

1 Germany is developing its nuclear energy programme.
2 There is a town in northern Russia that stores nuclear waste.
3 Politically unstable countries have developed nuclear weapons.
4 On ecological grounds, France does not approve of fracking.
5 Renewable energy will eventually replace all other forms of energy.

3 🅖 Re-read the text *La destruction de la planète* on page 114. Find and note down the French for these five phrases. In each one, underline the verb in the subjunctive.

1 Before it is too late
2 Although more than 150 countries sign this agreement
3 Provided it is not too cold
4 Although it is inconvenient
5 Although it is not the easy solution

4 ✏️ Write three short paragraphs about the three environmental problems you think are the most serious. Explain the causes of these problems and suggest at least one solution to each problem.

Je trouve / pense que le problème le plus grave, c'est …
La cause de …, c'est …
Pour protéger l'environnement, il faut / il ne faut pas …
La solution à ce problème, c'est de …
On doit / On devrait / On pourrait …

Expressions followed by the subjunctive

Grammaire — page 186

Several expressions in French require the verb that follows to be in the form called the subjunctive. The way it is formed is explained on page 186: the key ones to note are *ce soit* and *il y ait* – the subjunctives of *c'est* and *il y a*.

Below are three such expressions that you should learn.

avant que	before
bien que	although
à condition que	provided that

*Il est important de faire quelque chose **avant qu'il ne soit** trop tard.* – It is important to do something before it is too late.

Also learn about emphatic pronouns (e.g. *moi, toi, lui*).

See page 120 ➡

Varying your language

Stratégie 4

Try to vary your language whenever possible, e.g. *La solution à ce problème est de … / Pour résoudre ce problème, il faut … / Ce qu'on devrait faire, c'est de …*

To say what needs to be done, you can use *il faut que* + subjunctive or *il faut* + infinitive.

6.2 F Une ville propre

Objectifs

Local issues and actions

Faire: present and perfect tenses

Recognising new words

1 ⓥ Solve these anagrams. The definitions should help you.

1 **none pête in oz** – c'est pour les gens à pied
2 **blue poles** – c'est pour les déchets non recyclables
3 **yet roten** – rendre propre
4 **re space vests** – les parcs et les jardins publics
5 **rare quit** – une partie de la ville

Troyes: ville propre

Ici à Troyes on a fait beaucoup pour l'environnement …

1 Le centre-ville est une zone piétonne où les véhicules sont interdits.
2 On a introduit un système de pistes cyclables.
3 On a installé des poubelles dans les espaces verts.
4 Il y a des centres de recyclage dans les parkings.

Pour recycler vos déchets …

Il y a des centres de recyclage pour les bouteilles, le papier et pour toutes sortes de choses recyclables. Cette initiative a eu beaucoup de succès: il y a trois ans, les habitants de Troyes recyclaient 10 pour cent de leurs déchets, aujourd'hui c'est 30 pour cent.

Pour avoir une ville propre …

On a installé des poubelles dans tous les espaces verts. Dans le quartier St-Julien, le club des jeunes a organisé l'opération «Nettoyage du jardin public». Ils l'ont vraiment transformé. Un grand merci à tous ces jeunes!

Pour pédaler sans polluer …

Une autre mesure qu'on a introduite dans la région est la construction de pistes cyclables. C'est surtout bon pour la santé des jeunes. On les encourage à prendre le vélo pour aller à l'école.

2a 📖 🎧 Decide which symbol (A–D) goes with each numbered point (1–4) in the first section.

2b 📖 🎧 Read the whole leaflet and decide whether the following sentences are true (**T**), false (**F**) or not mentioned (**?**).

1 They have installed recycling facilities.
2 Garden waste is collected from homes.
3 Young people are encouraged to cycle to school.
4 The city has done little to improve the environment.
5 There are initiatives for young people.
6 The park in St-Julien is dirty.

Recognising new words

You are often able to recognise new words from those you already know. For example, from the verb *recycler*, you can recognise the noun *recyclage*. Find the verb from the noun *pollution* and the noun from the verb *nettoyer* in the leaflet.

Stratégie 2a–2b

3a 🎧 Listen to the interviews. Match the people (1–3) with the right pictures (A–C).

1 Alex 2 Juliette 3 Zoé

3b 🎧 Who says what? Write Alex, Juliette or Zoé for each sentence.

1 I refuse plastic bags.
2 I'm doing something good for my health.
3 We had to clear up after the party.
4 I use public transport.
5 Mum used to take me to school.
6 You have to pay for a plastic bag.
7 We recycled everything.

4 **G** Copy the sentences and fill in each gap using the verb *faire* in the <u>perfect</u> tense. Then start each sentence with *d'habitude* (usually) instead of *hier* (yesterday) and do the activity again, this time using the <u>present</u> tense of the verb *faire*.

1 Hier, j' _____ du recyclage.
2 Hier, mon frère _____ des économies d'eau.
3 Hier, mes copains _____ du nettoyage.
4 Hier, nous _____ du vélo.
5 Hier, on _____ le trajet en utilisant les transports en commun.
6 Hier, mes parents _____ les courses avec des sacs en coton.

> **Grammaire** page 195
>
> ***Faire*: present and perfect tenses**
>
> It is important to be able to use the common verb *faire* (to do) correctly.
>
> ***Je fais*** *du nettoyage.* – I am doing some cleaning.
>
> ***J'ai fait*** *du nettoyage.* – I did some cleaning.
>
> If you can't remember how to form the present tense or the perfect tense of *faire*, look it up in the verb tables (page 195), or refer back to Topic 3 (page 61) and Topic 4 (page 77).
>
> Also learn how to use *on*.
> See page 120 ➡

5 🗨 Work with a partner. Prepare answers to the following questions, then take turns to ask and answer.

1 Quels sont les problèmes de l'environnement dans votre ville?
2 Est-ce que la ville fait assez pour la protection de l'environnement?
3 Personnellement, qu'est-ce que vous faites pour protéger l'environnement? Qu'est-ce que vous avez fait récemment?
4 Qu'est-ce que vous recyclez?
5 Économisez-vous l'eau? le gaz? l'électricité?

Il y a trop de …	
Il n'y a pas assez de …	
Dans notre ville,	il y a … on peut …
Moi,	j'utilise … j'économise … je recycle … j'ai nettoyé … j'ai fait …

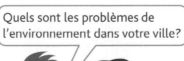
Quels sont les problèmes de l'environnement dans votre ville?

Dans notre ville, il y a trop de circulation et il n'y a pas assez de pistes cyclables.

Lien
6.2 Groundwork is available in the Foundation book.

6.2 H L'environnement et ma ville

Des conseils écologiques

A Le dentifrice en flacon pompe, les déodorants en aérosol et les biscuits sont emballés dans de l'aluminium, puis dans du carton et finalement dans du plastique. Les emballages coûtent cher. De plus, tout cela finit inutilement dans nos poubelles et contribue aux montagnes de déchets que l'on voit dans les décharges publiques. Personne n'aime habiter à proximité d'une de ces décharges. Pour éviter qu'elles ne se multiplient, il faut limiter les déchets qu'on met à la poubelle.

B
- D'abord, pour faire ses achats, il faut qu'on emporte un sac recyclable au lieu de prendre les sacs en plastique des supermarchés (dont 170 millions ont été distribués aux caisses françaises l'année dernière!).
- Puis, quand on boit un café pendant la pause au travail, on devrait prendre une tasse en porcelaine au lieu d'utiliser trois ou quatre gobelets en plastique. Le plastique est pratiquement indestructible.
- On peut mettre un panneau «Pas de publicité, merci!» sur sa boîte aux lettres pour éviter les prospectus et les journaux gratuits. Si vous en recevez quand même, n'oubliez pas de les recycler.
- Ensuite, on doit recycler tous ses déchets et ordures (papier, magazines, emballages, bouteilles). Afin de faciliter le recyclage, chaque ville a des centres de recyclage et souvent les éboueurs ramassent aussi les sacs de choses recyclables posés devant la maison.
- Finalement, on peut recycler les résidus alimentaires qu'on peut utiliser plus tard dans le jardin sous forme de compost. On peut alors cultiver des légumes biologiques.

1a Find in the leaflet above the French terms to match these definitions.

1 Something to make you smell nice
2 What is used to wrap products
3 Where you take your non-recyclable rubbish
4 What you should carry your shopping in
5 What you should drink your coffee in
6 Annoying stuff that comes through the letter box
7 People whose job it is to collect rubbish
8 Something that you can compost

1b Read the leaflet again and answer the questions in English.

1 What is the environmental problem highlighted in Section A?
2 What, according to the leaflet, causes the problem?
3 In Section B, what are you advised to take to the supermarket, and why?
4 Why is it better to use a china cup than a plastic cup?
5 Why would you put a sign on your letter box?
6 What two things do local councils do to encourage people to recycle?
7 What should you do with leftover organic waste?

Reading the whole text first

Stratégie 1b

Although the order of the questions often follows the order of the text, some questions aim to test gist comprehension, for example question 1. When you are dealing with questions like this, it is advisable to read the whole text first.

2a 🎧 You are attending an open meeting on how to improve the local environment chaired by the Mayor of Troyes. Listen to the proceedings (Sections A–D) and answer these questions.

1 Why did the first speaker want to raise the issue of a pedestrian area? (Section A)
2 According to the second speaker, what is the consequence of creating a shopping centre outside town? (Section B)
3 How would the third speaker solve the traffic problems that exist in town? (Section C)
4 What point does the fourth speaker make? (Section D)

2b 🎧 Listen again and note what the mayor thinks of the following. Is his attitude positive (**P**), negative (**N**) or both positive and negative (**P + N**)?

1 a pedestrian area
2 the shopping centre outside town
3 park-and-ride facilities
4 a tram line
5 more recycling points

> **Stratégie 2b**
>
> **Tackling 'P, N or P + N' tasks**
>
> Look out for conjunctions such as *mais, pourtant, cependant, par contre* after positive phrases such as *j'aime, c'est super*, etc. They may well lead you to a 'P + N' answer.

3 Ⓖ Rewrite these sentences, replacing the infinitive with the subjunctive form.

Exemple: Il faut consommer moins d'énergie. → Il faut qu'on consomme moins d'énergie.

1 Il ne faut pas jeter les déchets par terre.
2 Il faut recycler les bouteilles.
3 Il faut utiliser le vélo.
4 Il faut aller au lycée à pied.
5 Il faut être prudent.
6 Il faut faire plus d'efforts.

> **Grammaire** pages 186, 188
>
> **Il faut + infinitive or subjunctive**
>
> After *il faut* (you have to) you can use either the infinitive or the form called the subjunctive.
>
> The subjunctive form of *-er* verbs is the same as the present tense, e.g. *il faut qu'on recycle.*
>
> But *-ir* and *-re* verbs change. You need to learn some irregular subjunctive forms.
>
> | Infinitive | Subjunctive |
> |---|---|
> | *Il faut …* | *Il faut …* |
> | *aller* | *qu'on aille* |
> | *être* | *qu'on soit* |
> | *jeter* | *qu'on jette* |
> | *faire* | *qu'on fasse* |
> | *construire* | *qu'on construise* |
>
> Also learn when to use an infinitive. *See page 121* ➡

4 ✏ Write an article about environmental issues in your local area and what can be done about them. Mention:

■ what the concerns are
■ what the solutions to those concerns are
■ what you do to help with some of those concerns
■ what else you intend to do in the future to help the situation.

Il y a trop de …
Il n'y a pas assez de …
Il y a / il n'y a pas de …
C'est un problème parce que …

La solution à ce problème serait de …
On pourrait / on devrait / il faut que …

Moi, je …
Pour la protection de l'environnement, je …
En ce qui me concerne, je …
Pour améliorer la situation, je …

À l'avenir, je …

Environment

1a How can we save the planet? Copy the sentences and fill in each gap with *personne ne / n'* or *tout le monde*, to describe an environmentally friendly world.

Exemple: <u>Personne</u> ne pollue les rivières.

1 _____ a un vélo.

2 _____ va au collège en voiture.

3 _____ utilise de sacs en plastique.

4 _____ prend des sacs en papier.

5 _____ recycle le papier.

6 _____ économise l'eau.

> ### Indefinite pronouns: *tout le monde, personne*
> The French for 'everybody' is *tout le monde* and 'nobody' is *personne*.
>
> Both are followed by a verb in the singular. Note that in front of a verb, *personne* is followed by *ne* (or *n'* before a vowel).
>
> *Tout le monde économise l'énergie.* – Everyone saves energy.
>
> *Personne ne jette ses déchets ici.* – Nobody throws their rubbish away here.
>
> *Grammaire* (page 180)

1b Select sentences from Activity 1a as captions for these pictures.

2 Write these verb forms in French, using *on*.

1 we recycle

2 we pollute

3 we use

4 we travel

5 we go

> ### On
> Remember that *on* is often used to mean 'we' instead of saying *nous*. Verbs used with *on* take the same endings as *il* or *elle*.
>
> *On voyage en avion.* – We travel by plane.
>
> *Grammaire* (page 178)

3 Copy the sentences and fill in each gap with the correct emphatic pronoun from the grammar box.

1 _____, j'utilise des sacs en coton.

2 Mais _____, tu prends des sacs en plastique.

3 _____, il va à l'école en voiture.

4 Mais _____, elle prend le bus.

5 _____, nous éteignons la lumière.

6 _____, vous dépensez trop d'énergie.

7 _____, ils jettent leurs déchets sur le trottoir.

8 _____, elles les mettent à la poubelle.

> ### Emphatic pronouns
> In English if you want to emphasise something you do or don't do, you just say it a bit more forcefully. When you write it you sometimes put it in italics or underline it. French people put 'me', 'you', 'him' or 'her' at the beginning of the sentence to emphasise it. For example:
>
> *Moi, je recycle toutes mes bouteilles.* – I recycle all my bottles.
>
> *Toi, tu ne recycles rien.* – You don't recycle anything.
>
> Use the following pronouns for emphasis:
>
> *moi* with *je*, *toi* with *tu*, *lui* with *il*, *elle* with *elle*, *nous* with *nous*, *vous* with *vous*, *eux* with *ils*, *elles* with *elles*.
>
> *Grammaire* (page 179)

4 Find in the *Des conseils écologiques* leaflet (page 118), the French for these English phrases.

1 in order to avoid
2 instead of taking
3 we should take
4 instead of using
5 we must recycle
6 we can then grow

> ### When to use an infinitive
> The infinitive is used to translate 'to do something':
>
> *parler* = to talk
>
> However, it is also used after prepositions such as *à*, *de*, *pour*, *au lieu de*:
>
> *au lieu de prendre les sacs en plastique* – instead of taking plastic bags
>
> It is also used when a verb immediately follows another. The second verb is an infinitive:
>
> *On peut recycler.* – We can recycle.

Grammaire page 181

5 Translate the following sentences into French. Choose from the regular infinitives below, and use the verb tables to check for the correct ending of the tense that you need.

1 She was watching TV.
2 I am listening to a CD.
3 We get washed.
4 I used to catch the bus.
5 Today, I got up at eight o'clock.
6 You spoke to Marc yesterday. (*tu* form)
7 Will you work tomorrow? (*vous* form)
8 He will choose a car.

| écouter | prendre | parler | choisir |
| travailler | regarder | se laver | se lever |

> ### Using regular verb tables
> Many verbs in French follow one of three patterns of endings. You can usually tell from the infinitive which pattern they follow. The infinitive will either end in -er, e.g. *parler*; -ir, e.g. *finir*; or -re, e.g. *vendre*.
>
> The first page of the verb tables gives examples of four tenses of these regular verbs, which you can use to work out the endings for other verbs that follow the same pattern. There is also an example of a reflexive verb, to remind you of the extra pronoun needed with these verbs.

Grammaire page 193

6 Copy and complete the table with the correct forms of the infinitives given in column 1. Some have been done for you.

infinitive	*je* – present	*il* – perfect	*nous* – imperfect	*ils* – future
avoir	j'ai			
être			nous étions	
aller				
faire		il a fait		
pouvoir				
venir				ils viendront
vouloir				

> ### Using irregular verb tables
> There are a number of irregular verbs in French that you need to be able to use. The tables of irregular verbs on pages 194–197 enable you to see how they change in the present, perfect, imperfect and future tenses, which you should be able to use at Higher level. Make sure that you know how to use these tables, so that you can make your work as accurate as possible.

Grammaire pages 194–197

Environment

Topic 6.1 Current problems facing the planet

6.1 F Les problèmes de l'environnement
➡ *pages 112–113*

	affreux(-euse)	horrible, awful
l'	avion (m)	plane
	conduire	to drive
les	déchets (m)	rubbish
la	destruction	destruction
	économiser	to save
l'	électricité (f)	electricity
	fondre	to melt
la	forêt	forest
le	gaz	gas
le	glacier	glacier
l'	habitat (m)	habitat
	monter	to go up
le	niveau	level
la	planète	planet
des	produits bio (m)	organic products
	protéger	to protect
	sauver	to save, to rescue
la	tempête	storm
la	tornade	tornado

6.1 H Planète en danger ➡ *pages 114–115*

	abandonner	to abandon
	baisser	to lower
le	besoin	need
le	changement climatique	climate change
la	consommation	consumption
	contaminé(e)	contaminated
	écologique	ecological, green
l'	effet de serre (m)	greenhouse effect
	fabriquer	to make
l'	inondation (f)	flood

	gênant(e)	inconvenient, annoying
	menacer	to threaten
la	moitié	half
	nucléaire	nuclear
	propre	clean
le	réchauffement de la planète	global warming
	réduire	to reduce
	remplacer	to replace
	renouvelable	renewable
	sauvegarder	to save
le / la	scientifique	scientist
le	siècle	century
la	vague	wave

Topic 6.2 Local issues and actions

6.2 F Une ville propre ➡ *pages 116–117*

le	carton	cardboard
le	club des jeunes	youth club
	emporter	to take (something with you)
l'	environnement (m)	environment
les	espaces verts (m)	parks, green spaces
	gratuit(e)	free (of charge)
l'	habitant (m)	inhabitant
	interdit(e)	forbidden
	introduire	to introduce
	marcher	to walk
	nettoyer	to clean
le	nettoyage	cleaning
	propre	clean
la	protection	protection
	protéger	to protect
le	quartier	district
le	sac en coton	cotton bag
	sans	without

le	trajet	journey
le	trottoir	pavement

6.2 H L'environnement et ma ville

➡ *pages 118–119*

	à mon avis	in my opinion
	au lieu de	instead of
	construire	to build
la	décharge publique	rubbish dump
les	déchets (m)	rubbish
se	déplacer	to get around
l'	éboueur (m)	refuse collector
l'	emballage (m)	packaging
	emballer	to pack, to wrap
	être en train de	to be in the process of
	évidemment	obviously
les	grandes surfaces (f)	hypermarkets
les	ordures (f)	rubbish
le	panneau	sign
la	poubelle	dustbin
	pourtant	however
	ramasser	to pick up, to collect
se	rappeler	to remember
le	parking relais	park-and-ride
	sans doute	no doubt, without doubt

Learning frequently used words

Stratégie

The words in the two 'frequently-used words' lists are some of the most common words in the French language. They come up in every single GCSE Topic and you will find that it is a really good investment of your time to learn them all by heart.

1 Frequently used words

alors	so, then
après	after
assez	quite, fairly
au revoir	goodbye
aussi	also
avant	before

avec	with
avant	before
beaucoup	a lot
bien	well
bientôt	soon
bon(ne)	good
bonjour	hello
car	because
combien	how much
comme	as, like
comment	how
d'abord	first of all
dans	in
enfin	finally

2 Frequently used words

grand(e)	big
ici	here
mais	but
ou	or
où	where
par exemple	for example
parce que	because
petit(e)	small
plus	more
pour	for
pourquoi	why
puis	then
quand	when
que	that, which
qui	who
sans	without
souvent	often
sur	on
tout(e) / tous / toutes	all, every
très	very

Higher – Exam practice

ⓘnfo
These pages give you the chance to try GCSE-style practice exam questions at grades B–A* based on the AQA Context of Home and environment.

Lien
Foundation practice exam questions (grades D–C) are available at the end of this Context in the Foundation Book.

Problèmes sur la côte de l'Afrique

Obasi, un jeune journaliste nigérien, décrit l'environnement où il habite.

A La côte ici, près de Calabar, est interdite au public à cause du niveau de pollution. La fumée des usines pollue l'atmosphère et ces usines rejettent des produits chimiques dans la rivière près d'ici. Résultat: le ciel est toujours gris, l'eau est toxique et dangereuse. Il y a aussi des déchets plastiques partout sur la plage. Ce sont des emballages qu'on pourrait recycler. Et, en plus, le bruit des trains qui transportent les marchandises des usines jour et nuit est insupportable! Dans cet environnement, la santé des habitants se dégrade et des poissons sont morts.

B Le gouvernement dit que c'est la faute des patrons américains qui dirigent les usines installées ici. Ce sont les patrons qui autorisent le déversement de produits toxiques dans la rivière et dans l'atmosphère. Avant, les patrons ne venaient jamais ici et ne s'intéressaient pas à ces problèmes, mais récemment il y a eu la visite d'un nouveau directeur. Quand il a vu les problèmes, il a promis d'investir de l'argent pour moderniser les usines. Il y a quelques semaines, un ingénieur est arrivé des États-Unis. Il va organiser ces changements:

«Nous allons commencer par les problèmes de la rivière. En installant un équipement moderne, contrôlé par ordinateur, il n'y aura plus de produits chimiques rejetés dans la rivière. Dans deux ans, vous reverrez des oiseaux et des poissons dans cette région.»

La réponse de la mairie?

«Bien qu'on soit heureux de recevoir cette aide, nous devons continuer à demander aux patrons de ne pas oublier leur responsabilité envers nos habitants. J'ai peur que ce soit une action isolée. Nous avons aussi besoin d'un air propre et d'une plage sans déchets.»

1a 📖 Read Section A of the report about a heavily polluted area of the West African coast. Answer the questions in English.

1 How do local factories pollute the air?
2 What happens to chemical residues from the factories?
3 What sort of plastic waste is found on the beach?
4 When do the trains run?
5 How are the local people and fish affected by the pollution? (2)

Total = 6 marks

1b 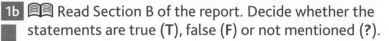 Read Section B of the report. Decide whether the statements are true (**T**), false (**F**) or not mentioned (**?**).

1 The government takes responsibility for the pollution.
2 The American owners used to take an active role in the running of the factories.
3 New ICT systems will monitor the factory's output into the river.
4 Wildlife has already started to return to the area.
5 The mayor gives the changes a cautious welcome.
6 The beach will be clear of rubbish in two years' time.

Total = 6 marks

2a 🎧 Listen to Section A of a radio report at a recycling centre. Which of the slogans below applies to each person interviewed (1–5)?

a Turn all your garden waste into compost!
b A tonne of recycled plastic saves more than 700 kilos of crude oil!
c Our recycling centre is near the shops. Arrive with your rubbish! Leave with your shopping!
d Cardboard can be recycled up to ten times!
e Old textiles are still useful!

Total = 5 marks

2b 🎧 Listen to Section B and choose the correct ending for each sentence.

1 When the interviewee turns down the heating, his wife is likely to …
  a put on extra clothes.
  b turn it up again.
  c agree with what he has done.

2 He will save water in the summer by …
  a recycling washing up water in the garden.
  b installing a shower.
  c washing clothes less often.

3 He tries to encourage his children to …
  a watch less television.
  b spend less time on the computer.
  c switch off equipment that they are not using.

4 He thinks low-energy bulbs are …
  a expensive.
  b attractive.
  c a waste of time.

5 He uses his daughter's old bed as an example of …
  a how he recycles everything.
  b how he would like to recycle more.
  c why he thinks recycling is pointless.

6 He also argues with his family about …
  a how often they go out.
  b using the car to go out.
  c using public transport.

Total = 6 marks

Total for Reading and Listening = 23 marks

Higher – Speaking

Chez moi

You are talking to your French friend about your house and your town. Your teacher will play the part of your friend and will ask you:

1 where you live and what your house is like
2 who lives in your house
3 what your room is like
4 about meal times
5 what you do to help round the house
6 what your local town is like.
7 !

! Remember, you will have to respond to something that you have not yet prepared.

1 Where you live and what your house is like
- Say where you live and what you think of the area.
- Say what your house is like and how long you have lived there.
- Say how many rooms it has and which is your favourite.
- Describe your ideal house.

2 Who lives in your house
- Say who lives in the house and give physical descriptions.
- Describe their characters and say who you get on with.
- Say who you don't get on with and why.
- Talk about your pets and say who looks after them.

3 What your room is like
- Describe your room and say what you like about it.
- Say whether you share your room and what you think of this arrangement.
- Give details of what is in your room and what you would like to have in your room.
- Say what you like doing in your room and why.

4 About meal times

- Say at what times you have meals and what you like eating.
- Say whether you have your meals as a family and who prepares them.
- Say what your favourite meal is and what you don't like eating.
- Talk about the last time you went out for a meal (when, where, what you ate, your opinion of it).

Stratégie

Suggested words for your plan: *quand, quoi, famille, préféré.*
Add a maximum of two words to this list.
Use *prendre* + food or drink as an alternative to using *manger* or *boire*. Take care, as it is an irregular verb.
For the last point, you will need to use the perfect tense – see the grammar section pages 183–184. To say what it was like, use the imperfect, e.g. *c'était, il y avait.*
Show initiative by saying whether you would recommend that place to others. See Exam technique S10.

5 What you do to help round the house

- Describe what you do to help round the house and how frequently you do it.
- Say whether you get pocket money for helping and, if so, how you like to spend it.
- Say what other members of the household do to help and whether the workload is shared fairly.
- Say what you did and didn't do to help in the house last weekend.

Stratégie

Suggested words for your plan: *quoi, fréquence, poche.*
Add a maximum of three words to this list.
Some of the verbs you will need have irregular past participles, e.g. *faire, mettre,* so make sure you learn them.
If *sortir* is followed by a direct object, it takes *avoir* instead of *être* in the perfect tense, e.g. *J'ai sorti la poubelle.*

6 What your local town is like

- Describe the town centre and say what you like about it.
- Say what facilities there are for young people and also for tourists.
- Say when you intend to go to town next and what you would like to do.
- Talk about your ideal town and compare it to where you live.

Stratégie

Suggested words for your plan: *activités – jeunes.*
Add a maximum of four words to this list.
As an alternative to *il y a,* use *pouvoir* in different forms, e.g. *on peut / les touristes peuvent / les jeunes peuvent.*
Use the conditional to talk about your ideal town, e.g. *dans ma ville idéale, il y aurait …* (see the grammar section page 185).
See also Exam technique S11.

7 ! At this point you may be asked …

- if there are environmental problems in your local town and, if so, what they are and what could be done to solve them.
- if you prefer living in town or in the countryside and what the advantages and disadvantages of each are.
- if you intend to continue living in the same area or if you would like to move, and what you would gain and lose if you moved.
- if you prefer living in a small town or a large town and why.

Stratégie

Choose the **two** options that you think are the most likely. In your plan, write **three** words for each of the two options you have chosen. For the first option you might choose: *circulation, déchets, recyclage.* Learn these two options using your reminder words.
Remember to check the total number of words you have used. It should be 40 or fewer.

Lien

Foundation sample assessment tasks for this Context can be found in the Foundation Book.

Higher – Writing

L'environnement

Your French friend Yannick has been asked to participate in a debate on the environment at school. He is keen to have an international perspective, and he has asked you:

1 what your local town is like
2 if there are any environmental problems
3 what you think the solutions to those problems are
4 what you do that makes environmental problems worse
5 what the main problems of the environment are in today's world
6 what we as individuals can do about it
7 if we should stop going on holiday by plane.

1 What your local town is like
 - Write about where your local town is situated and what sort of town it is.
 - Describe the town centre and the suburbs.
 - Include what you think of your local town and why.
 - Mention whether you prefer to live in town or in the country and why.

Stratégie

Start your plan. Here are some suggested words for bullet point 1: *où, industries, centre, banlieue, opinion, préférence*.
Use *se trouve / est située dans le* (county), *dans le* (compass direction) *de l'* (country – for Wales, you would say *du pays de Galles*).
Use *je pense / je trouve / je crois que … parce que …* to give your opinion and justify it.

2 If there are any environmental problems
 - Describe the litter and graffiti situation and give your opinion.
 - Explain to what extent the town suffers from pollution.
 - Give details of how much traffic there is in the town and whether it is a problem.
 - Give your opinion of whether there is enough green space in the town.

Stratégie

Suggested words for your plan: *sale, papiers, pollution, circulation, espaces verts*.
Vary the ways in which you give your opinion.
Use *à mon avis / selon moi, c'est …*
Use *la circulation* for 'traffic'.
In your plan, use words that generate other ideas or words, e.g. *sale* leads you to say what is dirty (e.g. the pavement) and what makes it dirty (e.g. litter).

3 What you think the solutions to those problems are
 - Write about what should be done about litter and graffiti.
 - Say what can be done to improve the traffic situation.
 - Say what can be done to reduce pollution.
 - Say what can be done to improve the town for pedestrians.

Stratégie

Suggested words for your plan: *poubelles, amendes, voitures électriques, zones piétonnes*.
Use *on devrait / il faudrait* + verb in the infinitive to say what we should do.
Use *pour réduire la pollution, on pourrait …* to say what could be done to reduce industrial or traffic pollution.

4 What you do that makes environmental problems worse
- Say whether you occasionally drop litter.
- Say whether you always cycle or walk to your destination and what the benefits of doing so are.
- Mention what you recycle and how you do it.
- Say whether you sometimes travel by car when you shouldn't and say why.

Suggested words for your plan: *papiers, transport localement, recyclage.*
Add a maximum of two words to this list.
Use *laisser tomber* for 'to drop'. Change the ending of the first verb only, e.g. *je laisse tomber ...*
Use *je vais* + destination + *à pied / à vélo* to say that you walk or cycle to a place.

5 What the main problems of the environment are in today's world
- Mention climate change and give an example of its effects.
- Say how the weather has changed, comparing it to what it used to be.
- Write about pollution and give an example of its effects.
- Write about the need to look at renewable sources of energy.

Suggested words for your plan: *climat, pollution, exemple.*
Add a maximum of three words to this list
Use *le changement climatique* for 'climate change'.
Use the imperfect tense to say what the weather used to be like, e.g. *avant, il faisait ...* and the future tense for the last sub-division, e.g. *à l'avenir, nous devrons développer ...* See Exam technique W5.
In your plan, use grammatical markers, e.g. *avant,* to remind yourself that you will be writing in the past tense at that point.

6 What we as individuals can do about it
- Write about cycling, walking and public transport.
- Write about recycling and saving energy.
- Write about new technology, e.g. electric or solar-powered cars.
- Mention what else you are going to do to protect the environment.

Suggested words for your plan: *transport, recyclage.*
Add a maximum of four words to this list.
Use *on peut / on doit / il est possible de* + infinitive.
Extend your answers by saying what you have done in the past to be environmentally friendly.
Use the future tense or *je vais* + infinitive to start the last sub-division. See Exam technique W8.
In your plan, use cognates if you can, e.g. *transport, énergie, nouvelle technologie, protection.* You can be sure of knowing what these words mean! See Exam technique W2.

7 If we should stop going on holiday by plane
- Say if you sometimes go on holiday by plane, where and how often.
- Say whether you agree that flying should be more expensive and why.
- Include how often you holiday in Britain, where you go and how you travel.
- Describe the effects of flying on the environment.

Add up to six words to your plan.
In French, words that express frequency, e.g. *quelquefois, souvent, rarement,* are placed immediately after the verb in the present tense.
You could expand on what you write for the first and third sub-divisions by referring to a specific holiday you have had.
Remember to check the total number of words you have used in your plan. It should be 40 or fewer.

Lien

Foundation sample assessment tasks for this Context can be found in the Foundation Book.

Exam technique – Speaking

S7 Ideas for practising

Treat each bullet point as a mini-task. Practise your answer to one bullet point at a time. Look at one word on your plan and say aloud all the things that the word is reminding you to say. Repeat the process for each word on your plan. Next, try to account for two words, then for three words, etc. Time your answer for one whole bullet point. Repeat the process for each bullet point. Record yourself if possible.

You can also practise with a partner. Together, work out the questions that your teacher might ask you in the exam and practise your answers to these questions in turn.

S8 Info about Interaction and Fluency

Interaction is about your ability to contribute to the conversation. To gain good marks, you will need to show initiative (see Exam technique S10).

Fluency is your ability to speak without hesitation. Try to speak with fluency but not too fast. If you are likely to be nervous when performing the task, practise it and practise it again. Time your whole response. Make a point of slowing down if you feel that you are speaking too fast. Practise with your plan in front of you so that you know what you are going to say next and therefore do not hesitate in the exam itself.

S9 Info about Communication, Range of language and Accuracy

The marks that you get for Communication are for getting the message over to the teacher who is examining you. The marks for Range of language are awarded if you have a good variety of vocabulary and grammatical structures in your responses. The marks that you get for Accuracy will be linked to how well you know and use the rules of French grammar and pronunciation. These three are closely linked because if you get the grammar wrong, it can change the meaning of your message. If this happens, you lose both Communication / Range of language, and Accuracy marks.

Grade booster

To reach grade B, you need to …

- Give a good amount of information for every question and answer generally without hesitation, e.g. for bullet point 1 of the sample Controlled Assessment on page 126, give a lot of details about your town and your house: size, type of town, number of rooms in your home, details about the garage and garden.
- Include some complex structures and a variety of tenses which clearly communicate, e.g. for bullet point 4, show that you know a range of tenses. Use present, perfect and imperfect here.

To reach grade A, you need to …

- Develop nearly all your answers and sometimes show initiative, e.g. for bullet point 5, show initiative by developing the last sub-division, comparing what you did last weekend with what others did. You could also extend your answer to the first sub-division of bullet point 5 by saying what you think of doing different chores.
- Use a good range of vocabulary and your pronunciation must generally be good, e.g. for bullet point 2, use different words to describe different people. Vary your vocabulary, including verbs and phrases. Do not overuse *est* + adjective.

To reach grade A*, you need to …

- Present your ideas and points of view with confidence and sustain a conversation at a reasonable speed, e.g. for bullet point 3, give your opinion of your room, say whether you share a room (or not), what is in your room and what you do in your room. Explain your points of view by saying why (not) each time.
- Use a variety of verb tenses and other structures with accuracy, e.g. for bullet point 6, by following the detailed plan, you will show that you can use the present, the future and the conditional. Focus on accuracy.

Exam technique – Writing

W7 Marking of the tasks

AQA examiners will mark your work. A senior examiner will check the work of the examiner. This is to ensure that candidates are given the correct mark for their work.

The pair of Writing tasks count for 30% of the whole GCSE French exam, so each of the Writing tasks is worth 15%. Your work will be marked in terms of Content, Range of language, and Accuracy. Each task will be marked out of 30 marks. Fifteen of these marks are for Content, 10 are for Range of language and 5 are for Accuracy.

W8 Info about Range of language

If you are aiming at grade A, you must use a wide variety of vocabulary and structures. You must also include more complex sentences and use different verb tenses (see Exam technique W5).

W9 Info about Content

You will be awarded marks under the heading 'Content' for:

■ the amount of relevant information you give
■ expressing and explaining ideas and points of view
■ developing the points you make
■ producing a well-structured piece of work.

Refer to Exam technique W6 for the number of words you should aim to write.

Grade booster

To reach grade B, you need to ...

■ Use a good variety of vocabulary and structures, e.g. for bullet point 3 of the sample Controlled Assessment on page 128, use a variety of ways to say what could or should be done, such as *on devrait / on pourrait / il faudrait / il serait possible / il est essentiel de ...*
■ Convey a lot of information clearly, e.g. for bullet point 1, give many details about your town: location, size, places to visit, suburbs, industry, etc.

To reach grade A, you need to ...

■ Express and explain ideas and points of view with clarity, e.g. for bullet point 2, explain the problems and take a pro-environment stance. With regard to public parks / green spaces, give your opinion and justify it.
■ Develop the majority of the points you make, while being accurate, particularly with regard to verb and tense formations, e.g. for bullet point 6, use past, present and future tenses in your answer. Focus on accuracy.

To reach grade A*, you need to ...

■ Give a fully relevant and detailed response to the task which is largely accurate, e.g. for bullet point 7, write at least 50 words to cover all the sub-divisions that are suggested for this bullet point.
■ Handle complex sentences with confidence, making very few errors in the process, e.g. for bullet point 5, include different tenses in your answer: what the weather used to be like (imperfect), how it has changed (perfect), what it is like now (present), and the need to develop renewable forms of energy (future).

7.1 F   La vie au collège

1 **V** Match the French with the English.

1	la rentrée	a	a study period (when one of your teachers is away)
2	une heure d'étude	b	a personal diary
3	un carnet de notes	c	a school book
4	une carte de sortie	d	a school diary (booklet with your marks / grades)
5	un journal intime	e	an exit pass (to leave the school premises)
6	un livre scolaire	f	the first day of the school year
7	le professeur principal	g	the form tutor

Manon, élève de sixième, écrit dans son journal intime

Mon journal intime

Lundi

Aujourd'hui, c'était la rentrée. Ma mère m'a accompagnée au collège et je n'ai pas aimé ça. Je ne suis plus un bébé! À huit heures, j'ai rencontré mon professeur principal et il est plutôt sévère. Puis, on a eu cours jusqu'à midi. Je suis allée à la cantine. Ce qu'on mange à la cantine, ce n'est jamais bon.

Mardi

Aujourd'hui, j'ai eu dessin, anglais et informatique. J'adore ces matières. J'ai aussi retrouvé trois de mes copines de l'école primaire qui sont aussi en sixième mais dans des classes différentes. On a beaucoup parlé à la récréation. Hier, elles n'étaient pas contentes non plus, mais aujourd'hui, ça va mieux.

Mercredi

Il n'y a pas de cours cet après-midi. Ça, c'est bien. Je dois sortir avec ma mère pour aller acheter mes livres scolaires et mes cahiers. Plus tard, Hélène va venir chez moi. C'est une nouvelle copine qui est dans ma classe. On va faire nos devoirs ensemble.

Jeudi

On n'a commencé les cours qu'à dix heures. C'est bien parce que je suis restée au lit jusqu'à neuf heures. Cet après-midi, entre trois heures et quatre heures, on a eu une heure d'étude parce qu'il n'y avait pas de professeur de sciences. Il était absent. L'étude, c'est une salle de classe où on fait ses devoirs si un professeur est absent.

Vendredi

J'ai trouvé la semaine plutôt longue. Je suis assez fatiguée parce qu'aujourd'hui, j'ai eu cours de huit heures à midi et de deux heures à cinq heures. Heureusement, c'est le week-end maintenant.

2a 📖🎧 Read Manon's diary and decide whether these statements are true (T), false (F) or not mentioned in the text (?).

1 Manon did not enjoy her first day in secondary school.
2 She is in the same class as three of her primary school friends.
3 She only had one lesson on Wednesday afternoon.
4 She has to buy her own school books.
5 Hélène likes the same subjects as Manon.
6 On Thursday, Manon did her homework at lunch time.
7 She likes French and geography.
8 She was tired on Friday as she had a lot of homework to complete during the week.

2b 📖🎧 Read Manon's diary again. Which three of these aspects of school life does Manon not like?

1 the canteen
2 being taken to school by her mother
3 English lessons
4 starting lessons at 10 a.m.
5 Wednesday afternoons
6 her Friday timetable

3a 🎧 Zoë has just come back from her exchange visit to a school in the UK. Listen to her talking to her friend Hélène about her day at the comprehensive school. Decide whether the statements below are true (**T**), false (**F**) or not mentioned (**?**).

1 Zoë and Hélène would happily wear a school uniform.

2 There is no morning registration in French schools.

3 Zoë did not like the assembly she attended.

4 In the UK school, students have five lessons a day.

5 French students have to buy their own school equipment.

6 French students have more homework than British students.

3b 🎧 Listen again and answer these questions in English.

1 What school uniform do students in the UK school wear?

2 What happens before lessons in the UK school?

3 How many lessons do students have every afternoon?

4 At what time do lessons start and finish?

5 What equipment is not given to students in French schools?

6 What is likely to cause French students to have to repeat a school year?

4 **G** Transform these positive sentences into negative ones as indicated in brackets. The ones marked * have an extra factor to think about, as you will need to use *de / d'*.

Exemple: Elle achète des livres scolaires. (**never**)*
Elle n'achète jamais de livres scolaires.

1 Je prends un repas à la cantine. (**never**)*
2 Manon a trois amis dans sa classe. (**only**)
3 Je suis contente de mes notes. (**not**)
4 Hélène a des devoirs à faire. (**no more**)*
5 Elle a une carte de sortie. (**not**)*
6 Elle a une heure d'étude. (**never**)*

> **Using different negatives** *Grammaire*
>
> When you change a sentence from positive to negative, you must change *un, une* or *des* to *de* or *d'*. You must remember to do this with all of the negative forms, e.g. *ne … plus, ne … jamais* as well as *ne … pas*.
>
> *J'ai des devoirs. → Je n'ai plus de devoirs.* (I haven't got any more homework.)
>
> Also learn about linking phrases with *qui*. *See page 144* ➡
>
> *page 188*

5 🗨 Work with a partner to compare life in your school to life in a typical French school. Partner A plays the part of an interviewer from a French school. Partner B talks about life in a British school and makes comparisons. Below are some suggested questions.

■ Tu vas au collège quels jours de la semaine?
■ À quelle heure est-ce que tu es arrivé(e) au collège ce matin?
■ La pause-déjeuner dure combien de temps?
■ À quelle heure est-ce que tu vas quitter le collège cet après-midi?
■ Est-ce que tu as acheté tes livres scolaires?
■ Tu aimes ton uniforme?
■ Est-ce que tu aimes ton collège?

> **Making longer sentences** *Stratégie 5*
>
> When speaking, try to make your sentences longer by joining up simpler ones.
>
> Useful words are *et* (and), *mais* (but), *parce que* (because) and *qui* (who).
>
> Think of some simple sentences about your school and join them together.

> **Lien**
>
> 7.1 Groundwork is available in the Foundation book.

7.1 H   Des écoles différentes

L'école: c'est mieux en France ou en Grande-Bretagne?

Il y a bien sûr des différences entre les collèges français et leurs équivalents britanniques.

En France, la journée scolaire commence plus tôt qu'en Grande-Bretagne (à huit heures) et peut continuer jusqu'à dix-sept heures. La pause-déjeuner est plus longue en France et peut durer deux heures, ce qui explique que pas mal d'élèves rentrent chez eux à midi. Il y a donc moins de demi-pensionnaires français.

Les vacances sont plus longues en France. Les élèves ont une semaine fin octobre, deux semaines à Noël, une semaine en février, deux semaines en avril et deux mois en été.

Comme la pause-déjeuner est longue, il y a toutes sortes d'activités sportives et artistiques organisées pour occuper les élèves. Cependant, après les cours, il n'y en a pas. Tout le monde rentre chez soi.

Dans la plupart des écoles secondaires britanniques, les élèves portent un uniforme scolaire, ce qui n'est pas le cas en France. Les directeurs d'école sont contre l'idée d'imposer

aux familles des dépenses inutiles. L'éducation est gratuite et c'est un principe important dans la société française.

En France, si on n'a pas fait assez de progrès, on redouble l'année, c'est-à-dire qu'on refait exactement la même chose l'année scolaire suivante. Les élèves détestent ça parce que leurs copains sont alors dans une autre classe. De plus, ceux qui redoublent sont dans une classe avec de plus jeunes élèves et trouvent ça un peu humiliant. Ces élèves dont nous parlons doivent refaire le même programme scolaire ce qui est aussi plutôt ennuyeux. En Grande-Bretagne, personne ne redouble.

1a 📖🎧 Read the text and put these headings into the order in which the topics are mentioned.

1 Holidays
2 The repetition of a school year
3 The length of the school day
4 School uniform
5 Going home for lunch
6 Extra-curricular activities

1b 📖🎧 Read the text again and answer these questions in English.

1 In which country is the school day longer? What about the holidays?
2 Why do many pupils go home for lunch in France?
3 Why don't pupils wear a school uniform in France?
4 Identify two things that French pupils dislike about repeating a school year.

2a 🎧 Listen to Section A, in which Mani Mustafa talks about his school in Senegal. Which three statements are correct?

1 There weren't enough books.
2 The classes were small.
3 He didn't fail his exams.
4 He didn't have to repeat a year.
5 He didn't like his teachers.

2b 🎧 Listen to Section B. Which three statements are true, according to Mani?

1 Having good teachers was more important than having good equipment.
2 At primary school he used to eat in the canteen.
3 As a secondary school pupil, he was a boarder.
4 The school rules were quite different from the rules in France.
5 He is going to raise funds for the school in Senegal.

3 Ⓖ Select the correct word to complete each sentence.

1 J'ai écrit une rédaction **que / qui / où** s'appelait «Les collèges écossais».
2 La rédaction **que / qui / où** j'ai écrite était excellente.
3 Je suis allé à un cours **que / qui / où** était nul.
4 L'uniforme **que / qui / où** je porte est super.
5 Je suis allé à la cantine, **que / qui / où** j'ai mangé.
6 Le repas **que / qui / où** j'ai mangé était délicieux.

4 ✏ Write a short article that explains at least three differences between French and British schools. Include your own opinion and give reasons for your opinion.

Au collège en France, …	
Par contre, en Grande-Bretagne, …	
À mon avis, / je pense que / je crois que / je trouve que …	parce que …
On doit / il faut / on est obligés de …	
Il est interdit de / on n'a pas le droit de …	

Inferences and deductions

In listening and reading tasks, sometimes the answer to a question will not be specifically stated in the text. You will have to identify the implied meaning of what is being said in order to get to the answer required. For example:

Oui, bien sûr, je fais mes devoirs mais j'aime être libre le week-end pour faire ce que je veux.

Question: When does he do his homework?

Answer: During the week.

The answer is not specifically stated in the text, but by implication, if he does his homework (*je fais mes devoirs*) but doesn't do it at the weekend because he likes being free to do what he wants (*mais j'aime être libre le week-end pour faire ce que je veux*), then he must do his homework during the week.

Relative pronouns: *qui, que* and *où*

qui means 'who', 'which' or 'that'. It is usually followed by a verb.

J'ai un prof d'anglais qui s'appelle Monsieur Smith. – I have an English teacher who is called Mr Smith.

que (qu') means 'which' or 'that'. It is usually followed by a person or a thing.

C'est une matière que j'aime bien. – It's a subject that I like.

où means 'where'.

Le café où on va d'habitude est près de chez moi. – The café where we usually go is near my home.

Don't mix it up with *ou* with no accent (same pronunciation), which means 'or'.

Also learn how to recognise the relative pronoun *dont*.

See page 145 ➡

7.2 F Problèmes scolaires

1 **V** Sort these sentences into three groups: school work, school rules or facilities.

Les examens sont difficiles.

Il faut arriver en cours à l'heure.

Il faut porter un uniforme.

Il y a trop de devoirs.

Il n'y a pas assez d'ordinateurs.

Les bâtiments sont vieux.

Problèmes scolaires – Tante Hélène répond

Problèmes

1 Quand je vois des garçons ou des filles de ma classe qui portent des vêtements très chics, je suis jalouse. Moi aussi, je voudrais porter des vêtements comme ça, mais ils sont trop chers! *Pascale, 14 ans*

2 Beaucoup de cours sont barbants et je ne les aime pas. Je n'aime pas beaucoup les profs non plus. Si on leur demande de faire des activités amusantes, ils se fâchent. Moi, je ne fais pas assez attention en classe, donc j'ai de mauvaises notes! *Laurence, 15 ans*

3 Comme il n'y a pas assez d'ordinateurs dans notre collège, une copine a demandé à notre prof principal s'il était possible d'utiliser son ordinateur portable. Il lui a dit que non. On n'a pas le droit de s'en servir en cours. *Sanja, 16 ans*

4 On n'a pas le droit de porter de bijoux au collège et je trouve ça vraiment bête. Si je porte mon bracelet ou ma boucle d'oreille, quel problème est-ce que ça pose? *Marc, 14 ans*

Réponses

A Je trouve que les profs devraient te permettre de l'utiliser. Mais tu peux quand même t'en servir pour faire tes devoirs et pour réviser.

B Je sais que c'est bien de porter des vêtements à la mode, mais la mode, ce n'est pas vraiment important. Il ne faut pas être jalouse, ça ne change rien.

C Aucun problème. Je ne comprends pas pourquoi ils interdisent d'en porter. Je te recommande cependant de respecter le règlement. Les bijoux, ce n'est pas très important.

D Je comprends, c'est difficile et quelquefois ennuyeux, mais il faut faire un effort. C'est ton avenir qui en dépend. Je suppose que plus tard, tu voudrais un travail intéressant? Penses-y, ça va te motiver.

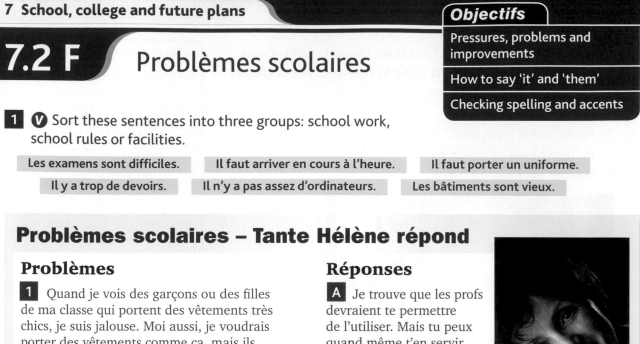

2a Read the text and match the students' problems (1–4) with Tante Hélène's replies (A–D).

2b Read the text again. Which three sentences are correct?

1 Tante Hélène says that laptops are not as good as school computers.
2 Fashion is an issue for Pascale.
3 Tante Hélène suggests thinking of a future career as a way to get more motivated.
4 Not being allowed to wear jewellery bothers Marc.
5 There is excellent IT provision in Sanja's school.

3a 🎧 📹 Watch the video and / or listen to Section A of the conversation. The French Education minister is visiting a London comprehensive school, where he interviews a brother and sister. Their family moved from France a few years earlier and they are now fully integrated into British school life. Answer the questions in English.

1 What are the **two** advantages of wearing a school uniform, according to Justine?

2 What does she not like about her uniform?

3 Which three rules does she not agree with?

3b 🎧 📹 Watch the video and / or listen to Section B. Answer the questions in English.

1 How much homework does Romain get each week?

2 How long does he take to complete it?

3 What does he complain about?

4 How does the minister conclude the interview?

4 🄶 Match these questions with the correct answers.

1 Tu portes ton uniforme en voyage scolaire?

2 Tu fais tes devoirs au collège?

3 Tu aimes le chewing-gum?

4 Tu connais mon professeur principal?

5 Tu as acheté ton ordinateur récemment?

a Non, je ne l'ai jamais rencontré.

b Non, je le mets seulement au collège.

c On me l'a donné pour mon anniversaire.

d Non, je les fais chez moi.

e Non, je ne l'aime pas.

> **How to say 'it' and 'them'** *Grammaire page 179*
>
> The French words *le, la, l', les* (meaning 'the') have a different meaning when you see them immediately before a verb. They are then called direct object pronouns.
>
> | him | *le, l'* | *Je le vois souvent.* |
> | her | *la, l'* | *Je la connais.* |
> | it | *le, la, l'* | *Le bus? Je le prends matin et soir.* |
> | them | *les* | *Nos professeurs? Oui, je les aime bien.* |
>
> Also learn about indirect object pronouns. *See page 144* ➡

5 ✏ Write an article about school pressures and problems, based on your school or an imaginary school. Don't forget to give your opinions and offer possible solutions wherever you can. Include your views on:

■ school uniform   ■ school rules   ■ homework.

Je pense que / qu'	certains cours sont barbants.
À mon avis,	il y a trop de devoirs.
Je trouve que / qu'	les examens sont (trop) difficiles.
On n'a pas le droit de / il est interdit de	porter des bijoux / fumer au collège.
Les bâtiments sont vieux / modernes.	
On n'a pas assez de / d'	ordinateurs
On a trop de / d'	tableaux interactifs.
Il faut / on doit	porter un uniforme scolaire.

> **Checking spelling and accents** *Stratégie 5*
>
> Although infinitives and past participles often sound the same, they need different endings, e.g. *on doit utiliser* (you have to use) but *j'ai utilisé* (I used).
>
> Make sure you know the difference between *ou* (or) and *où* (where) – they also sound the same.
>
> Check that you have remembered circumflexes (e.g. *hôpital*) and cedillas (e.g. *français*).

🔗 **Lien**

7.2 Groundwork is available in the Foundation book.

7.2 H Améliorer la vie scolaire

At the last meeting of the student council at the Collège Charlemagne, students discussed how to make the school a better place. Here is an extract from the minutes of the meeting.

Le Conseil des élèves

Le Conseil des élèves est arrivé aux conclusions suivantes lors de sa dernière réunion:

A Afin d'aider les élèves à faire leurs devoirs dans de bonnes conditions de travail, on devrait avoir une salle de classe réservée à cela, ouverte pendant une heure en fin de journée, après les cours. Cette classe aurait un professeur qui serait là pour faciliter la tâche de ceux qui trouvent leurs devoirs difficiles à faire.

B La pause-déjeuner est trop longue pour la majorité des élèves. Il devrait y avoir un cours supplémentaire pour aider les élèves qui ont des difficultés dans certaines matières. L'école offrirait une matière différente chaque jour de la semaine.

C L'école devrait employer des professeurs de langues qui ne sont pas enseignées dans notre collège actuellement, par exemple des professeurs de russe et de chinois. Les cours ne seraient pas obligatoires. Les élèves que ça intéresse pourraient y assister et donc avoir la possibilité d'apprendre d'autres langues.

D Notre collège devrait devenir partenaire d'une école du Tiers-Monde. Le côté éducatif pour nos élèves est évident. Nos élèves pourraient également aider cette école en lui envoyant des livres et d'autres choses dont elle a besoin. Le collège pourrait aussi, par exemple, organiser une fête payante à laquelle les parents d'élèves seraient invités. On pourrait envoyer l'argent à l'école partenaire.

E Récemment, un groupe de nos élèves a fait un échange scolaire avec une école anglaise. Ils ont remarqué des différences importantes entre nos écoles, par exemple leur uniforme scolaire, l'absence de redoublement, la durée courte de leur pause-déjeuner et aussi de leurs retenues. On devrait discuter de certaines de ces différences avec le directeur et lui recommander des changements qui contribueraient à améliorer la vie scolaire ici à Charlemagne.

1a 📖 🎧 Read the meeting minutes and match the five resolutions (A–E) with these headings.

1 Using another school's ideas
2 Extra optional subjects
3 Pairing up with a school in a developing country
4 Extra tuition
5 A homework room

1b 📖 🎧 Read the minutes again and answer the questions in English.

1 Why would there be a teacher in the homework room?
2 How would the extra tuition be organised?
3 What extra opportunities would there be for pupils who are keen on languages?
4 In what two ways would students help their partner school?
5 What are the four differences between the British and French schools that were noted during the last exchange visit?

2 🎧 Listen to the students discussing with their teacher what could be done to make their school better. Complete each statement with the correct person: Kemal (**K**), Marine (**M**), Frédérique (**F**) or Bruno (**B**).

> *Qu'est ce qu'on pourrait faire pour améliorer le collège?*

Section A

1 _____ thinks there is too much assessment.

2 _____ would prefer to see fewer books in schools.

3 _____ would like to be able to email completed homework to the teachers.

4 _____ would like students to be more involved in discussing their progress.

Section B

5 _____ suggests showing real school life on the website.

6 _____ suggests asking students to improve the website.

7 _____ thinks that students should each have their own laptop.

8 _____ thinks that examples of students' work should be displayed on the website.

3 🄶 Copy the sentences and fill in each gap with the correct conditional form of *pouvoir* or *devoir*, as indicated in brackets.

1 On _____ travailler dans le CDI. (**could**)

2 On _____ faire nos devoirs. (**should**)

3 Sascha _____ acheter un appareil numérique. (**should**)

4 Laure _____ acheter un ordinateur. (**could**)

5 Les profs _____ être plus stricts. (**could**)

6 Ils _____ préparer leurs cours. (**should**)

4 🗨 In groups, discuss how your school could be improved.

- Start by suggesting a problem or situation that could be improved.
- Give one possible way of improving it.
- Give another possible way of improving it.
- Say which is the best solution and why.

> *Qu'est-ce qu'on pourrait faire pour améliorer la vie scolaire?*

> *On pourrait aider les élèves à faire leurs devoirs plus facilement.*

Qu'est-ce qu'on pourrait faire pour améliorer la vie scolaire?	On pourrait …
	On devrait …
Quelle est la solution?	On devrait / pourrait … parce que …
Il y a d'autres possibilités?	Les élèves devraient / pourraient …
Quelle est la meilleure solution? Pourquoi?	Je pense que la première / la deuxième solution est meilleure parce que …

Grammaire — page 185

On pourrait, on devrait

Je pourrais (I could) and *on devrait* (you / we / they ought to) are examples of modal verbs in the conditional. They are always followed by another verb in the infinitive.

Don't forget that the conditional is formed from a future stem and imperfect endings.

***pouvoir* – to be able to / can**

je pourrais	*nous pourrions*
tu pourrais	*vous pourriez*
il / elle / on pourrait	*ils / elles pourraient*

The future stem of *devoir* (to have to / must) is *devr-*. Can you work out its conditional forms?

Also revise a range of question words. *See page 145* ➡

Stratégie 4

Giving extra information

If you want to do well in speaking and writing, you need to offer extra information and use different tenses.

Give examples of situations you have been involved in using *par exemple*, *quand* … and the perfect tense.

Suggest different possibilities using *peut-être* (perhaps) and the conditional.

Give your opinion using *à mon avis* or *je pense* / *trouve que* and justify it using *car* or *parce que* and the present tense.

7.3 F Continuer ses études ou non?

1 **V** Read the speech bubbles. Who …

1 will look for an apprenticeship?
2 will go to university?
3 is going to stay on at school?
4 will sit the bac (equivalent to A-levels)?
5 would like a work experience placement?
6 will not stay on at school?

a Je vais continuer mes études.

b Je chercherai un apprentissage.

c Je voudrais un placement en entreprise.

d Je passerai le bac.

e J'irai à l'université.

f Je ne continuerai pas mes études.

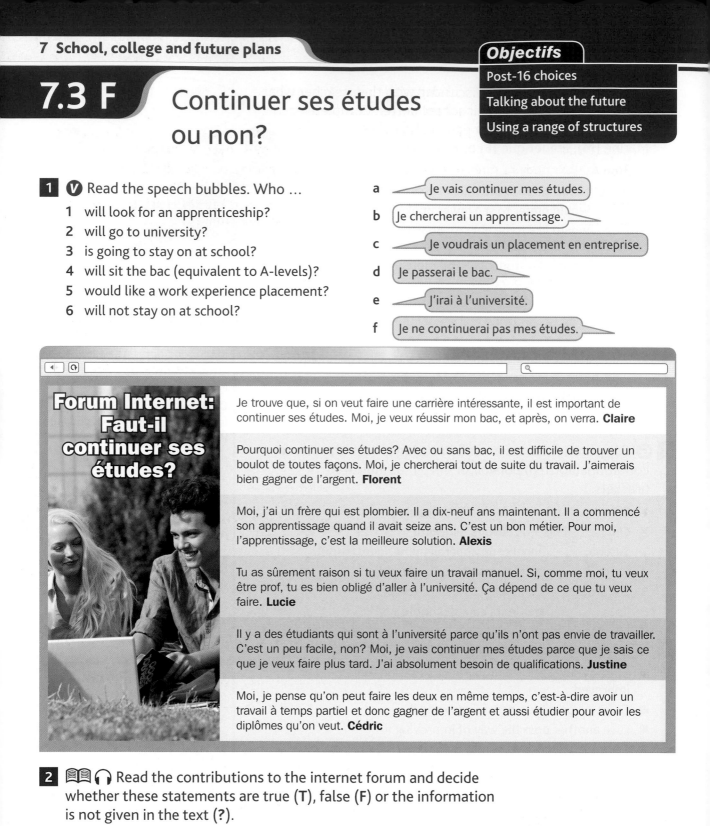

Forum Internet: Faut-il continuer ses études?

Je trouve que, si on veut faire une carrière intéressante, il est important de continuer ses études. Moi, je veux réussir mon bac, et après, on verra. **Claire**

Pourquoi continuer ses études? Avec ou sans bac, il est difficile de trouver un boulot de toutes façons. Moi, je chercherai tout de suite du travail. J'aimerais bien gagner de l'argent. **Florent**

Moi, j'ai un frère qui est plombier. Il a dix-neuf ans maintenant. Il a commencé son apprentissage quand il avait seize ans. C'est un bon métier. Pour moi, l'apprentissage, c'est la meilleure solution. **Alexis**

Tu as sûrement raison si tu veux faire un travail manuel. Si, comme moi, tu veux être prof, tu es bien obligé d'aller à l'université. Ça dépend de ce que tu veux faire. **Lucie**

Il y a des étudiants qui sont à l'université parce qu'ils n'ont pas envie de travailler. C'est un peu facile, non? Moi, je vais continuer mes études parce que je sais ce que je veux faire plus tard. J'ai absolument besoin de qualifications. **Justine**

Moi, je pense qu'on peut faire les deux en même temps, c'est-à-dire avoir un travail à temps partiel et donc gagner de l'argent et aussi étudier pour avoir les diplômes qu'on veut. **Cédric**

2 Read the contributions to the internet forum and decide whether these statements are true (**T**), false (**F**) or the information is not given in the text (**?**).

1 Claire is not sure what career she would like to have.
2 Florent wants to continue with his studies.
3 Alexis wants to be a plumber.
4 Lucie want to go to university.
5 Justine wants to start working as soon as possible.
6 Cédric will have a part-time job while continuing with his education.

Lien

7.3 Groundwork is available in the Foundation book.

3a 🎧 Listen to two 16-year-old students talking about what they intend to do next year. Which three statements below are true?

1 Romain's parents would like him to study for a 'bac littéraire'.
2 Romain likes studying foreign languages.
3 Although Romain has not quite made up his mind what he intends to study next year, Guillaume has done so.

4 Guillaume wants to stay on at school in order to study for a 'bac professionnel'.
5 Guillaume would not like to become an electrician, like his dad.
6 Guillaume is keen to secure a job for which he has been trained.

3b 🎧 Listen again and decide what Romain and Guillaume would like to do next year. Select your answers from the options below.

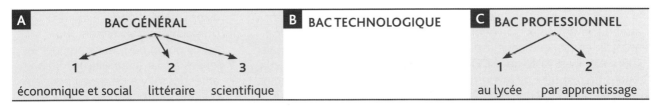

A BAC GÉNÉRAL	**B** BAC TECHNOLOGIQUE	**C** BAC PROFESSIONNEL
1 économique et social 2 littéraire 3 scientifique		1 au lycée 2 par apprentissage

4 **G** These sentences are all written in the future tense. Rewrite each of them using the immediate future (*aller* + infinitive).

Exemple: Je gagnerai de l'argent → <u>Je vais gagner</u> de l'argent.

1 Je ferai un bac général.
2 Il passera un bac professionnel.
3 Il apprendra un travail.
4 Je déciderai de mon avenir moi-même.
5 Qu'est-ce que tu choisiras?

5 💬 Work with a partner. Take turns to ask and answer questions about your partner's intentions regarding future studies. Answer fully, giving explanations and reasons whenever possible.

Qu'est-ce que tu vas étudier l'année prochaine?		
Tu voudrais aller à l'université?		
Pour étudier quoi?		
J'aimerais	étudier ...	parce que ...
Je voudrais	aller ...	
Je veux	devenir ...	
Je vais		

See page 144 ➡

Talking about the future

The future can be referred to in different ways.

■ Using the **immediate future tense**: use the present tense of *aller* followed by an infinitive to say 'what is going' to happen, e.g. *Je vais faire un apprentissage* – I am going to do an apprenticeship.

■ Using the **future tense**. The endings of the future tense are: *-ai, -as, -a, -ons, -ez, -ont*. For the stem of the verb, use the infinitive for *-er* and *-ir* verbs and the infinitive without the final *e* for *-re* verbs:

je mangerai   je finirai   j'attendrai

Note that, at Foundation, you are expected to recognise the future tense but do not need to use it yourself.

Also learn how to recognise some irregular future tense verbs.

Grammaire *page 185*

Qu'est-ce que tu vas étudier l'année prochaine?

Je vais étudier le français et l'espagnol parce que j'adore les langues étrangères. Et toi?

Using a range of structures

Show off your knowledge by using a wide range of ways of referring to future events.

■ the immediate future: *je vais étudier ...*
■ phrases such as *j'aimerais / je voudrais* (I would like), *je veux* (I want) *étudier...*
■ the future tense: *j'étudierai ...*

Stratégie 5

7.3 H L'orientation

Objectifs
Talking about post-16 studies
Si + imperfect, + conditional
Recognising word families

L'orientation après seize ans

Que faut-il conseiller aux jeunes? Continuer leurs études ou entrer dans le monde du travail?

Il y a bien sûr certains jeunes qui finissent leur scolarité dès que possible pour pouvoir suivre un apprentissage et donc entrer dans la vie active. Cependant, ce qui attend souvent ceux qui voudraient avoir un emploi immédiat est le chômage. Il est triste de voir des jeunes ne rien faire de la journée.

La plupart des jeunes continuent leurs études et préparent un bac général, technologique ou professionnel. Ceux qui veulent faire une carrière dans l'enseignement ou toute profession qui demande au moins une licence, doivent aller à l'université. Pour devenir dentiste, il faut cinq ans d'université – pour devenir médecin, il en faut sept. Les jeunes qui commencent aujourd'hui des études universitaires doivent être certains de leur choix car cela va leur coûter très cher!

En comparaison avec les jeunes Anglais, qui doivent payer neuf mille livres par an simplement pour avoir le droit d'assister à leurs cours, les jeunes Français ont de la chance, car chez eux, les cours sont beaucoup moins chers et même gratuits pour certains étudiants. Cependant, il ne faut pas oublier que la plupart des étudiants n'habitent pas une ville universitaire. Il leur faut donc payer un loyer et il y a aussi les frais de nourriture et de sorties. Si l'étudiant a des parents qui peuvent l'aider, ça va, sinon il faut emprunter de l'argent à la banque.

À la fin de leurs études universitaires, beaucoup d'étudiants ont des dettes. C'est aussi le moment où ils ont peut-être rencontré la personne avec qui ils veulent passer le reste de leur vie, mais ils n'ont pas assez d'argent pour se marier ou s'acheter une maison. Alors, est-ce qu'on devrait encourager les jeunes à aller à l'université? Bien entendu, s'il y a du travail pour eux quand ils auront fini leurs études. Malheureusement, le nombre de personnes titulaires d'une licence se trouvant actuellement au chômage est important. Alors, que faut-il conseiller aux jeunes?

1a 📖 Read the magazine article about post-16 choices and find in it phrases similar in meaning to these:

1 commencer un travail / une carrière
2 faire le métier de professeur
3 un examen universitaire
4 avoir la permission d'être en cours
5 le prix d'une chambre / d'un logement au mois
6 ce qu'il faut payer pour manger
7 le résultat quand on a emprunté de l'argent
8 bien sûr

1b 📖🎧 Read the article again and answer these questions in English.

1 The article starts and finishes with the same question. What does it mean?
2 According to the article, why is it not advisable to leave school at sixteen?
3 What warning is given to young people who want to go to university?
4 In what way is studying at university cheaper in France than it is in Britain?
5 How do French students often end up with a large debt?
6 What does the debt prevent some students from doing?
7 What makes the author of the article unsure that young people should be encouraged to go to university?

Recognising word families

You can often work out the meaning of new words from words you already know. Study the list below and guess the meaning of the second French word each time:

l'apprenti (the apprentice)
l'apprentissage

la profession (the profession)
professionnel

étudier (to study)
l'étudiant

une licence (a university degree)
un licencié

les conseils (advice)
conseiller

Stratégie 1a–1b

2a 🎧 Listen to a parents' evening interview and answer the questions in English.

Section A

1   Give four reasons why Julien's performance at school is not as good as it could be.

Section B

2   With regard to Julien's part-time job, what useful advice does the teacher give Monsieur and Madame Blanc?

Section C

3   What practical advice does the teacher give to encourage Julien to be more organised?

2b 🎧 Listen to the interview again and correct the errors in these statements.

Section A

1   Julien's teacher is confident that he will do well in his exams.

2   Julien's father helps him with his homework and explains to him what he does not understand.

Section B

3   After the summer holiday, Julien will be able to work full time.

4   Julien thinks that his friends are as important as his school work.

Section C

5   Monsieur and Madame Blanc should discuss Julien's future with his other teachers.

6   Julien's parents intend to follow some of his teacher's advice.

3 Ⓖ Copy these sentences and fill in each of the gaps with the correct tense of the verb in brackets.

1   S'il _____ ses devoirs (**faire**), je serais content.

2   Si vous lui expliquiez le problème, il _____. (**comprendre**)

3   Si j'_____ à votre place (**être**), je _____ une solution au problème. (**trouver**)

4   S'il _____ dur (**travailler**), il _____ son examen. (**réussir**)

5   S'il _____ (**échouer**), ce _____ vraiment dommage. (**être**)

4 🖉 Write about your own ambitions in terms of your education. Explain what you hope to achieve in the next two years and beyond. Mention university studies. Say what will happen if you cannot achieve your goals.

Si + imperfect, + conditional

In the listening task, you heard several examples of this grammatical construction:
Si + imperfect, + conditional, i.e. 'If X happened, Y would follow':

*S'il **faisait** plus attention en classe, il **ferait** plus de progrès.*
– If he paid more attention in class, he would make better progress.

Note that, in such sentences, the imperfect tense is used after *si*.

Also practise sentences that contain indirect object pronouns.
See page 145 ➡

Ⓖrammaire   *page 185*

L'année prochaine, je voudrais étudier …

J'espère passer …

À l'âge de dix-huit ans, j'aimerais …

Je veux devenir …

Si j'échoue, je …

School, college and future plans

1 Use *qui* to turn each pair of sentences into one sentence.

Exemple: J'étudie une matière. Elle est intéressante.

J'étudie une matière <u>qui est</u> intéressante.

1 Il y a des élèves. Ils m'énervent.

2 Il y a des matières. Elles sont difficiles.

3 Elle a une prof de maths. Elle explique bien.

4 Il y a des professeurs. Ils encouragent beaucoup leurs élèves.

5 Nous avons une pause-déjeuner. Elle dure une heure et demie.

6 J'ai compris l'exemple. Il est au tableau.

> **Linking phrases with *qui***
>
> ■ *Qui* (meaning 'who' or 'that') can refer to either people or objects, and is used to link phrases together.
>
> *Tu as un prof. Il est gentil.*
>
> *Tu as un prof qui est gentil.*
>
> You have a teacher who is kind.
>
> *Il y a un livre. Il est intéressant.*
>
> *Il y a un livre qui est intéressant.*
>
> There is a book that is interesting.
>
> ■ Remember you will score higher marks in Speaking and Writing if you use longer sentences that have linking words like *qui*.

Grammaire (page 180)

2 Choose the correct translation for each sentence, a or b.

1 Je ne lui réponds jamais.

  a I never answer him.

  b I never answer you.

2 Il te pose une question.

  a He is asking me a question.

  b He is asking you a question.

3 Est-ce que tu leur as demandé?

  a Did you ask them?

  b Did you ask her?

4 Mes parents m'ont acheté un dictionnaire.

  a My parents bought us a dictionary.

  b My parents bought me a dictionary.

5 Elle nous a dit qu'on ne travaillait pas assez.

  a She told them that we work enough.

  b She told us that we didn't work enough.

6 Le professeur vous donne de bonnes notes.

  a The teacher gives them good grades.

  b The teacher gives you good grades.

> **Indirect object pronouns**
>
> These are used to say 'to me', 'to you', etc. Like direct object pronouns, they come before the verb in French.
>
> ■ Singular: *me* (to me), *te* (to you), *lui* (to him / her / it).
>
> *Elle me donne un stylo.* – She gives a pen to me. (She gives me a pen.)
>
> ■ Plural: *nous* (to us), *vous* (to you), *leur* (to them).
>
> *Elle leur donne un livre.* – She gives a book to them. (She gives them a book.)

Grammaire (page 179)

3 What do these sentences mean? Translate them into English.

1 Demain, il fera beau.

2 En décembre, j'aurai seize ans.

3 On aura deux semaines de vacances à Noël.

4 Je serai dentiste à l'avenir.

5 Elle ira à l'université si c'est possible.

> **Irregular future tense verbs**
>
> There are no irregular endings in the future tense. Only some verb stems are irregular. Learn to recognise these verbs in the future tense:
>
> | | |
> |---|---|
> | *je ferai* | I will do |
> | *j'irai* | I will go |
> | *j'aurai* | I will have |
> | *je serai* | I will be |

Grammaire (page 185)

4 Translate the following sentences into English.

1. J'étudie les matières dont j'ai besoin.
2. Elle aime les élèves dont elle s'occupe.
3. Tu connais la fille dont je suis amoureux?
4. Il déteste le garçon dont la mère est prof de maths.
5. Ils vont passer les examens dont je t'ai parlé.
6. Il y a quelques résultats dont elle est fière.

Relative pronoun: *dont*

Dont is used to link phrases together. It is usually needed instead of *qui / que* when the verb in the second phrase is constructed with *de* (*avoir besoin de, s'occuper de, être fier de,* etc.). *Dont* can be translated by 'that' or 'of which', but in English these words can often be left out.

la note dont je suis fier – the grade (that) I am proud of / the grade of which I am proud

le prof dont j'ai besoin – the teacher (that) I need

Grammaire page 180

---

5 Select the correct word from the list to complete each question.

1. _____ livre choisit-il?
2. _____ matière préfères-tu?
3. _____ étudiez-vous le français?
4. _____ d'élèves y a-t-il dans ta classe?
5. _____ est la salle d'informatique?
6. _____ vas-tu passer l'examen?
7. _____ va réussir?
8. _____ tu vas faire ce soir?

Qui	Qu'est-ce que	Quel
Où	Quand	Combien
Quelle	Pourquoi	

Question words (revision)

Make sure you know the following words and use them to introduce questions.

combien? — how much? / how many?
où? — where?
pourquoi? — why?
quand? — when?
qu'est-ce que? — what?
qui? — who?
quel? — which? / what?

Remember that *quel* agrees with the noun it goes with.

masculine singular: *quel livre?* (which book?)
feminine singular: *quelle matière?* (which subject?)
masculine plural: *quels stylos?* (which pens?)
feminine plural: *quelles affaires?* (which things?)

Grammaire pages 188–189

---

6 Rewrite each of these sentences using the appropriate French pronoun, as indicated in brackets. Remember to place the pronoun in the correct position.

1. Elle a prêté de l'argent … (**to him**)
2. Ils ont envoyé une carte postale … (**to them**)
3. J'écris souvent … (**to her**)
4. Explique le problème … (**to them**)
5. Ils ont offert un nouveau portable … (**to me**)

Indirect object pronouns (revision)

Indirect object pronouns are: *me / m'* (to me), *te / t'* (to you), *lui* (to him / to her), *nous* (to us), *vous* (to you), *leur* (to them).

In French, they are placed before the verb:

*Je **lui** enverrai un mail.* – I'll send him / her an email.

However, when they are used with a verb in the perfect tense, they are placed before the part of *avoir / être*:

*Je **lui** ai écrit.* – I've written to him / her.

When they are used with an imperative, they are placed after the verb:

*Donnez-**nous** votre adresse.* – Give us your address.

Note the added hyphen between the verb and pronoun.

Grammaire page 179

School, college and future plans

Topic 7.1 Comparing schools

7.1 F La vie au collège ➡ *pages 132–133*

	accompagner	to accompany
l'	*appel (m)*	registration
l'	*assemblée (f)*	assembly
la	*cantine*	canteen
le	*carnet de notes*	record booklet for grades
la	*carte de sortie*	exit pass
la	*chemise*	shirt
le	*cours*	lesson
la	*cravate*	tie
les	*devoirs (m)*	homework
l'	*élève (m / f)*	pupil
	ensemble	together
	expliquer	to explain
	fatigué(e)	tired
l'	*heure d'étude (f)*	study period
le	*journal intime*	personal diary
le	*livre scolaire*	school book
la	*matière*	subject
le	*pantalon*	trousers
la	*pause-déjeuner*	lunch break
	porter	to wear
le	*professeur principal*	form tutor
le	*redoublement*	repeating a school year
	rencontrer	to meet
la	*rentrée*	first day of the school year
en	*sixième*	in Year 7

7.1 H Des écoles différentes ➡ *pages 134–135*

le	*car de ramassage*	school bus
	c'est-à-dire	that is to say
	collecter des fonds	to collect funds
	de plus	moreover
le / la	*demi-pensionnaire*	student who stays at school for lunch

la	*dépense*	expense
le	*directeur d'école*	head teacher (m)
la	*directrice d'école*	head teacher (f)
	doué(e)	gifted, clever
	échouer à	to fail
	équipé(e)	equipped
	humiliant(e)	humiliating
	interdit(e)	forbidden
	inutile	useless
la	*plupart de*	most (of)
	plutôt	rather
	redoubler	to repeat a school year
le	*règlement*	rules
	rentrer chez soi	to go home
	tôt	early
	travailleur(-euse)	hard-working

Topic 7.2 Addressing school pressures and problems

7.2 F Problèmes scolaires ➡ *pages 136–137*

	à la mode	in fashion
	avoir le droit de	to have the right to, to be allowed to
	barbant(e)	boring
	bête	stupid
la	*boucle d'oreille*	earring
	chic	smart
la	*couleur*	colour
	discipliné(e)	well-behaved
	faire attention à	to pay attention to
	interdit(e)	forbidden
	jaloux(-ouse)	jealous
	motiver	to motivate
l'	*ordinateur portable (m)*	laptop
	pauvre	poor
le	*point de vue*	viewpoint
la	*règle*	rule

	riche	rich
les	vêtements (m)	clothes
le	voyage scolaire	school trip

7.2 H Améliorer la vie scolaire ➡ pages 138–139

	afin de	so as to
	améliorer	to improve
l'	appareil numérique (m)	digital camera
	assistera	to be present at, to attend
le	chinois	Chinese
la	connaissance	knowledge
	court(e)	short
la	durée	duration
	enseigner	to teach
	faire des recherches	to do research
	mettre à jour	to update
	obligatoire	compulsory
	parfait(e)	perfect
le	redoublement	repeating a school year
	remarquer	to notice
la	retenue	detention
la	réunion	meeting
le	russe	Russian
le	sujet	subject, topic
	supplémentaire	extra
la	tâche	task
le	Tiers-Monde	developing world

Topic 7.3 Present and future studies

7.3 F Continuer ses études ou non?
➡ pages 140–141

	à l'avenir	in future
	à temps partiel	part time
	apprendre	to learn
l'	apprentissage (m)	apprenticeship
	au chômage	unemployed
	avoir envie de	to feel like, to want
le	bac	exam equivalent to A-levels

le	bac général / professionnel / technologique	the three main options for le bac
le	bac économique et social / littéraire / scientifique	the three choices within le bac général
	chercher	to look for
le	diplôme	diploma
les	études (f)	studies
l'	entreprise (f)	company
	gagner	to earn
le	lycée	secondary school (for 15 to 18 year olds)
le	métier	job, profession
	passer un examen	to sit an exam
le / la	plombier / plombière	plumber
	réussir un examen	to pass an exam
le	travail	job, profession
l'	université (f)	university
la	voie	path

7.3 H L'orientation ➡ pages 142–143

à	temps plein	full time
	bien entendu	of course
la	connaissance	knowledge
	conseiller	to advise
la	dette	debt
le	doute	doubt
	dur(e)	hard
	emprunter	to borrow
l'	enseignement (m)	teaching, education
	être en train de	to be in the process of
l'	explication (f)	explanation
la	faculté	university
les	frais (m)	expenses
la	licence	university degree
le / la	licencié(e)	university graduate
le	loyer	rent
	ne … aucun	not any, none
	promettre	to promise
	repasser un examen	to resit an exam

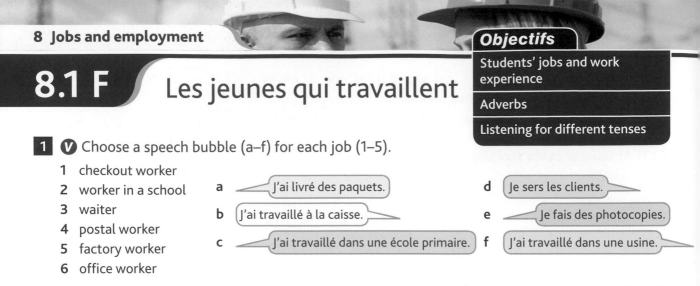

8.1 F Les jeunes qui travaillent

1 Ⓥ Choose a speech bubble (a–f) for each job (1–5).

1 checkout worker
2 worker in a school
3 waiter
4 postal worker
5 factory worker
6 office worker

a J'ai livré des paquets.
b J'ai travaillé à la caisse.
c J'ai travaillé dans une école primaire.
d Je sers les clients.
e Je fais des photocopies.
f J'ai travaillé dans une usine.

Quatre jeunes qui travaillent

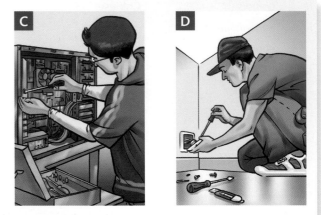

Pendant les vacances scolaires, Juliette travaille toujours comme caissière dans un magasin. Elle travaille bien et elle est assez bien payée, mais elle dit que c'est un peu ennuyeux.

Comme Jérôme fait un stage, il n'est pas payé. Il est dans l'entreprise d'un électricien au centre-ville. Il voudrait être électricien un jour parce qu'il veut gagner un bon salaire.

Xavier voudrait travailler comme mécanicien à la fin de ses études. Mais pour son stage, il n'a pas trouvé de place de mécanicien, alors il a travaillé comme technicien dans une entreprise d'informatique. Il a bien travaillé parce qu'il adore les ordinateurs.

Zoé travaille tous les samedis comme vendeuse chez un boucher. C'est mal payé mais malheureusement elle n'a pas pu trouver autre chose. Elle espère bientôt trouver quelque chose de plus intéressant et surtout de mieux payé.

2a 📖 🎧 Read the article and match each picture (A–D) with the correct name.

2b 📖 🎧 Complete each of these sentences with the name of the person being referred to.

1 The job _____ wants is well paid.
2 _____ always has the same holiday job.
3 _____ worked for an IT company.
4 _____ has a Saturday job.
5 _____ is doing this job because it's the only one she could get.

Lien

8.1 Groundwork is available in the Foundation book.

3 🎧 Listen to these people talking about their jobs in Sections A and B, and about their work experience in Sections C and D. Choose the correct answer to complete each sentence.

Section A

1 Nicolas works in **a bakery / a butcher's / an office**.
2 He works **every Sunday / every Saturday / in the holidays**.

Section B

3 Émilie **works in a shop / works in an office / delivers the post**.
4 She **writes / sends / opens** letters.

Section C

5 Mehmet **has done / is doing / is going to do** his work experience.
6 He found the work **easy / hard / boring**.

Section D

7 Dominique worked **with horses / for a firm / on a farm**.
8 One day she wants to **go on the stage / work in agriculture / work with race horses**.

4 Ⓖ Complete these sentences with an adverb, as indicated in brackets.

1 J'ai travaillé _____. (**quickly**)
2 _____, je n'ai pas pu trouver de travail. (**unfortunately**)
3 _____, j'ai gagné beaucoup d'argent. (**luckily**)
4 _____, je reste chez moi le dimanche. (**normally**)
5 J'étais _____ payé. (**well**)
6 Et moi, j'étais _____ payé! (**badly**)

5 🗨 Work with a partner. Prepare answers to the following questions, then take turns to play the part of a teacher carrying out a debrief with a pupil after work experience.

■ Où as-tu fait ton stage?
■ Qu'est-ce que tu as fait?
■ C'était comment?

■ Est-ce que tu as aussi un petit job / un emploi le soir ou le week-end?
■ Est-ce que tu voudrais un emploi permanent comme ça plus tard?

Pour mon stage, j'ai travaillé	dans un bureau / dans un magasin / dans une usine / dans une école.
Le (samedi), je travaille	
Je fais / J'ai fait	des photocopies.
Je sers / J'ai servi	les clients.
C'est / C'était	barbant / dur / fatigant / pas mal / amusant parce que ...
J'ai trouvé le travail	
Un jour, je voudrais travailler	dans un bureau / ...

Stratégie 3

Listening for different tenses

Sometimes a listening passage has a section in the present tense and another in the perfect tense. Listen for auxiliaries (*avoir / être*) and past participles (*sorti, travaillé*). This tells you that the section is in the past tense.

Which section is in the present / past tense here?

Grammaire — *page 177*

Adverbs

French adverbs are usually formed by adding *-ment* (which is the equivalent of the English ending '-ly') to the feminine form of the adjective.

Normalement, heureusement, malheureusement, facilement have been used in either the reading or the listening activities on these pages. What do you think they mean?

Many adverbs are irregular including: *vite* (quickly), *bien* (well), *mal* (badly).

Also learn to recognise and understand verbs in the passive form:

Il est bien payé. He is well paid.
See page 160 ➡

Où as-tu fait ton stage?

Dans un bureau, près de chez moi.

C'était comment?

C'était barbant. J'ai fait des photocopies toute la journée!

8.1 H Comment gagner de l'argent

Les jeunes Français aiment gagner de l'argent!

Bien qu'il y ait des jeunes qui ont un travail à temps partiel pendant les vacances ou même pendant l'année scolaire, ce n'est pourtant pas la majorité. De nos jours, on ne trouve pas un travail facilement. Ceux qui ont un petit boulot travaillent à la caisse des supermarchés ou dans un restaurant, un café ou un hôtel. Le job le plus populaire, c'est de faire du baby-sitting.

Quand on leur demande pourquoi ils ont un travail en plus de leurs études, plus de quatre-vingts pour cent des jeunes disent qu'ils veulent avoir plus d'argent de poche et donc la possibilité de sortir le soir ou de s'acheter les dernières baskets par exemple.

Cependant, le ministre de l'Éducation n'est pas d'accord. Il a publié un communiqué officiel en exprimant ce que pensent beaucoup de parents d'élèves:

«Je comprends bien que les jeunes d'aujourd'hui veuillent gagner de l'argent. On vit dans une société de consommation où les adolescents pensent qu'il est essentiel d'avoir les mêmes vêtements et jeux vidéo que leurs amis. Mais en travaillant le soir et le

Le job le plus populaire est le baby-sitting

week-end, leur travail scolaire va certainement en souffrir parce que les élèves seront fatigués et n'auront pas assez de temps pour faire leurs devoirs. On retrouvera cette fatigue le lendemain en cours. Ces élèves feraient bien de se rappeler qu'on ne fait son éducation qu'une fois et que leur avenir en dépend.

La recommandation gouvernementale est de ne pas travailler pendant le trimestre scolaire. Les grandes vacances sont suffisamment longues dans notre pays et les élèves qui souhaitent gagner de l'argent devraient s'en satisfaire. Je demande donc aux parents d'élèves d'encourager ces jeunes à se concentrer sur leurs activités scolaires. C'est ce qui compte le plus à leur âge.»

1a 📖 🎧 Read the article and decide whether the sentences are true (**T**), false (**F**) or not mentioned (**?**).

1 Most young people have a part-time job.
2 80% of young people who have a job do babysitting.
3 The usual reason for wanting to work is to earn more pocket money.
4 The Minister of Education understands the reasons why young people want to work.
5 He recommends that young people should not work at all.
6 He thinks that young people should only work as preparation for their chosen career.

1b 📖 🎧 Read the article again and answer the questions in English.

1 How do young people spend their pocket money? Note two ways that are mentioned.
2 According to the minister, when young people work, in what way does their school work suffer?
3 How does the minister then stress the importance of education?
4 What is the government's recommendation with regard to young people working?

Distinguishing -*ant* and -*ment*

Don't confuse words ending in -*ant* and -*ment*.

Words that end in -*ant* are present participles (see the grammar section page 186).

Words that end in -*ment* are adverbs (like English words ending in '-ly').

There are two examples of each in the article. Re-read it and find them.

Stratégie 1a–1b

2a 🎧 Listen to four students discussing the importance of work experience. Decide whether these statements are true (**T**), false (**F**) or the information is not given (**?**).

Section A

1 Guillaume thinks that work experience should be optional.

2 He thinks that work experience should be done in the summer holidays.

Section B

3 Amina's work experience was very successful.

4 She preferred being on work experience to being at school.

Section C

5 According to Julien, the timing of work experience is the real issue.

6 He thinks that every student should be made to do work experience.

Section D

7 Manon thinks that the nature of work experience placements is the key issue.

8 She was not happy with her own work experience.

2b 🎧 Listen again. Who might have said …?

1 I don't need a work experience placement.

2 I would like to do work experience in the Easter holiday.

3 I learnt a lot about the world of work.

4 If your work experience placement is not relevant to your choice of career, it is a waste of time.

3 **G** Copy the sentences and fill in each gap with *en* + the present participle of an appropriate verb from the list.

1 J'ai cherché du travail _____ dans le journal.

2 J'ai gagné 20 euros _____ dans un magasin.

3 Laurent s'est blessé _____ au travail.

4 J'ai gagné de l'expérience _____ un stage.

5 Je suis arrivée au bureau de bonne heure _____ l'autobus.

| prendre | travailler | aller | regarder | faire |

4 🖋 Write an account of your work experience. Include:

■ where you worked and what you did

■ how long you worked and when you started and finished

■ what you thought of your work experience and why

■ how your working day was compared to a school day

■ whether this is a job that you would like to do later.

> **Present participles**
>
> The French present participle ends in *-ant* ('-ing' in English). Take the *nous* form of the present tense, remove *-ons* and replace it with *-ant*.
>
> Use *en* + present participle when two actions happen together:
>
> *Il fait ses devoirs en écoutant de la musique.* – He does his homework while listening to music.
>
> *En travaillant le soir, je gagne de l'argent.* – By working in the evening, I earn money.
>
> Also learn about object pronouns with negatives. *See page 161* ➡
>
> **Grammaire** *page 186*

> **Make it up!**
>
> If you don't want to write about your own work experience for your exam, feel free to make it up. Remember that in the writing test it is the quality of your French that counts, not whether you're telling the truth!
>
> **Stratégie 4**

J'ai travaillé	dans un magasin / bureau / centre sportif.
J'ai	servi des clients / travaillé à la caisse.
Il a fallu que	je fasse le café / aille à la poste.
Ça m'a plu / C'était ennuyeux	parce que …
Je trouve que le travail était	barbant / dur / intéressant / fatigant / amusant / mal payé.
C'était plus / moins intéressant	qu'une journée au collège parce que …
Ce genre de travail	m'intéresse / ne m'intéresse pas pour l'avenir parce que …

8.2 F Au travail

1 **V** Unjumble these French words for jobs and translate them into English. Add accents where they are needed.

1 fire in mire
2 nice musi
3 rut face

4 i erase trec
5 i reli cop
6 teach run

7 chore bu
8 i can mince e

9 dr venue
10 free rim

Offres d'emploi

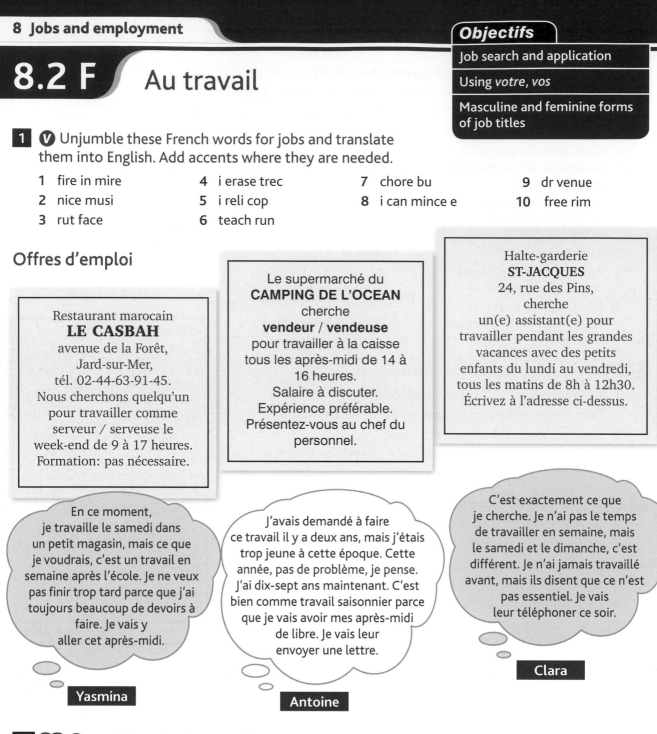

Restaurant marocain
LE CASBAH
avenue de la Forêt,
Jard-sur-Mer,
tél. 02-44-63-91-45.
Nous cherchons quelqu'un
pour travailler comme
serveur / serveuse le
week-end de 9 à 17 heures.
Formation: pas nécessaire.

Le supermarché du
CAMPING DE L'OCEAN
cherche
vendeur / vendeuse
pour travailler à la caisse
tous les après-midi de 14 à
16 heures.
Salaire à discuter.
Expérience préférable.
Présentez-vous au chef du
personnel.

Halte-garderie
ST-JACQUES
24, rue des Pins,
cherche
un(e) assistant(e) pour
travailler pendant les grandes
vacances avec des petits
enfants du lundi au vendredi,
tous les matins de 8h à 12h30.
Écrivez à l'adresse ci-dessus.

En ce moment,
je travaille le samedi dans
un petit magasin, mais ce que
je voudrais, c'est un travail en
semaine après l'école. Je ne veux
pas finir trop tard parce que j'ai
toujours beaucoup de devoirs à
faire. Je vais y
aller cet après-midi.

Yasmina

J'avais demandé à faire
ce travail il y a deux ans, mais j'étais
trop jeune à cette époque. Cette
année, pas de problème, je pense.
J'ai dix-sept ans maintenant. C'est
bien comme travail saisonnier parce
que je vais avoir mes après-midi
de libre. Je vais leur
envoyer une lettre.

Antoine

C'est exactement ce que
je cherche. Je n'ai pas le temps
de travailler en semaine, mais
le samedi et le dimanche, c'est
différent. Je n'ai jamais travaillé
avant, mais ils disent que ce n'est
pas essentiel. Je vais
leur téléphoner ce soir.

Clara

2a 📖 🎧 Read the job adverts and also what each person is thinking in the thought clouds underneath. Which three sentences are true?

1 No experience is necessary if you want to work at Le Casbah.
2 The job at St-Jacques crèche is for afternoons only.
3 To work at the supermarket, they'd rather you had experience.
4 Antoine worked at St-Jacques crèche two years ago.
5 Yasmina wants to finish work early so as to have enough time to do her homework.
6 Clara needs to send a letter of application.

2b 📖 🎧 Read the adverts and thought clouds again. Who is best suited to each job?

1 Restaurant Le Casbah
2 Halte-garderie St-Jacques
3 Supermarché Océan

3a 🎧 Listen to Yasmina's interview (Section A) and choose the correct answers.

1 Yasmina's family name is **Farik / Fariq / Feriq**.
2 She is **15 / 16 / 17** years old.
3 She is offered a salary of **10 / 11 / 12** euros an hour.
4 She can start work next **Monday / Tuesday / Wednesday**.

3b 🎧 Listen to Antoine's interview (Section B) and choose the correct answers.

1 Antoine's age is **16 / a problem / no longer a problem**.
2 He has **two brothers and one sister / two brothers and two sisters / one brother and two sisters**.
3 He is offered a salary of **100 / 120 / 200** euros a week.
4 He can start work on **1 July / 1 June / 1 August**.

4 **G** Transform these questions, using *vous* instead of *tu*.

1 Comment est ton travail?
2 Quel est ton salaire?
3 Tu habites chez tes parents?
4 Tu fais du baby-sitting pour tes parents?
5 Ta journée de travail commence à quelle heure?

5 🗨 Work with a partner to carry out an imaginary job interview. Partner A asks the questions and notes down Partner B's answers. Then swap roles, using different details. Ask and answer questions about the following:

- the type of job being applied for
- name and age, including spelling
- experience
- salary
- when you can start work.

C'est à propos du poste / de la place	d'assistant(e) / de vendeur(-euse).
J'ai de l'expérience. Je n'ai pas d'expérience.	
J'ai déjà travaillé	avec les enfants / dans un bureau.
Je gagne	dix / onze euros de l'heure / par semaine.
Je peux commencer	lundi / mardi, etc.

🔗 **Lien**

8.2 Groundwork is available in the Foundation book.

Stratégie 2b

Masculine and feminine forms of job titles

Most words for jobs have a masculine and a feminine version:

employé / employée

caissier / caissière

vendeur / vendeuse

acteur / actrice

However, *professeur* (teacher), and *médecin* (doctor) don't change. For more on this, see page 173.

Make a list of jobs with their male and female versions. Use a dictionary if you like.

Grammaire page 176–177

Using *votre*, *vos*

When addressing someone politely with *vous*, the verb forms are different from those used for *tu*:

Tu fais tes devoirs le soir? but *Vous faites vos devoirs le soir?*

Note that *tes devoirs* has become *vos devoirs*.

To say 'your' in French, *ton* (masculine singular), *ta* (feminine singular), *tes* (masculine and feminine plural) become *votre* (masculine <u>and</u> feminine singular) or *vos* (masculine and feminine plural) when used with the *vous* form of the verb.

Also learn to recognise the pluperfect tense. *See page 160* ➡

C'est à propos de quel poste?

C'est à propos du poste de vendeuse.

Vous avez de l'expérience?

Oui, j'ai déjà travaillé dans un petit magasin.

8.2 H   Le monde du travail

Métiers: les avantages et les inconvénients

A Nathalie Chevet a commencé sa carrière de mannequin à un très jeune âge. À huit ans, elle dansait déjà en public comme pom-pom girl avant le début des matchs de basket à Lyon, où elle a grandi. Actuellement, sa place est plutôt sur les podiums des plus grandes maisons de mode parisiennes. Mais ce métier a tout de même ses inconvénients. On peut être photographié à n'importe quel moment. Il faut aussi faire attention à ce qu'on mange de manière à rester mince. En plus, c'est un métier extrêmement fatigant. «Mais les avantages sont plus importants», explique-t-elle. «Après avoir voyagé partout dans le monde et rencontré des vedettes de film et de musique, je suis devenue une célébrité et on me voit souvent à la télé. Je dois aussi dire que ce n'est quand même pas mal payé.»

B Cédric Timplet vient de déménager à Bruxelles où il travaille pour l'Union européenne. Il avait déjà décidé de devenir interprète quand il était adolescent. En effet, après avoir passé un an en Allemagne, les langues étrangères sont petit à petit devenues ses matières préférées. Pour devenir interprète, il faut faire de longues études: trois ans d'université pour obtenir une licence de langues et deux ans d'école d'interprète. C'est un métier toutefois qui offre beaucoup d'avantages. Pour commencer, c'est assez bien payé et on est souvent en contact avec le public. De temps en temps, on a l'occasion de voyager et comme Cédric habite près de son bureau, il peut y aller à pied. Mais il y a aussi des inconvénients. On doit vraiment se concentrer sur ce qu'on fait et avoir suffisamment de confiance en soi pour faire une traduction simultanée. Les journées de travail sont quelquefois longues et on doit souvent se lever de très bonne heure.

1a 📖 Read the text and find in it phrases similar in meaning to these.

1 ce travail a quand même ses désavantages
2 pour ne pas grossir
3 le salaire n'est tout de même pas mauvais
4 a récemment changé de maison
5 avoir assez d'assurance pour traduire les choses instantanément
6 il faut se réveiller très tôt

Beware of *faux amis*!

Faux amis are words that look the same as or similar to English words, but that do not mean what you expect them to mean. Some examples are :

actuellement	at present
passer	to spend time
le bureau	office
la journée	day

Stratégie 1a–1b

1b 📖🎧 Read Section A. List three advantages and three disadvantages of Nathalie's job.

1c 📖🎧 Read Section B. List three advantages and three disadvantages of Cédric's job.

2a 🎧 Listen to Section A. Note an advantage and a disadvantage of each person's job: Élodie's father and Monsieur Collin.

2b 🎧 Listen to Section B and read the statements. Decide whether they apply to Daniel's mother (**D**), Malika (**M**) or to both of them (**D + M**).

1 She has just started her job.
2 She has / had a boring job.
3 Her salary is / was not good.
4 She regrets not having been given responsibilities.
5 She works / worked for a charity.
6 She gets / got on well with her colleagues.

3a Ⓖ Copy the sentences and fill in each gap with the correct verb, as indicated in brackets.

1 Je _____ _____ faire mon stage. (**have just**)
2 Je _____ _____ rentrer d'Afrique. (**have just**)
3 Mon père _____ _____ téléphoner. (**has just**)

3b Ⓖ Transform each pair of sentences into one sentence by linking them with *après avoir* or *après être*.

Exemple: Elle a téléphoné à son patron. Elle a perdu son emploi. →
           Après avoir téléphoné à son patron, elle a perdu
           son emploi.

1 Elle est devenue danseuse. Elle est souvent passée à la télé.
2 Il a appris l'allemand. Il est devenu interprète.
3 Il est allé en Namibie. Il a pratiqué la médecine.
4 Il a quitté son emploi d'ouvrier d'usine. Il est allé travailler dans un supermarché.

4 🖉 Describe the jobs of two members of your family, or of two other adults you know.

Mention:
- the kind of job they do
- what they think of their jobs
- where they work
- something that happened recently at their workplace
- one advantage and one disadvantage.

Mon père / ma mère est	employé(e) de banque / professeur.
Il / elle pense / trouve que son travail est	très / assez / plutôt … parce que …
Il / elle travaille	dans un hôpital / un lycée / un supermarché.
	comme médecin / secrétaire / ouvrier / ouvrière.
La semaine dernière, au travail	on a dû … / il a fallu … / il y a eu …
L'avantage, c'est que / qu'	c'est … / il y a … / on peut … / il faut …
L'inconvénient, c'est que / qu'	on doit … / il / elle n'aime pas … / ce n'est pas …

Venir de and après avoir / être — Grammaire page 182

- *Venir de* + infinitive, in the present tense, means 'to have just done something':
  Je viens de finir mon travail. – I have just finished my work.
- Use *après avoir / être* + past participle for perfect tense sentences where you want to give the order of events:
  Après avoir fini le travail, il est allé à la maison. – After finishing work, he went home

Don't forget the agreement with *être*:
  Après être rentrée du travail, elle a regardé la télé. – After returning home from work, she watched TV.

Also learn about uses of definite and indefinite articles.
See page 161 ➡

Checking grammar in your writing — Stratégie 4

Before handing in written work, always check your grammar carefully.

Have you remembered plural endings on nouns and adjectives? Do your verbs have the correct endings?

If a past participle ends in é, have you remembered the accent?

If you have used an *être* verb in the perfect tense, does the past participle agree?

8.3 F   La vie professionnelle

1 Ⓥ Choose the correct ending for each of the following sentences.

1 Je voudrais devenir acteur. Je travaillerai …
2 Je veux être professeur. Je travaillerai …
3 Je serai hôtesse de l'air. Je travaillerai …
4 Je deviendrai secrétaire. Je travaillerai …
5 Je veux être fermier. Je travaillerai …
6 J'ai décidé que je serai policier. Je travaillerai …

a avec des adolescents
b dans un théâtre
c en plein air
d dans le tourisme
e dans un bureau
f avec le public

Qu'est-ce que tu feras dans la vie?

A Fabrice ira passer une année aux États-Unis. Il travaillera peut-être dans le tourisme, comme guide. Comme ça, il apprendra l'anglais. À son avis, c'est essentiel pour la carrière qu'il veut faire.

Catherine a déjà commencé son boulot. Elle travaille comme hôtesse de l'air. C'est un travail très dur. Elle ne peut pas rentrer chez elle tous les soirs et doit très souvent dormir dans un hôtel à l'étranger.

B Tina ira à l'université l'année prochaine. Pour le moment, elle est toujours au lycée et elle espère réussir son bac au mois de juin. Après ça, elle dit qu'elle a l'intention de devenir ingénieur, parce qu'elle pense que c'est un travail plus varié que d'autres professions. Elle a déjà fait un stage chez un ingénieur et elle a bien aimé ça.

Roger a décidé de devenir plombier. Il a choisi ça parce qu'il trouve que c'est un métier très pratique. «Tout le monde a besoin d'un plombier de temps en temps» dit-il. «En plus, on peut gagner beaucoup d'argent si on travaille bien. J'ai passé six mois en Irlande, où j'ai fait un stage de plombier. C'était vraiment intéressant.»

2a 📖 🎧 Read Section A and decide whether Fabrice (**F**) or Catherine (**C**) is being referred to.

1 _____ va aller en Amérique.
2 _____ passe beaucoup de temps en avion.
3 _____ n'est pas souvent à la maison.
4 _____ pense que les langues sont importantes.

2b 📖 🎧 Read Section B and decide whether Tina (**T**) or Roger (**R**) is being referred to.

1 _____ veut être étudiante.
2 _____ a travaillé à l'étranger.
3 _____ aimerait avoir un travail pratique.
4 _____ n'a pas de travail en ce moment.
5 _____ sera ingénieur un jour.

⊂⊃⊂⊃ *Lien*

8.3 Groundwork is available in the Foundation book.

3a 🎧 Listen to Section A and write down the letter of the job (A–D) each person would like.

| A | B | C | D |

1 Nicolas ⚬
2 Mehmet ⚬
3 Olivier ⚬
4 Émilie ⚬

3b 🎧 Listen to Section B and match the beginnings and endings of the sentences.

1 Jérémy wants to be
2 He thinks it is
3 He likes the idea of working in
4 Charlotte wants to be
5 She thinks it is
6 She likes the idea of working in

a the open air.
b well paid.
c an office.
d a PE teacher.
e a programmer.
f not well paid.

4 **G** Copy the sentences and fill in each gap with the correct verb from the list.

1 Après les examens, Éric _____ dans un magasin.
2 Je _____ au bureau jusqu'à six heures.
3 Nicolas _____ au Canada.
4 Après le travail, je _____ le bus pour aller chez moi.
5 Mon père _____ à la maison à cinq heures.
6 Nous _____ nos devoirs avant le repas.
7 Vous _____ travailler du lundi au vendredi.
8 Tu _____ gagner beaucoup d'argent

| arrivera | ira | prendrai | ferons | devrez |

| travaillera | resterai | pourras |

5 🖊 Write an email to your French penfriend, explaining your future plans:

■ say what you will do as soon as you leave school
■ say what career you hope to follow later and why
■ mention advantages and disadvantages of this career.

Je travaillerai / je vais travailler	à l'étranger / en plein air. avec les enfants / adolescents. dans le tourisme / un bureau / l'informatique.	
Je voudrais travailler comme / être / devenir	professeur / infirmier(-ière) / chauffeur / caissier(-ière) / …	
J'ai choisi ce métier	parce que c'est	intéressant / bien payé / varié / …
Je ne veux pas être …		dur / ennuyeux / mal payé / …

Grammaire *page 185*

The future tense

You have already worked on aspects of the future tense in Topic 7. Here is a summary of what you should be able to do.

At Foundation level you don't need to use the future tense itself, but you have to be able to recognise it when someone uses it. Its endings are: *-ai, -as, -a, -ons, -ez, -ont*. There are no exceptions to this.

At Higher level you need to show that you can use the future tense.

To form the future tense of a regular **-er** or **-ir** verb, you need the infinitive form of the verb and then add the future tense endings, e.g. *je commencerai* (I will start), *ils finiront* (they will finish).

For regular *-re* verbs, delete the final e is from the infinitive before adding the endings, e.g. *il répondra* (he will reply),

Make sure you learn the verbs that are irregular in the future tense, e.g. *j'aurai* (I will have), *ils seront* (they will be).

Also practise expressing your hopes and intentions. *See page 160* ➡

Checking your written work **Stratégie 5**

Before handing in written work, always make sure you have checked it carefully. Think about accents (for example é on a past participle), plural endings on nouns (*les parents*) and correct verb endings (*ils regardent*).

8.3 H La vie commence

L'avenir des jeunes. Qui fait quoi?

Maëlle espère trouver un métier dans le monde du théâtre, peut-être comme actrice. Elle pense que si on travaille avec le public, la vie n'est jamais monotone ou ennuyeuse. «Comme actrice, on peut voyager et gagner beaucoup d'argent si on a du succès» dit-elle, mais la réalité est que la plupart des actrices sont au chômage.

Rajid a seize ans et s'est toujours intéressé à tous les aspects du droit. Il espère faire une carrière d'avocat. Les études universitaires durent quatre ans et sont suivies de dix-huit mois de formation professionnelle. À la fin de chaque année, il y a des examens difficiles auxquels, malheureusement, beaucoup de candidats échouent. Si on réussit, on passe dans l'année supérieure, sinon on doit refaire l'année que l'on n'a pas réussie. Ceux qui arrivent au bout deviennent avocat et reçoivent un très bon salaire. C'est l'ambition de Rajid. Il ne veut pas être homme au foyer ou avoir un travail qui ne l'intéresse pas.

Anjelica trouve qu'aller à l'université coûte trop cher. Elle a toujours aimé le plein air et son rêve est de devenir jardinière paysagiste. Bien qu'elle puisse faire un bac professionnel ou un bac techno, la formation professionnelle en apprentissage est la meilleure solution. Comme elle aimerait être indépendante le plus vite possible, elle pense à l'apprentissage qui lui permettra de se former en même temps que de gagner un peu d'argent. Anjelica, comme tout le monde, voudrait faire quelque chose qui lui plaît, donc, être femme de ménage ou femme au foyer, ça ne l'intéresse pas.

1a 📖 Read the article and find in it phrases similar in meaning to these.

1 pense avoir un boulot
2 sans emploi
3 pas mal d'étudiants ne réussissent pas
4 il faut redoubler si on a échoué
5 son ambition est d'être
6 quoiqu'elle ait la possibilité de
7 aimerait faire un métier qu'elle aime
8 ça ne lui dit rien

1b 📖 🎧 Read the first two paragraphs and decide who the statements are about. Write **M** (Maëlle) or **R** (Rajid) depending on who is being referred to.

1 _____ doesn't want a boring life.
2 _____ intends to study for four years.
3 _____ wants to have an interesting job.
4 _____ is unlikely to be working all the time.
5 _____ is a 'people person'.

1c 📖 🎧 Read about Anjelica and decide whether the statements are true (**T**), false (**F**) or not mentioned in the text (**?**).

1   Anjelica doesn't intend to go to university.
2   Her dream is to be a gardener in a different country.
3   She will do an apprenticeship as she can earn money while learning on the job.
4   She would like to find a job in a public park or garden.
5   If she fails to be a gardener, she will be a housewife.

2a 🎧 Listen to what Julien, Camille, Pauline and Alexandre say when asked if they intend to go into further education. Is their view of further education (**P**), negative (**N**) or both positive and negative (**P + N**)?

2b 🎧 Listen to each section (A–D) again and answer the questions in English.

1   What two reasons does Julien give to justify his answer?
2   What is Camille's main concern?
3   How has Pauline's older sister's recent experience helped her decide on her future?
4   Why is Alexandre against apprenticeships?

3 🄖 Copy the sentences and fill in the first gap in each of them with *celui, celle, ceux* or *celles*, then the second gap with *qui*, *que* or *qu'*.

1   _____ _____ elle a choisie est la meilleure.
2   Laquelle? _____ _____ est à Marseille.
3   _____ _____ il étudie sont intéressantes.
4   Quel boulot? _____ _____ je fais en ce moment.
5   Quel diplôme? _____ _____ permet de devenir technicien.
6   Quelles entreprises? _____ _____ offrent des places d'apprentis.

4 🗨 Work with a partner. Take turns to tell one another about your plans for the future.

- Say whether you intend to further your studies and why (not).
- Say that you want to go to university (or not). Give your reasons.
- Say what career you would like to have. Explain what training / qualifications are necessary.
- Say what your long-term professional ambitions are.
- Explain what you will do if you can't achieve your professional goals.

Qu'est-ce que tu veux faire comme métier?

J'aimerais devenir professeur de langues.

Grammaire page 180

Demonstrative pronouns + *qui / que*

Study the table below.

masculine sing.	*celui* (the one)
feminine sing.	*celle* (the one)
masculine plural	*ceux* (the ones)
feminine plural	*celles* (the ones)

When demonstrative pronouns *celui / celle / ceux / celles* are followed by *qui / que / qu'*, they mean 'the one(s) which / that' or 'those who', as in the reading text: *Ceux qui arrivent.*

When they are followed by *-ci*, they mean 'this one / these ones'. When they are followed by *-là*, they mean 'that one / those ones':

Tu préfères celui-ci ou celui-là? – Do you prefere this one or that one?

Remember that *qui* replaces the subject of the verb and *que / qu'* replaces the object of the verb.

Also learn about comparative and superlative adverbs.

See page 161 ➡

Using modal verbs

Stratégie 4

To help you get a high grade, show that you can use modal verbs (*pouvoir, devoir, vouloir*). They are usually followed by another verb in the infinitive, e.g. *Je voudrais devenir pilote.*

Jobs and employment

1 In the paragraph below, find phrases that mean the following:

1 are bought
2 are sent
3 are done
4 are served
5 is forgotten
6 are delivered
7 is prepared

> Je suis bien payée et mon assistante est super. Quand j'arrive au bureau, le café est préparé et les croissants sont achetés. Ensuite les clients sont servis rapidement, les photocopies sont faites et les paquets sont envoyés et sont livrés sans problème. Rien n'est oublié. C'est fantastique!

Understanding the passive

The passive is used to say what is done to someone or something. It is formed from *être* followed by a past participle.

active form	passive form
Elle écrit la lettre.	*La lettre est écrite.*
She writes the letter.	The letter is written.
Il prépare le thé.	*Le thé est préparé.*
He prepares tea.	Tea is prepared.

Grammaire page 186

2 Each of sentences 1–6 contains an example of the pluperfect tense. Each verb in the pluperfect is made up of two words – copy them. Then match four of these sentences with the pictures below.

1 Il savait que j'avais oublié le paquet.
2 Je pensais que tu n'avais pas trouvé de travail.
3 Elle était arrivée au bureau à huit heures ce matin-là.
4 Elle était très contente parce que j'avais préparé du bon café.
5 On m'a dit que tu n'avais pas aimé ton stage l'année dernière.
6 Elle m'a dit qu'elle avait travaillé dans un hôtel pendant trois ans.

The pluperfect tense

The pluperfect tense is used to refer to something further back in the past than the perfect or the imperfect. It is used to say what someone **had** done or **had been** doing. It is formed using the imperfect of *avoir* or *être* followed by a past participle:

*Je savais **qu'il avait travaillé** chez un boulanger.* – I knew he **had worked** in a bakery.

Grammaire page 184

A

B

C

D

3 What would these people say about their ambitions? Write a sentence in French that starts with *je* for each of them.

1 Arnaud hopes to work in an office.
2 Élodie intends to be an air hostess.
3 Thomas hopes to work as a postman.
4 Marine intends to be a musician.
5 Maxime does not intend to work in a restaurant.

Expressing hopes and intentions

To say what you hope / intend to do as a job, use *j'espère* (I hope) or *j'ai l'intention de* (I intend), followed by a verb in the infinitive:

J'espère être médecin. – I hope to be a doctor.

You can also make these two verbs negative if you wish:

je n'espère pas être …

je n'ai pas l'intention d'être …

Grammaire page 181

4 Transform these positive sentences into negative ones, then translate them into English.

1 Ils lui disent la vérité.
2 Je leur donne les certificats.
3 Le jardinier nous demande de l'aider.
4 La secrétaire vous permet de téléphoner.
5 On te demande la permission.
6 Le patron les paie bien.

> ### Object pronouns with negatives
> Think carefully about the word order when using negatives with verbs that take an object pronoun. In the present tense, the word order is: subject + *ne* + pronoun + verb + *pas*.
> *Il ne me regarde pas.* – He is not looking at me.
> *Je ne lui parle pas.* – I am not speaking to him / her.
>
> *Grammaire* page 188

5 Match the captions with the pictures. Then decide which nouns need an article and which ones don't. Copy the captions and fill in each gap with *un, une, le, la* or *les* if necessary.

1 C'est _____ jardinier qui cultive de bons légumes.
2 Je vais appeler _____ plombier pour qu'il répare la douche.
3 Il adore _____ animaux et il a trouvé un stage chez _____ vétérinaire.
4 Elle adorait _____ maths au lycée et maintenant elle est _____ comptable.
5 Ma mère aimait _____ dessin et elle est devenue _____ architecte.
6 _____ mode m'intéresse et je rêve d'être _____ mannequin!

> ### Use of definite and indefinite articles
> Remember not to use the indefinite article (*un, une*) when stating what someone's job is in French:
> *Ma sœur est architecte.* – My sister is an architect.
> It is needed in all other cases:
> *C'est un très bon professeur.* – He is a very good teacher.
> However, use the definite article (*le, la, les*) when talking about likes and dislikes, even though it is not needed in English.
>
> *Grammaire* page 174

A · B · C · D · E · F

6a Copy the sentences and fill in each gap with the correct French phrase, as indicated in brackets.

1 Ma mère finit le travail _____ mon père. (**later than,** *tard*)
2 Le vétérinaire le voit _____ avant. (**as often as,** *souvent*)
3 Je joue au football _____ toi. (**as well as,** *bien*)
4 Il travaille _____ Amina, sa collègue. (**less fast than,** *vite*)
5 Le médecin parle _____ l'infirmière. (**louder than,** *fort*)

6b Find in the email the French for these superlative phrases.

1 the best paid
2 the most often
3 the loudest
4 the fastest
5 the best

> ### Comparative and superlative adverbs
> Comparisons can be made using adverbs, as with adjectives:
> *Je travaille moins vite que le chef* – I work less fast than (don't work as fast as) the boss.
> *Elle parle aussi bien que sa sœur.* – She speaks as well as her sister.
> Note that the French for better (as an adverb) is *mieux*:
> *Il chante mieux que son frère.* – He sings better than his brother.
> **Superlative adverbs**
> Superlatives can be expressed with adverbs as well as with adjectives:
> *C'est moi qui travaille le moins vite.* – I'm the one who works the least fast.
> Note that the French for best (as an adverb) is *le mieux*:
> *Qui chante le mieux?* – Who sings the best?
>
> *Grammaire* page 177

Dans ma famille, tout le monde chante, mais c'est ma mère qui chante le mieux! Mon père et ma sœur sont tous les deux plombiers. C'est ma sœur qui travaille le plus vite et c'est elle qu'on appelle le plus souvent. Pourtant, c'est mon père qui est le mieux payé. C'est bizarre! C'est peut-être parce que c'est lui qui crie le plus fort …

(V) # Jobs and employment

Topic 8.1 Part-time and casual work

8.1 F Les jeunes qui travaillent ➡ pages 148–149

	autre chose	something else
	barbant)e)	boring
	bientôt	soon
le / la	client(e)	customer
	dur(e)	hard, difficult
	en bois	made of wood
l'	entreprise (f)	company
	faire un stage (en entreprise)	to do work experience
les	grandes vacances (f)	summer holidays
l'	informatique (f)	IT
	livrer	to deliver
le	meuble	piece of furniture
	mieux payé(e)	better paid
le	paquet	parcel
	pas tellement	not much
le	patron	boss
la	place	job, position
	quelque chose	something
	servir	to serve
un	peu	a little
la	vache	cow
	vite	quickly, fast

8.1 H Comment gagner de l'argent
➡ pages 150–151

	avoir de la chance	to be lucky
	avoir envie de	to want
	avoir raison	to be right
la	carrière	career
	ce qui / ce que	what (in a statement)
le / la	comptable	accountant
	de plus	moreover
	exprimer	to express

le	lendemain	next day
	lier	to link
	manquer	to miss
	passer un examen	to take an exam
la	perte de temps	waste of time
	pourtant	however
se	rappeler	to remember
	rien à voir avec	nothing to do with
	souhaiter	to wish
	souffrir	to suffer
le	travail à temps partiel	part-time work

Topic 8.2 The world of work

8.2 F Au travail ➡ pages 152–153

	à lundi	see you (on) Monday
la	caisse	cash desk, till
le	chef du personnel	personnel manager
	chez le boulanger	at the baker's
	comme	as
	demander	to ask
	discuter	to discuss
	écrire	to write
	en semaine	during the week
	envoyer	to send
la	formation	training
	jeune	young
	libre	free
	maintenant	now
	oublier	to forget
	parfait(e)	perfect
	quelqu'un	someone
	par semaine	per week
	téléphoner	to phone
	trop	too

8.2 H Le monde du travail ➡ *pages 154–155*

l'	*association caritative (f)*	charity
	aucun(e)	not any, none
la	*confiance en soi*	self-confidence
	déménager	to move house
	doué(e) en	good at
	embaucher	to recruit
	enrichissant(e)	enriching
l'	*inconvénient (m)*	disadvantage
l'	*interprète (m / f)*	interpreter
la	*langue étrangère*	foreign language
la	*licence*	university degree
le	*mannequin*	model
	non plus	neither
	offrir	to offer
l'	*ouvrier*	worker (m)
l'	*ouvrière*	worker (f)
s'	*occuper de*	to look after, to deal with
	toucher un salaire	to receive a salary
la	*traduction*	translation
	traduire	to translate

Topic 8.3 Looking to the future

8.3 F La vie professionnelle ➡ *pages 156–157*

	à l'étranger	abroad
	apprendre	to learn
	avoir l'intention de	to intend
le	*bac*	exam equivalent to A-levels
le	*boulot*	job
	choisir	to choose
	devenir	to become
	devoir	to have to, must
	dur(e)	hard
	en plein air	in the open air
	espérer	to hope
	gagner	to earn, to win
l'	*hôpital (m)*	hospital
l'	*ingénieur (m / f)*	engineer

l'	*informatique (f)*	IT
le	*lycée*	secondary school (for 15 to 18 year olds)
le	*métier*	profession
la	*pratique*	practice
le	*programmeur*	programmer
le	*stage*	work experience, placement
	varié(e)	varied

8.3 H La vie commence ➡ *pages 158–159*

	actuel(le)	present
l'	*apprenti(e)*	apprentice
l'	*apprentissage (m)*	apprenticeship
l'	*avocat(e)*	barrister, lawyer
	dépenser	to spend (money)
	échouer à	to fail
l'	*entreprise (f)*	company
l'	*entretien (m)*	(job) interview
les	*études universitaires (f)*	university studies
la	*femme de ménage*	cleaning lady
la	*formation professionnelle*	professional training
se	*former*	to train (for a job)
l'	*homme au foyer (m)*	house husband
le	*jardinier*	gardener (m)
la	*jardinière*	gardener (f)
	inquiéter	to worry
le / la	*licencié(e)*	graduate
la	*plupart de*	most of
le	*poste*	position (at work)
	redoubler	to repeat a school year
	renvoyer	to sack
	réussir	to succeed
	rêver de	to dream of

Higher – Exam practice

info

These pages give you the chance to try GCSE-style practice exam questions at grades B–A* based on the AQA Context of Work and education.

Lien

Foundation practice exam questions (grades D–C) are available at the end of this Context in the Foundation Book.

Un four marocain ouvert à tous!

Nadège Gahinet, une étudiante française de Rouen, passe une année sabbatique au Maroc. Un jour, elle a visité une boulangerie marocaine. Voilà sa description de la visite:

A «J'étais à Assilah, une petite ville historique. Un dimanche matin, j'ai vu un groupe de femmes. Chaque personne portait une grande assiette sur la tête. Elles portaient leurs morceaux de pâte à pain chez le boulanger. Elles sont entrées dans le petit bâtiment, le boulanger a mis la pâte dans un grand four. Il m'a invitée à passer quelques heures avec lui.

Il a continué son travail. Un peu plus tard, les clientes sont revenues chercher leur pain. Beaucoup des clientes ont aussi acheté des gâteaux traditionnels préparés par la femme du boulanger.

J'ai comparé son système avec la boulangerie de mon père en France. Mon père utilise des machines pour préparer la pâte. Le pain aussi est différent. On ne voit pas de baguettes françaises au Maroc, mais un pain rond et plat.»

B Ibrahim, le boulanger, m'a expliqué la tradition du four communal. «Il y a longtemps, il y avait seulement un four pour tout le village. Chaque matin, on commençait avec le pain, et après, comme le four était toujours chaud, on apportait des plats de viande ou de poisson. Maintenant, je n'accepte que le pain et seulement le week-end.

De nos jours, beaucoup de familles préfèrent acheter du pain et des gâteaux, comme en France. Mais le week-end, quand les gens ne travaillent pas, il y a des familles qui continuent à préparer le pain selon la tradition, mais seulement celles qui ne préfèrent pas rester au lit! Pour les autres, on prépare du pain et on le leur vend.

Je fais tout à la main. C'est très fatigant car je dois aussi chauffer le four. Ce qui n'est pas typique, c'est que ma femme travaille avec moi, et elle fait de bonnes pâtisseries. Les gâteaux sont importants pour attirer les clients, surtout les touristes, qui sont plus nombreux maintenant.»

1a 📖 Read Section A. Which five of the pictures could illustrate the scene at the Moroccan bakery?

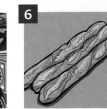
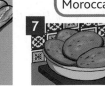

Using details, rather than gist

All the pictures are in some way connected to the article. The trick is to sort out the ones that are a perfect fit from those that do not quite fit. For example, look out for negatives and references to other places – clues such as these will help you work out whether the item shown applies to the Moroccan bakery or not.

Stratégie 1a

Total = 5 marks

1b 📖 Read Section B. Answer the questions in English.

1 What used to be cooked first in the communal oven?

2 What can villagers no longer bring to his oven? (2)

3 What disadvantage does he mention of bringing bread to cook in his oven?

4 Which two factors does he mention that make his job tiring?

5 What does his wife do to attract tourists?

> **Total** = 7 marks

2a 🎧 Listen to Section A of an interview with Youenn, who has just finished his gap year in Mauritania, West Africa. Choose the correct ending for each sentence in English.

1 Youenn took a break from his studies in **ICT / maths / accountancy**.

2 In Mauritania, he was able to use his skills in the classroom and in the **school office / post office / sports centre**.

3 He was usually woken by **the other people in his house / noise from the café / noise of dogs barking**.

4 They worked hard to make **music / art / maths** lessons more interesting.

5 He escaped the heat at lunchtime by **staying indoors / sitting in the garden / going to the beach**.

6 In the afternoon, he found it quite easy to **work until three o'clock / install the new computer system / explain the new system to the staff**.

> **Total** = 6 marks

2b 🎧 Listen to Section B. Which four of these statements are true?

1 They have enough computers in the school in Mauritania.

2 The children appreciate the most basic equipment.

3 The children lack energy.

4 There is overcrowding in many homes.

5 Youenn would like to spend more time in the desert.

6 He would like to work with homeless children.

7 He wants to pursue his career in France.

8 He has changed his ambition for the future since going to Mauritania.

> **Total** = 4 marks

> **Total for Reading and Listening** = 22 marks

Using your knowledge of tenses

Section B is typical of a Higher level recording, in that it uses a range of tenses. You need to use your knowledge of verbs and their endings to sort out where, for example, Youenn is referring to the future. Then you can more easily work out if statements 5 to 8 are true.

Stratégie 2b

Higher – Speaking

Au travail

You are talking to your French friend Aurore about part-time jobs, work experience, future careers and your free time. Your teacher will play the part of your friend and will ask you:

1 what part-time job you do and when
2 further details about your part-time job
3 details about your work experience
4 the possibilities for when you leave school
5 what career you envisage for yourself
6 what you do with your leisure time.
7 !

! Remember, you will have to respond to something that you have not yet prepared.

info

Important information:
This sample task is for practice purposes only and should not be used as an actual assessment task. Study it to find out how to plan your Controlled Assessment efficiently to gain maximum marks and / or work through it as a mock exam task before the actual Controlled Assessment.

1 What part-time job you do and when
- Say what job you do and give details of your activities.
- Say how long you have had your job for, how long you intend to keep it for and why.
- Mention your hours of work and say whether they are convenient.
- Say which days you work and say whether you would prefer other times.

Stratégie

Start your plan. Here are some suggested words for bullet point 1: *activités, depuis, heures (opinion), jours – préférences*.
If you don't have a part-time job, be creative and make one up!
For the second sub-division suggested here, use the present tense with *depuis* and a phrase that refers to a future event, e.g. *je fais ce travail depuis … et je vais continuer à …* See Exam technique S9.
Use *je voudrais / j'aimerais commencer à … / finir à …* to say what working hours you would prefer

2 Further details about your part-time job
- Say where you work and how far it is from home and school.
- Say how you get to work and how long it takes using different means of transport.
- Say how much you earn and what you think of your wages.
- Say what you think of the job and give reasons for your opinion.

Stratégie

Suggested words for your plan: *où?, loin?, transport, opinion (salaire – travail)*.
Use *le trajet dure …* to say how long it takes to travel.
Vary the ways in which you give your opinion, e.g. *je pense que … / je trouve que … / à mon avis, c'est … parce que …*

3 Details about your work experience
- Say when it took place and how long it lasted.
- Say what work you did, including three different tasks.
- Say what you enjoyed doing and comment on the value of work experience in general.
- Say whether you preferred a day of work experience to a typical day at school and ask Aurore if she has done work experience herself.

Stratégie

Suggested words for your plan: *dates, travail (détails), bien?, comparaison – collège*.
Most of this section refers to something that happened in the past. See the grammar section pages 183–184.
Use *plus / moins / aussi … que …* to make comparisons, e.g. *plus utile que …*

4 The possibilities for when you leave school
- Say that you can take up an apprenticeship and give an example.
- Say that you can continue at school, then go to university, mentioning costs.
- Say that you can go straight into a job, giving an advantage and a disadvantage of doing that.
- Talk about what you intend to do and give reasons.

Suggested words for your plan: *apprentissage, université, travail – avantage*.
Add a maximum of two words to this list.
Use *faire un apprentissage* for 'to take up an apprenticeship'.
Use *on peut / tu peux / il est possible de* + infinitive to say what you can do.

5 What career you envisage for yourself
- Say what career you envisage for yourself and what you will have to do to achieve it.
- Say what the advantages of that career are.
- Say what the disadvantages are.
- Say what career you will have if that proves impossible.

Suggested words for your plan: *médecin, université, avantages*.
Add a maximum of three words to this list.
Use *je dois* + infinitive to say what you have to do.
Use the present tense to say what the advantages and disadvantages are, e.g. *c'est assez bien payé*.
Use the future tense to cover the last sub-division suggested here.

6 What you do with your leisure time
- Say how much leisure time you have now and how the rest of your time is accounted for.
- Say what you do when you stay at home on weekdays and say what you did last weekend.
- Say what you do when you go out on weekdays and say what you will do next weekend.
- Say what you think you will do with your free time when you have a career.

Suggested words for your plan: *libre, quand*.
Add a maximum of four words to this list.
There are references to past, present and future in this bullet point; the clues are 'now', 'last', 'next' and 'will'. Take care and check the relevant pages in the grammar section as necessary. See Exam technique S11.
Use *quand j'aurai commencé ma carrière* … to introduce the last sub-division suggested here.
Use grammatical markers on your plan to help you, e.g. *maintenant, dernier, prochain*. See Exam technique S2.

7 ! At this point you may be asked …
- if you are prepared to move to another area and, if so, what you would gain and lose.
- about holidays – where you normally go, what you will do this year and if it will be different when you have a career.
- whether when you have a career, you will settle down, get married and have children.
- what you think of the idea of a gap year, what you would do, where you would go and how you would fund it.

Choose the **two** options that you think are the most likely. In your plan, write **three** words for each of the two options you have chosen, e.g. for the third option suggested here you might choose: *s'installer, mariage, enfants*.
Learn these two options using your reminder words.
Remember to check the total number of words you have used. It should be 40 or fewer.

Lien

Foundation sample assessment tasks for this Context can be found in the Foundation Book.

Higher – Writing

Mon collège

Your French friend Myriam has asked you to write an article in French for her school magazine entitled *La vie scolaire en Grande-Bretagne, c'est comment?* You could include:

1 the facilities in your school

2 your school routine

3 your subjects and teachers

4 your friends

5 extra-curricular activities

6 your school uniform

7 your ambitions for the future.

ℹ️ info

Important information:
This sample task is for practice purposes only and should not be used as an actual assessment task. Study it to find out how to plan your Controlled Assessment efficiently to gain maximum marks and / or work through it as a mock exam task before the actual Controlled Assessment.

---

1 The facilities in your school

- Introduce your school (name, location, what you think of it).
- Mention the size of the school, comparing it to the primary school you went to.
- Say a little about its organisation (mixed or single sex, age range, options in Year 10).
- Mention the buildings and their purposes, what the facilities are and what you think of them.

Stratégie

Start your plan. Here are some suggested words for bullet point 1: *informations générales, grand, primaire, organisation, bâtiments.*

Use *plus / moins* + adjective when you compare schools.

Use the imperfect tense to describe what your primary school was like, e.g. *c'était, il y avait.*

Use *on peut choisir …* to introduce options in Year 10.

Choose words for your plan that suggest more than six details to you, e.g. *primaire* could suggest your entire primary school experience: which school, where, when, what it was like, how it compares to your secondary school experience, etc. See Exam technique W2.

---

2 Your school routine

- Include when you arrive, what you do then, when lessons start, the number of lessons.
- Mention at what time morning break is, how long it lasts and what you do at break.
- Describe what you eat, where you eat and what else you do at lunchtime.
- Mention at what time school finishes, how you get home, how long it takes and how much homework you get.

Stratégie

Suggested words for your plan: *cours, récréation, heure déjeuner, retour, devoirs.*

Although there are only four sub-divisions suggested for bullet point 2, there are actually 14 different ideas. See Exam technique W9. However, don't write 14 sentences. Use connectives to link up sentences, e.g. *et, mais.*

Use *on me donne …* to introduce how much homework you get.

---

3 Your subjects and teachers

- Write about compulsory subjects and options and say what you think of your school's options system.
- Say which subject is your favourite and why.
- Say which subject is your least favourite and why. Say what you would prefer to study.
- Describe your favourite teacher, saying why you like him / her.

Stratégie

Suggested words for your plan: *obligatoires, options, préférée, détestée, prof préféré.*

Use *les matières obligatoires* for 'compulsory subjects'.

Use *si j'avais le choix, je voudrais …* to say what you would like to study.

Justify your opinion whenever possible.

4 Your friends
- Mention who your friends at school are and why you are friends with them.
- Describe your best friend (physically and also their character).
- Write about when and where you meet and what you like talking about.
- Mention what you did with him / her yesterday and what you thought of it.

Suggested words for your plan: *qui, pourquoi, Ann* (name of friend), *récréation*.
Add a maximum of two words to this list.
If your best friend is a girl, make sure that you make the adjectives you use to describe her feminine, e.g. *intelligente*.
Use *se retrouver* to say that you meet.
Using names in your plan, e.g. your best friend's name, is sometimes the most economical way of summarising what you want to write.

5 Extra-curricular activities
- Write about the extra-curricular activities that are on offer and when they take place.
- Write about an activity that you are involved in, who runs it, where, when and if it is well attended.
- Describe the last time you went.
- Say which activity (not currently on offer) you would like to do and say why.

Suggested words for your plan: *choix, quand, photographie.*
Add a maximum of three words to this list.
Use *avoir lieu* or *se passer* to say where or when something takes place: *ça a lieu … / ça se passe …*
Use *je fais partie d'un club de …* to say what you are involved in.
Use the conditional to cover the last sub-division suggested here. See Exam technique W5.

6 Your school uniform
- Describe what you wear at school, and say what you think of it and why.
- Describe what you wear when not at school and say why.
- Give your opinion of the school rules regarding what pupils can and cannot wear.
- French students do not wear a school uniform. Say whether you think British schools should have the same policy.

Suggested words for your plan: *description, opinion.*
Add a maximum of four words to this list.
Use *on a le droit de … / on n'a pas le droit de …* to introduce what you are allowed / not allowed to wear.
Use *on devrait* + infinitive to say whether British schools should have uniforms or not.

7 Your ambitions for the future
- Mention whether you intend to continue with your education in September, giving details.
- Mention whether you intend to go to university and why / why not.
- Say what job you would like to do in the future and give reasons for your choice.
- Say in which town / area you would like to work in the future and say why.

Add up to six words to your plan.
Remind yourself of the various ways of referring to a future event, e.g. *je vais / j'espère / j'aimerais / je voudrais / j'ai l'intention de* + infinitive, and the future tense itself. See the grammar section pages 181 and 185.
All the phrases above can be made negative by placing *ne … pas* around the verb. Take care: *j'ai l'intention de …* becomes *je n'ai pas l'intention de …*
Remember to check the total number of words you have used in your plan. It should be 40 or fewer.

Lien
Foundation sample assessment tasks for this Context can be found in the Foundation Book.

Exam technique – Speaking

S10 Showing Initiative

'Showing Initiative' does not mean that you suddenly ask your teacher 'What about you, where did you go on holiday?' (although you could do that!). You are generally expected to answer questions. For instance, if you are asked the question *Tu aimes le foot?*, you should first answer it directly and then try to develop your answer, e.g. *Oui, j'aime le foot. J'y joue trois fois par semaine avec mes copains.*

'Showing Initiative' means that you take the conversation elsewhere in a way that is connected to your answer and still relevant to the original question, e.g. *J'aime aussi jouer au basket. En fait, c'est mon sport préféré.* You were not asked about basketball, but you decided to add it to your response. It is relevant, linked to what you were asked and follows your developed answer quite naturally. That is 'Showing Initiative'. Use it to extend your answers and therefore show off extra knowledge of French.

S11 Using different tenses

If you are aiming at grade A, as well as a knowledge of the present, past and immediate future, you should also show that you know the future tense, the pluperfect and the conditional.

S12 Checklist for Speaking success

You will score well in the Speaking task if:

- you say a lot that is relevant to the question
- you have a good range of vocabulary
- you can include complex structures
- you can refer to present, past and future events
- your French accent is good
- you can speak fluently
- you can show initiative
- you can speak with grammatical accuracy.

Grade booster

To reach grade B, you need to …

- Develop most of your answers well, using some complex sentences, e.g. for bullet point 4 of the sample Controlled Assessment on page 167, go through each of the suggested sub-divisions, adding extra details each time. For example, you could add details about A-levels, which subjects, etc. when talking about continuing at school. Link up your sentences with appropriate connectives.

- Answer without hesitation, using a good range of vocabulary, e.g. for bullet point 2, use a variety of ways of expressing an opinion and provide different reasons each time.

To reach grade A, you need to …

- Attempt a variety of verb tenses, e.g. for bullet point 6, use present, past and future tenses. If possible, show that you know irregular verbs such as *je ferai* and *je serai*, and also that you know which verbs take *avoir / être* in the perfect tense, e.g. *je suis allé(e), je suis resté(e).*

- Express ideas and points of view using complex sentences and a very good range of vocabulary, e.g. for bullet point 3, when giving an opinion, try to go beyond the usual phrases and include phrases such as *selon moi, …; je crois que …; ce qui me plaît, c'est …; le mieux / le pire, c'est que …*

To reach grade A*, you need to …

- Have a wide range of vocabulary and use a number of more complex structures, e.g. for bullet point 1, use the present tense with *depuis*, the future tense to say how long you intend to keep your job and the conditional to say whether you would prefer working at different times, e.g. *je préférerais …* Include other complex structures if you can.

- Respond readily and show initiative on several occasions, e.g. for bullet point 5, if you want to go to university to achieve the career that you envisage, explain how long the course will last and who will meet the costs. Mention some of the good and bad points of your second choice career.

Exam technique – Writing

W10 Info about Accuracy

If you are aiming at grade A, your writing should be generally correct, although there may still be mistakes, especially in your attempts at more complex sentences. Your use of different verb forms, in particular different tenses, must be virtually free of errors.

W11 Ideas for practising

Treat each bullet point as a mini-task. Write your answer to one bullet point at a time with the help of your plan. Ask your partner to take a critical look at your work. Take his / her suggestions on board and redraft your work. Study Exam technique W12, which lists what you should do in order to get the best possible mark, and try to improve your work using these hints.

Practise your writing using sample tasks from the AQA website or given to you by your teacher. Write a plan and attempt the task. As you are only allowed 60 minutes to complete the task in your exam, practise using approximately seven minutes for each bullet point, leaving you 10 minutes or so at the end for a final check. Use that time to check that what you have written makes sense and that it is as accurate as you can make it.

W12 Checklist for Writing success

You will score well if:

- you communicate a lot of relevant information clearly
- you can explain ideas and points of view
- you have a good range of vocabulary
- you can include complex structures
- you can write long sentences
- you can refer to past, present and future events
- you can write with grammatical accuracy
- you organise your ideas well.

Grade booster

To reach grade B, you need to …

- Be ready to explain ideas, using appropriate vocabulary and complex sentences, e.g. for bullet point 3 of the sample Controlled Assessment on page 168, explain the options system and what you think of it. Give your reasons for your opinions.
- Write with some accuracy. There may be errors in your attempt at more complex sentences but verb and tense formations should be usually correct. For example, although the language needed to cover bullet point 2 is fairly straightforward, it is important that it is as accurate as you can make it. Check verb endings in particular.

To reach grade A, you need to …

- Write 40 to 50 words per bullet point, conveying a lot of relevant information clearly. For example, although you could give a lot of information for bullet point 7, limit yourself to 50 words maximum and focus on the accuracy of the language you use, e.g. make sure that verb endings are correct.
- Be generally accurate in your attempts at complex sentences and verb tenses, e.g. for bullet point 5, use present, past and conditional. Again, focus on accuracy of verb endings.

To reach grade A*, you need to …

- Use a wide variety of vocabulary and structures with accuracy, e.g. for bullet point 6, show that you can use structures such as *on pourrait / on devrait / il faudrait* correctly (they are all followed by a verb in the infinitive). Try to avoid repetition of vocabulary, e.g. when writing about *uniforme scolaire*, use phrases such as *ce qu'on porte, nos vêtements, ce qu'on doit mettre* instead.
- Use more complex sentences and verb tenses successfully, e.g. for bullet point 4, give details of your best friend's personality and illustrate what you mean with examples. This should give you the opportunity to bring in the future or the conditional: *Elle est très intelligente, ce qui explique pourquoi elle aimerait devenir chirurgienne.*

(G) Grammaire

info

Key to colour coding on the grammar pages.

The grammar reference information is divided into four sections, indicated by different colour coding:

grammar to be learnt and used by all GCSE students

grammar to be learnt and used by students working at Higher level, and recognised by students working at Foundation level

grammar to be learnt and used by Higher students only

grammar to be recognised, but not necessarily used, by Higher students only.

■ Contents

■ Glossary of terms

Adjectives   *les adjectifs*

Words that describe somebody or something:
petit   small   *timide*   shy

Adverbs   *les adverbes*

Words that complement (add meaning to) verbs, adjectives or other adverbs:
très   very   *lentement*   slowly

Articles   *les articles*

Short words used before nouns:
un / une   a, an   *des*   some, any
le / la / les   the

The infinitive   *l'infinitif*

The verb form given in the dictionary:
aller   to go   *avoir*   to have

Nouns   *les noms*

Words that identify a person, a place or a thing:
mère   mother   *maison*   house

Prepositions   *les prépositions*

Words used in front of nouns to give information about when, how, where, etc.:
à   at   *avec*   with
de   of, from   *en*   in

Pronouns   *les pronoms*

Short words used to replace nouns:
je   I   *tu*   you
il   he   *elle*   she
moi   me   *toi*   you

Verbs   *les verbes*

Words used to express an action or a state:
*je **parle***   I **speak**   *il **est***   he **is**

A Nouns

Masculine and feminine nouns

All French nouns are either masculine or feminine.

In the singular, masculine nouns are introduced with *le, l'* or *un*:
le père   **the** father   *un livre*   **a** book
l'hôtel   **the** hotel

Feminine nouns are introduced with *la, l'* or *une*:
la mère   **the** mother   *une table*   **a** table
l'eau   **the** water

Some nouns have two different forms, masculine and feminine:

un copain   a male friend
une copine   a female friend
un coiffeur   a male hairdresser
une coiffeuse   a female hairdresser
un facteur   a postman
une factrice   a postwoman

Some nouns stay the same for masculine and feminine:

le prof   the male teacher
la prof   the female teacher
un enfant   a male child
une enfant   a female child

There are patterns to help you remember the correct gender of a noun.

■ All words ending in *-isme* are masculine:
l'alcoolisme, l'alpinisme, le racisme

■ Words ending in *-tion* are usually feminine:
la climatisation, la manifestation, la récréation, la station

There are many other patterns, e.g. nouns ending in *-age, -eau, -ment* (masculine); *-ie, -ière, -ité* (feminine). Look out for patterns when you are learning vocabulary, but make a note of exceptions.

Singular and plural forms

As in English, French nouns can be either singular (one) or plural (more than one).

Most plural nouns end in *-s*. Unlike English, the added *-s* is usually not pronounced.
un chat, deux chats   one cat, two cats

As in English, there are some exceptions.

■ With most nouns ending in *-al*, you change the ending to *-aux* in the plural:
un animal   an animal
des animaux   animals

■ With many nouns ending in *–au* or *-eu*, you add an *-x*:
un gâteau, des gâteaux   a cake, cakes
un jeu, des jeux   a game, games

■ Words already ending in *-s*, or in *-x* or *-z*, do not change:
le bras, les bras   arm, arms
le nez, les nez   nose, noses

■ A few nouns change completely:
un œil, des yeux   an eye, eyes

B Articles

Definite articles: *le, la, les* – the

The word for 'the' depends on whether the noun it goes with is masculine (m), feminine (f), singular or plural.

m singular	f singular	m + f plural
le	*la*	*les*

le grand-père	the grandfather
la grand-mère	the grandmother
les grands-parents	the grandparents

When a singular noun starts with a vowel or a silent *h*, *le* and *la* are shortened to *l'*:

l'ami	the friend
l'histoire	the story

In French, you often need to use *le, la* and *les* even when we wouldn't say 'the' in English:

- When talking about likes and dislikes:

J'adore **le** *poulet.*	I love chicken.
Elle déteste **les** *maths.*	She hates maths.

- When referring to abstract things:

La *musique est très importante.*	Music is very important.

Indefinite articles: *un, une, des, de* – a, an, some

Like the words for 'the' (*le / la / les*), the words for 'a / an' and 'some' depend on whether the noun they go with is masculine or feminine, singular or plural.

m singular	f singular	m + f plural
un	*une*	*des*

un *vélo*	a bike
une *moto*	a motorbike
une *orange*	an orange
des *voitures*	(some) cars

When talking about jobs, *un* and *une* are not used in French where 'a' or 'an' is used in English.

Il est professeur.	He is **a** teacher.

In negative constructions, *de* replaces *un, une* or *des* after *pas*:

J'ai un frère. – Je n'ai **pas de** *frère*.*	I don't have **any** brothers.
Il y a une piscine. – Il n'y a **pas de** *piscine.*	There is **no** swimming pool.

J'ai des sœurs. – Je n'ai **pas de** *sœur*.*	I don't have **any** sisters.

* Note that in French you use a singular noun after a negative construction, unlike English.

Change *de* to *d'* in front of a vowel or a silent *h*:

Je n'ai pas **d'**animal.	I don't have **any** pets.

Partitive articles: *du, de la, de l', des* – some, any

masculine	feminine	words beginning with a vowel or silent h	plural
de + le = du	*de + la = de la*	*de + l' = de l'*	*de + les = des*

du *café*	(some) coffee
de la *limonade*	(some) lemonade
de l'aspirine	(some) aspirin
des *chocolats*	(some) chocolates

- **du** always replaces *de + le*
- **des** always replaces *de + les*

Use *du, de la, de l', des* to mean 'some' or 'any':

Je voudrais **du** *poulet.*	I'd like **some** chicken.
Elle prend **de la** *limonade.*	She's having **(some)** lemonade.
Elle boit **de l'**eau.	She's drinking **(some)** water.
Avez-vous **des** *croissants?*	Do you have **any** croissants?

Also use *du, de la, de l', des* to talk about activities someone is doing or musical instruments someone is playing:

Je fais **du** *judo.*	I do judo.
Elle joue **de la** *guitare.*	She is playing the guitar.
Il fait **de l'**équitation.	He goes horse riding.
Ils font **des** *excursions.*	They go on trips.

After a negative, *de* or *d'* replaces these forms:

Je ne fais pas **de** *judo.*	I don't do judo.

C Adjectives

Feminine and masculine, singular and plural adjectives

In French, adjectives have different endings depending on whether they describe masculine, feminine, singular or plural nouns.

- The masculine singular form has no extra ending:

Mon frère est petit.   My brother is small.

- Add *-e* if the noun is feminine singular:

Ma sœur est petite.   My sister is small.

- Add *-s* to the masculine singular form if the noun is masculine plural:

Mes frères sont petits.   My brothers are small.

- Add *-s* to the feminine singular form if the noun is feminine plural:

Mes sœurs sont petites.   My sisters are small.

- When an adjective describes a group of masculine and feminine people or things, it has to be the masculine plural form:

Mes parents sont grands.   My parents are tall.

There are many exceptions in the feminine forms.

- With adjectives that already end in *-e*, don't add another *-e* in the feminine:

un vélo rouge   a red bike
une moto rouge   a red motorbike

- But with adjectives that end in *-é*, do add another *-e* in the feminine:

mon film préféré   my favourite film
ma chanson préférée   my favourite song

- With some adjectives, you double the final consonant before the *-e* in the feminine:

Il est italien.   He is Italian.
Elle est italienne.   She is Italian.

- Adjective endings *-eux* and *-eur* change to *-euse* in the feminine:

un garçon paresseux   ➡   *une fille paresseuse*
a lazy boy   a lazy girl
un garçon travailleur ➡   *une fille travailleuse*
a hard-working boy   a hard-working girl

- The adjective ending *-eau* changes to *-elle* in the feminine:

un nouveau vélo   a new bike
une nouvelle voiture   a new car

- The adjective ending *-if* changes to *-ive* in the feminine:

un copain sportif   a sporty (boy)friend
une copine sportive   a sporty (girl)friend

- The feminine of *blanc* is *blanche*:

Elle porte une robe blanche.
She is wearing a white dress.

- The feminine of *frais* is *fraîche*:

Je voudrais une boisson fraîche.
I would like a cool drink.

- The feminine of *gentil* is *gentille*:

Ma grand mère est gentille.
My grandmother is kind.

- The feminine of *sympa* is *sympa*:

Ma mère est sympa.   My mother is nice.

There are also some exceptions in the plural forms.

- Adjective endings *-al* and *-eau* change to *-aux* or *-eaux* in the masculine plural:

J'ai des poissons tropicaux.
I have got some tropical fish.
J'ai de nouveaux livres.
I have got some new books.

- With adjectives that end in *-s* or *-x*, don't add an *-s* in the masculine plural:

Mes frères sont paresseux.   My brothers are lazy.
Les nuages sont gris.   The clouds are grey.

Some adjectives, such as *marron* and *super*, do not change at all in the feminine or plural:

Elle porte des bottes marron.
She's wearing brown boots.

The position of adjectives

Most adjectives follow the noun they describe:

un prof sympa   a nice teacher
une copine intelligente   an intelligent friend
des idées intéressantes   interesting ideas

However, a few adjectives, such as *petit, grand, bon, mauvais, joli, beau, jeune* and *vieux*, usually come in front of the noun:

un petit garçon   a small boy
une jolie ville   a pretty town

A few adjectives that come in front of the noun have a special masculine form before a vowel or a silent *h*:

un bel endroit   a beautiful place
un vieil homme   an old man
un nouvel ami   a new friend

Adjectives of nationality

Adjectives of nationality do not begin with a capital letter:

Nicolas est français.   Nicolas is French.
Laura est galloise.   Laura is Welsh.

Like other adjectives, feminine adjectives of nationality have an -e at the end, unless there is one there already:

Sophie est française.   Sophie is French.
Juliette est suisse.   Juliette is Swiss.

Comparative and superlative adjectives

To make comparisons, use:

- *plus ... que*   more ... than / ...er than

  La Loire est plus longue que la Tamise.
  The Loire is **longer than** the Thames.

- *moins ... que*   less ... than

  Les vélos sont moins rapides que les trains.
  Bicycles are **less** fast **than** trains.

- *aussi ... que*   as ... as

  Les tomates sont aussi chères que les pêches.
  Tomatoes are **as** expensive **as** peaches.

For superlatives (the most ...), use:

- *le / la / les plus ...*   the most ... / the ...est

  C'est la chambre la plus chère.
  It is **the most** expensive room.
  C'est le plus petit vélo.
  It is **the smallest** bicycle.

- *le / la / les moins ...*   the least ...

  C'est le film le moins intéressant.
  It is **the least** interesting film.

The adjectives *bon* and *mauvais* have irregular comparatives and superlatives:

Ce CD est meilleur que l'autre.
This CD is **better** than the other one.

Elle est la meilleure!   She's the **best**!

Je suis pire que ma sœur.
I am **worse** than my sister.

Mon frère est le pire.   My brother is **the worst**.

Demonstrative adjectives: ce, cet, cette, ces – this, that, these, those

The French for 'this' or 'that' is *ce, cet* or *cette* and for 'these' or 'those' is *ces*.

masculine	feminine	masculine and feminine plural
ce	cette	ces

ce magasin	**this** / **that** shop
cette chemise	**this** / **that** shirt
ces baskets	**these** / **those** trainers

But *ce* changes to *cet* when the noun after it begins with a vowel or a silent *h*:

cet ami	**this** / **that** friend
cet hôtel	**this** / **that** hotel

Indefinite adjectives

The most common indefinite adjectives are:

autre(s)	other
certain(e)(s)	certain / some
chaque	each
même(s)	same
plusieurs	several
quelque(s)	some
tout / toute / tous / toutes	all

Chaque is always singular and *plusieurs* is always plural:

Il y a une télévision dans chaque chambre.
There is a television in **each room**.

Il a plusieurs voitures.   He has **several cars.**

Possessive adjectives, one 'owner'

mon / ma / mes	my
ton / ta / tes	your
son / sa / ses	his / her / its

There are three different ways of saying 'my' in French, as it depends on whether the noun is masculine or feminine, singular or plural. It is the same for 'your' and 'his' / 'her' / 'its'.

masculine singular	feminine singular	masculine and feminine plural
mon, ton, son	*ma, ta, sa*	*mes, tes, ces*

mon père	**my** father
ma mère	**my** mother
ton père*	**your** father
ta mère*	**your** mother
son pied	**his** / **her** / **its** foot
sa porte	**his** / **her** / **its** door
mes parents	**my** parents
tes parents*	**your** parents
ses fenêtres	**his** / **her** / **its** windows

* to someone you normally say *tu* to

French doesn't have three different words for 'his', 'her' and 'its'. The word changes according to whether the noun it is used with is masculine, feminine, singular or plural.

Possessive adjectives, several 'owners'

notre / nos   our
votre / vos   your
leur / leurs   their

masculine and feminine singular	masculine and feminine plural
notre, votre, leur	*nos, vos, leurs*

notre *père*	**our** father
notre *mère*	**our** mother
votre* *père*	**your** father
votre* *mère*	**your** mother
leur *frère*	**their** brother
leur *sœur*	**their** sister
nos *parents*	**our** parents
vos* *copains*	**your** friends
leurs *profs*	**their** teachers

* to several people **or** to someone you normally say *vous* to

Interrogative adjectives: *quel, quelle, quels, quelles*

Quel (meaning 'which' or 'what') agrees with the noun it refers to.

m singular	f singular	m plural	f plural
quel	*quelle*	*quels*	*quelles*

C'est **quel** *dessin?*	**Which** drawing is it?
Quelle *heure est-il?*	**What** time is it?
Quelles *sont tes matières préférées?*	**What** are your favourite subjects?

D Adverbs

Adverbs are used with a verb, an adjective or another adverb to express how, when, where or to what extent something happens.

Many French adverbs are formed by adding *-ment* (the equivalent of '-ly' in English) to the feminine form of the adjective.

m adjective	f adjective	adverb
doux	*douce*	*doucement* – gently
final	*finale*	*finalement* – finally
heureux	*heureuse*	*heureusement* – fortunately
probable	*probable*	*probablement* – probably

There are several exceptions, which are not formed from the feminine form of the adjective, including these:

m adjective		adverb
vrai	-	*vraiment* – really
évident	-	*évidemment* – obviously

Many common adverbs are completely irregular:

bien	well	*Elle joue* **bien**.	She plays well.
mal	badly	*Il mange* **mal**.	He eats badly.
vite	fast	*Tu parles* **vite**.	You speak fast.

Comparative and superlative adverbs

As with adjectives, you can make comparisons using *plus, moins* and *aussi ... que*:

Tu parles **plus** *lentement* **que** *moi.*
You speak **more** slowly **than** me.

Je mange **moins** *vite* **que** *ma sœur.*
I eat **less** quickly **than** my sister.

Elle joue **aussi** *bien* **que** *Paul.*
She plays **as** well **as** Paul.

The comparative of the adverb *bien* is an exception:

Elle joue **mieux** *que Paul.*
She plays **better** than Paul.

You can also use adverbs as superlatives:

Il joue **le mieux**.   He plays **the best**.

Il a fini son travail **le plus vite**.
He finished his work **the fastest**.

Adverbs of time, frequency, place, etc.

Adverbs of time include:

aujourd'hui	today
demain	tomorrow
hier	yesterday
après-demain	the day after tomorrow
avant-hier	the day before yesterday
déjà	already

Adverbs of frequency include:

quelquefois	sometimes
souvent	often
toujours	always
une fois par semaine / mois	once a week / month
encore	again
généralement	generally / usually
rarement	rarely
régulièrement	regularly

Adverbs of place include:

dedans	inside
dehors	outside
ici	here
là-bas	(over) there
loin	far
partout	everywhere

Adverbs of intensity and quantity (qualifying words) include:

assez	enough	*un peu*	a little
trop	too (much)	*très*	very
beaucoup	a lot		

Adverbs of sequence include:

d'abord	firstly	*enfin*	finally
après	afterwards	*puis*	then
ensuite	next		

E Pronouns

Subject pronouns: *je, tu, il, elle, on, nous, vous, ils, elles*

Subject pronouns usually come before the verb and express who or what performs the action.

singular	plural
je – I	*nous* – we
tu – you	*vous* – you
il – he / it	*ils* – they (m)
elle – she / it	*elles* – they (f)
on – we / you / they	

Je parle français.	**I** speak French.
Tu as quel âge?	How old are **you**?
Il s'appelle Théo.	**He** is called Théo.
Elle s'appelle Aïcha.	**She** is called Aïcha.
On se retrouve où?	Where shall **we** meet?
Nous habitons en ville.	**We** live in town.
Vous avez une chambre?	Do **you** have a room?
Ils s'appellent Do et Mi.	**They** are called Do and Mi.
Elles sont marrantes.	**They** are fun.

Je is shortened to *j'* if the word that follows begins with a silent *h* or a vowel:

J'aime les pommes.	**I** like apples.
J'habite en Écosse.	**I** live in Scotland.

There are two French words for 'you': *tu* and *vous*.

■ Use *tu* when talking to someone (one person) of your own age or someone in your family.

■ Use *vous* when talking to an adult not in your family (e.g. your teacher). The following phrases are useful to remember:

*Avez-**vous** ... ?*	Have **you** got ... ?
*Voulez-**vous** ... ?*	Do **you** want ... ?
*Voudriez-**vous** ... ?*	Would **you** like ... ?

■ Also use *vous* when talking to more than one person – whatever their age and whether you know them well or not.

Il and *elle* can both also mean 'it', depending on the gender of the noun they replace.

*L'hôtel est bien? – Oui, **il** est très confortable.*
Is the hotel good? – Yes, **it** is very comfortable.

*Je déteste ma chambre: **elle** est trop petite.*
I hate my bedroom: **it** is too small.

On can mean 'we', 'you' or 'they', depending on the context:

On *s'entend bien.*
We get on well.

*Comment dit-**on** «pencil» en français?*
How do **you** say 'pencil' in French?

On *parle français au Canada.*
They speak French in Canada.

There are two French words for 'they': *ils* and *elles*.

■ Use *ils* when all the people / things you are talking about are male, or it is a mixed group of males and females:

*J'ai un frère et une sœur, **ils** s'appellent Nicolas et Aurélie.*
I have a brother and a sister; **they** are called Nicolas and Aurélie.

■ Use *elles* when all the people / things you are talking about are female:

*J'ai deux copines espagnoles, **elles** habitent à Madrid.*
I have two Spanish friends; **they** live in Madrid.

Direct object pronouns: *me, te, le, la, nous, vous, les*

Direct object pronouns replace a noun that is not the subject of the verb.

singular	plural
me / m' – me	*nous* – us
te / t' – you	*vous* – you
le / l' – him / it (m)	*les* – them
la / l' – her / it (f)	

Direct object pronouns come in front of the verb, unlike in English:

*Je **le** prends.* — I'll take **it**.

*Je peux **vous** aider?* — Can I help **you**?

Le and *la* are shortened to *l'* in front of a vowel or a silent *h*:

*Mon petit frère a deux ans. Je **l'**adore!* — My little brother is two. I love **him**!

Indirect object pronouns: *me, te, lui, nous, vous, leur*

Indirect object pronouns are used to replace a noun that would be introduced with the preposition *à*.

singular	plural
me / m' – (to) me	*nous* – (to) us
te / t' – (to) you	*vous* – (to) you
lui – (to) him / her / it	*leur* – (to) them

Je donne du café à mon père.
➡ *Je **lui** donne du café.*
I give **him** some coffee.

Je parle à ma mère.
➡ *Je **lui** parle.* — I speak to **her**.

J'écris à mes grands-parents.
➡ *Je **leur** écris.* — I write to **them**.

Beware! Some French verbs are followed by a preposition when their English equivalents are not:

Je téléphone à mon père. — I ring my father.
*Je **lui** téléphone.* — I ring **him**.

Indirect object pronouns: *en* – of it / them; *y* – there

Use *en* to avoid repeating a noun that is introduced with *du, de la, de l'* or *des*:

Tu as des chiens? — Have you got any dogs?
*Oui, j'**en** ai trois.* — Yes, I've got three (**of them**).

Tu manges de la viande? — Do you eat meat?
*Oui, j'**en** mange.* — Yes, I do.

Y usually means 'there'. You can use *y* to avoid repeating the name of a place:

Tu vas à Paris? — Are you going to Paris?
*Oui, j'**y** vais demain.* — Yes, I'm going **there** tomorrow.

Order of object pronouns

When two object pronouns are used together in the same sentence, follow this sequence:

me		le		leur		y
te	come	la	come		come	
nous	before	l'	before	lui	before	en
vous		les				

*Je **te les** donne maintenant.*
I'm giving **them** to **you** now.

*Il **nous en** a parlé.*
He has talked to **us** about **it**.

Emphatic pronouns: *moi, toi, lui, elle, nous, vous, eux, elles*

These are also called disjunctive pronouns. Use them:

- for emphasis:

  Moi, j'adore les fraises. — I love strawberries.
  Toi, tu as quel âge? — How old are **you**?

- after *c'est*:

  *C'est **moi**.* — It's **me**.

- after a preposition:

*avec **moi***	with **me**
*avec **nous***	with **us**
*pour **toi***	for **you**
*pour **vous***	for **you**

chez **lui**	at **his** house	
chez **eux**	at **their** house	
*à côté d'***elle**	next to **her**	
*à côté d'***elles**	next to **them**	

- after a comparative:

Elle est plus sympa que **toi.**
She is nicer than **you.**

- with *à*, to express possession:

Possessive pronouns

m singular	f singular	m plural	f plural	
le mien	*la mienne*	*les miens*	*les miennes*	mine
le tien	*la tienne*	*les tiens*	*les tiennes*	yours
le sien	*la sienne*	*les siens*	*les siennes*	his / hers / its
le nôtre	*la nôtre*	*les nôtres*	*les nôtres*	ours
le vôtre	*la vôtre*	*les vôtres*	*les vôtres*	yours
le leur	*la leur*	*les leurs*	*les leurs*	theirs

C'est **le mien** *ou* **le tien**?   Is it **mine** or **yours**?

Il est **à toi**, *ce CD?*
Does this CD **belong to you?**

Relative pronouns: *qui, que, qu', dont*

Relative pronouns are used to link phrases together.

Use *qui* as the subject of the relative clause. It can refer to people and things, and means 'who', 'that' or 'which':

le copain **qui** *habite à Lyon*
the friend **who** lives in Lyon

le livre **qui** *est sur la chaise*
the book **that** is on the table

Use *que* (*qu'* before a vowel or a silent *h*) as the object of the relative clause. It means 'whom' or 'that':

le copain **que** *j'ai vu*
the friend (**that / whom**) I saw

le livre **qu'***il a acheté* the book (**that**) he bought

- Remember that *que* is not optional. Although it is often not translated in English, you cannot leave it out in French.

- If you cannot decide between *qui* and *que*, remember that *qui* is subject and *que* is object. If the relative clause already has a subject, then the pronoun you need must be *que*.

J'ai trouvé un job **qui** *me va.*
I have found a job **that** suits me.
– The subject of *va* is *qui*.

C'est une couleur **que** *je déteste.*
It's a colour (**that**) I hate.
– The subject of *déteste* is *je*, and *que* is object.

You will need to understand sentences containing the word *dont*. It is usually translated as 'whose' or 'of which'.

J'ai un ami **dont** *le père est espagnol.*
I have a friend **whose** father is Spanish.

J'ai cinq robes **dont** *trois sont rouges.*
I've got five dresses **of which** three are red.

Demonstrative pronouns: *ce, cela, ça, celui-ci*, etc.

Ce (shortened to *c'* before a vowel) means 'it', 'that' or 'those' and is usually followed with a form of *être*:

Ce *sont mes parents.*	**Those** are my parents.
C'est facile.	**It'**s easy.

Cela means 'that' and is often shortened to *ça*:

Cela *m'étonne.*	**That** surprises me.
Tu aimes **ça?**	Do you like **that**?

Ça is also used in various phrases:

Ça *va?*	Are you OK?
Ça *ne fait rien.*	It doesn't matter.
C'est **ça.**	That's right.

Celui (masculine), *celle* (feminine), *ceux* (masculine plural) and *celles* (feminine plural) are used with *-ci* or *-là* for emphasis or contrast, meaning 'this one', 'that one', 'these ones' or 'those ones':

Tu veux **celui-ci** *ou* **celui-là?**
Do you want **this one** or **that one**?

J'hésite entre **celles-ci** *et* **celles-là**.
I'm hesitating between **these** and **those**.

Indefinite pronouns: *quelqu'un, quelque chose, tout, tout le monde* and *personne*

The French for 'someone' is *quelqu'un*:

Il y a **quelqu'un** *à la maison.*
There's **someone** at home.

The French for 'something' is *quelque chose*:

Vous avez perdu **quelque chose?**
Have you lost **something**?

The French for 'all' is *tout / toute / tous / toutes*:

*C'est **tout**.*	That's **all**.
*Je les aime **tous**.*	I love them **all**.

The French for 'everybody' is *tout le monde*:

***Tout le monde** aime le chocolat.*
Everybody likes chocolate.

The French for 'nobody' is *personne*. In a sentence, it is followed by *ne* in front a verb or *n'* before a vowel, and it doesn't need *pas*:

***Personne ne** veut danser.*
Nobody wants to dance.

F Verbs

French verbs have different endings depending on who is doing the action and whether the action takes place in the past, the present or the future. The verb tables on pages 193–197 set out the patterns of endings for several useful verbs.

When using a name or a singular noun instead of a pronoun, use the same form of the verb as for *il / elle*:

*Martin **parle** espagnol.*   Martin **speaks** Spanish.

When using two names or a plural noun, use the same form of the verb as for *ils / elles*:

*Thomas et Lola **jouent** au basket.*
Thomas and Lola **are playing** basketball.

*Mes frères **écoutent** de la musique.*
My brothers **are listening** to music.

The infinitive

The infinitive is the form of the verb you find in a dictionary, e.g. *jouer, finir, être*. It never changes.

When two verbs follow each other, the second one is always in the infinitive.

- All verbs of liking, disliking and preferring (such as *aimer, adorer, préférer, détester*) are followed by the infinitive:

  *J'aime **jouer** de la guitare.*
  I like **playing** the guitar.
  *Je préfère **écouter** des CD.*
  I prefer **listening** to CDs.

- Modal verbs *vouloir, pouvoir* and *devoir* and the verb *savoir* are also followed by the infinitive:

  *Tu veux **aller** au cinéma?*
  Do you want **to go** to the cinema?

*On peut **faire** du shopping.*
You can **go** shopping.

*Je dois **faire** mes devoirs.*
I must **do** my homework.

*Je sais **conduire**.*
I know how **to drive**.

- Verbs expressing a future wish or intention are followed by the infinitive:

  *J'espère **partir** en vacances.*
  I hope **to go** on holiday.
  *Je voudrais **aller** en Italie.*
  I'd like **to go** to Italy.

The infinitive is used after *avant de* to mean 'before doing something':

*Je me lave les mains avant de **manger**.*
I wash my hands before **eating**.

Some verbs always need *à* between them and the infinitive:

*aider quelqu'un **à***	to help someone **to**
*apprendre **à***	to learn **to**
*arriver **à***	to manage **to**
*commencer **à***	to start **to**
*continuer **à***	to continue **to**
*s'intéresser **à***	to be interested **in**
*inviter quelqu'un **à***	to invite someone **to**
*réussir **à***	to succeed **in**
*Il **apprend à** nager.*	He is **learning to** swim.

Some verbs always need *de* between them and the infinitive:

*arrêter **de***	to stop
*décider **de***	to decide **to**
*essayer **de***	to try **to**
*être obligé(e) **de***	to be forced **to**
*oublier **de***	to forget **to**
*refuser **de***	to refuse **to**

*J'ai **oublié de** fermer la porte.*
I **forgot to** close the door.

Faire + infinitive

Faire + infinitive is used to say that someone is having something done:

> *Je **fais réparer** ma voiture.*
> I **have** my car **repaired**.

> *Il **se fait couper** les cheveux.*
> He **is having** his hair **cut**.

> *Ils **font construire** une maison.*
> They **are having** a house **built**.

The perfect infinitive: *après avoir / être* + past participle

The perfect infinitive is the infinitive of *avoir* or *être* (depending on which one the verb normally uses to form the perfect tense), plus the past participle of the verb. It is used after *après* to mean 'after doing something':

> ***Après avoir regardé** l'heure, il est parti.*
> **After looking** at the time, he left.

> *Il a lu le livre **après être allé** là-bas.*
> He read the book **after going** there.

> *Elle a mangé **après s'être levée**.*
> She ate **after getting up**.

The present tense

Use the present tense to describe:

- something that is taking place now:
  *J'**écoute** un CD.*
  I **am listening** to a CD.

- something that happens regularly:
  *J'**ai** maths le lundi.*
  I **have** maths on Mondays.

Present tense verb endings change depending on who is doing the action:

> ***Je** parle à ma grand-mère.*
> **I speak** to my grandmother.

> ***Nous** lavons la voiture.*
> **We wash** the car.

Most verbs follow a regular pattern.

Regular -*er* verbs

To form the present tense of -*er* verbs, remove the -*er* from the infinitive to form the stem, e.g. *parl* from *parler*. Then add the endings shown below.

parler – to speak / to talk	
je parle	nous parlons
tu parles	vous parlez
il / elle / on parle	ils / elles parlent

Some other regular -*er* verbs:

adorer	to love	*habiter*	to live
aimer	to like	*jouer*	to play
détester	to hate	*regarder*	to watch
écouter	to listen	*rester*	to stay

Regular -*ir* verbs:

To form the present tense of -*ir* verbs, remove the -*ir* from the infinitive to form the stem, e.g. *fin* from *finir*. Then add the endings shown below.

finir – to finish	
je finis	nous finissons
tu finis	vous finissez
il / elle / on finit	ils / elles finissent

Other regular -*ir* verbs:

choisir	to choose
remplir	to fill

Regular -*re* verbs:

To form the present tense of -*re* verbs, remove the -*re* from the infinitive to form the stem, e.g. *attend* from *attendre*. Then add the endings shown below.

attendre – to wait	
j'attends	nous attendons
tu attends	vous attendez
il / elle / on attend	ils / elles attendent

Other regular -*re* verbs:

descendre	to go down
répondre	to reply
vendre	to sell

Irregular verbs

Some verbs are irregular and do not follow these patterns. Turn to pages 194–197 for details of the most common ones.

Reflexive verbs

Reflexive verbs have an extra pronoun in front of the verb:

me	*je* **me** *réveille*	I wake up
te	*tu* **te** *lèves*	you get up
se	*il / elle* **s'***appelle*	he / she is called
	on **se** *lave*	we have a wash
nous	*nous* **nous** *amusons*	we have fun
vous	*vous* **vous** *couchez*	you go to bed
se	*ils / elles* **s'***excusent*	they apologise

Note that *me, te* and *se* are shortened to *m', t'* and *s'* in front of a vowel or a silent *h*.

Common reflexive verbs are:

s'amuser	to have fun
s'habiller	to get dressed
s'appeler	to be called
se laver	to have a wash
s'asseoir	to sit down
se lever	to get up
se coucher	to go to bed
se passer	to happen
s'ennuyer	to be bored
se promener	to go for a walk
s'excuser	to apologise
se réveiller	to wake up

The perfect tense

Use the perfect tense to talk about what somebody did or has done.

*Il **a mangé** un sandwich.*
He **ate** a sandwich. / He **has eaten** a sandwich.

To make the perfect tense of most verbs, use the present tense of *avoir* + past participle:

parler – to speak / to talk	
j'ai parlé	*nous **avons parlé***
*tu **as parlé***	*vous **avez parlé***
*il / elle / on **a parlé***	*ils / elles **ont parlé***

Some verbs use the present tense of *être* instead of *avoir*:

aller – to go	
*je **suis allé(e)***	*nous **sommes allé(e)s***
*tu **es allé(e)***	*vous **êtes allé(e)(s)***
*il **est allé***	*ils **sont allés***
*elle **est allée***	*elles **sont allées***
*on **est allé(e)(s)***	

Verbs that use *être* to form the perfect tense include:

aller	to go
arriver	to arrive
descendre	to go down
entrer	to enter
monter	to go up
mourir	to die
naître	to be born
partir	to leave
rentrer	to come back
rester	to stay
retourner	to return / to go back
sortir	to go out
tomber	to fall
venir	to come

All reflexive verbs use *être* to form the perfect tense. Don't forget the extra pronoun that comes before the part of *être*:

se lever – to get up	
*je **me suis levé(e)***	*nous **nous sommes levé(e)s***
*tu **t'es levé(e)***	*vous **vous êtes levé(e)(s)***
*il **s'est levé***	*ils **se sont levés***
*elle **s'est levée***	*elles **se sont levées***
*on **s'est levé(e)(s)***	

When using *être*:

- add -*e* to the past participle if the subject is female:

  *Elle est parti**e** en Écosse.*
  She went off to Scotland.

- add -*s* to the past participle if the subject is masculine plural:

  *Ils sont arrivé**s** en retard.*   They arrived late.

- add -*es* to the past participle if the subject is feminine plural:

  *Elles sont arrivé**es** en retard.*   They arrived late.

When making a negative statement in the perfect tense, *ne* comes before *avoir / être* and *pas* comes after it:

*Je **n'ai pas** mangé.*   I **haven't** eaten.
*Elle **n'est pas** sortie.* She **didn't** go out.

Past participles

The past participle of *-er* verbs ends in *-é*:

*aller – all**é***   gone
*donner – donn**é***   given
*parler – parl**é***   spoken

The past participle of regular *-ir* verbs ends in *-i*:

*choisir – chois**i***   chosen
*finir – fin**i***   finished

The past participle of regular *-re* verbs ends in *-u*:

*attendre – attend**u***   waited
*vendre – vend**u***   sold

Many common verbs have an irregular past participle:

*avoir – **eu***   had
*boire – **bu***   drunk
*devoir – **dû***   had to
*dire – **dit***   said
*écrire – **écrit***   written
*être – **été***   been
*faire – **fait***   done / made
*lire – **lu***   read
*mettre – **mis***   put
*pouvoir – **pu***   been able to
*prendre – **pris***   taken
*venir – **venu***   come
*voir – **vu***   seen
*vouloir – **voulu***   wanted

The imperfect tense

Use the imperfect tense:

- to describe what something or someone was like in the past:

*Il y **avait** une grande piscine.*
There **was** a big pool.

*C'**était** délicieux.*   It **was** delicious.

*J'**étais** triste.*   I **was** sad.

- to say what was happening at a certain time in the past:

*Je **regardais** la télé quand il a téléphoné.*
I **was watching** TV when he rang.

- to describe something that used to happen regularly in the past:

*Je **prenais** le bus tous les matins.*
I **used to catch** the bus every morning.

- after *si* to make a suggestion:

*Si on **allait** au cinéma?*
Shall we **go** to the cinema?

To form the imperfect tense, take the *nous* form of the verb in the present tense, remove *-ons* to form the stem, then add the correct endings:

finir – to finish	
(present tense: *nous* **finiss**ons)	
*je finiss**ais***	*nous finiss**ions***
*tu finiss**ais***	*vous finiss**iez***
*il / elle / on finiss**ait***	*ils / elles finiss**aient***

The verb *être* is the only exception. The endings are as above, but they are added to the stem *ét-*:

être – to be	
*j'ét**ais***	*nous ét**ions***
*tu ét**ais***	*vous ét**iez***
*il / elle / on ét**ait***	*ils / elles ét**aient***

Perfect or imperfect?

To help you decide between the perfect and the imperfect, remember that:

- the perfect tense usually describes single events in the past:

*Hier, je **me suis levée** à six heures.*
Yesterday, I **got up** at six.

- the imperfect describes what used to happen:

*Je **me levais** à huit heures.*
I **used to get up** at eight.

The pluperfect tense

This tense is used to refer to something further back in the past than the perfect or the imperfect, to say what someone had done or had been doing. You use the imperfect of *avoir* or *être*, plus a past participle:

*J'**avais** parlé.*   I **had spoken**.

*Il **était** parti.*   He **had left**.

*Vous **vous étiez habillés**.*
You **had got dressed**.

*Je savais qu'il **était allé** en Égypte.*
I knew that he **had gone** to Egypt.

The immediate future

Use the present tense of *aller* followed by an infinitive to say what you are going to do or what is going to happen:

je **vais pleurer**	I am going to cry
nous **allons manger**	we are going to eat
tu **vas partir**	you are going to leave
vous **allez boire**	you are going to drink
elle **va chanter**	she is going to sing
ils **vont dormir**	they are going to sleep

Je **vais continuer** mes études.
I'm **going to continue** studying.

Il **va neiger**. It's **going to snow**.

The future tense

The future tense expresses what will happen or will be happening in the future:

Qu'est-ce que vous **ferez** après l'école?
What **will you do** after school?

Vous **travaillerez** dans l'informatique?
Will you work in computing?

It is used for predictions such as weather forecasts:

Il **fera** beau / froid / chaud.
It **will be** fine / cold / hot.

Le temps **sera** pluvieux / nuageux.
The weather **will be** rainy / cloudy.

Il **neigera**.	It **will snow**.
Il **pleuvra**.	It **will rain**.
Il **gèlera**.	It **will freeze**.

To form the future tense, add the correct ending to the infinitive of the verb:

parler – to speak / to talk	
je parler**ai**	nous parler**ons**
tu parler**as**	vous parler**ez**
il / elle / on parler**a**	ils / elles parler**ont**

With some verbs, you add the same set of endings to an irregular stem instead of the infinitive:

aller – j'**ir**ai	pouvoir – je **pourr**ai
avoir – j'**aur**ai	savoir – je **saur**ai
être – je **ser**ai	venir – je **viendr**ai
faire – je **fer**ai	voir – je **verr**ai
falloir – il **faudr**a	vouloir – je **voudr**ai

The imperative

Use the imperative to give advice or instructions.

Use the *tu* form with a person your own age or a person you know very well:

Continue tout droit.	**Go** straight on.
Prends la première rue.	**Take** the first street.
Tourne à gauche.	**Turn** left.

Use the *vous* form with a person you don't know very well or to more than one person:

Continuez tout droit.	**Go** straight on.
Prenez la première rue.	**Take** the first street.
Tournez à gauche.	**Turn** left.

The imperative is the same as the *tu* or the *vous* form of the present tense, but without using a word for 'you' first. In the case of *-er* verbs, you miss off the *-s* of the *tu* form (unless the verb is followed by *y* or *en*):

Va au lit!	**Go** to bed!
Achète des pommes.	**Buy** some apples.
Vas-y!	**Go** on!
Achètes-en un kilo.	**Buy** a kilo (of them).

Note that all *vous* form imperatives end in *-ez* except for faire:

Faites vos devoirs! **Do** your homework!

Reflexive verbs in the imperative are hyphenated with their reflexive pronouns:

Lève-toi.	Stand up.
Asseyez-vous.	Sit down.

The conditional

You use the conditional in French when 'would' is used in English:

Je **voudrais** te voir.
I **would like** to see you.

Si j'étais riche, j'**achèterais** un piano.
If I **were** rich, I **would buy** a piano.

The conditional has the same stem as the future tense and the same endings as the imperfect:

	future	imperfect	conditional
aimer	j'**aimer**ai	j'**aim**ais	j'**aimer**ais
aller	j'**ir**ai	j'**all**ais	j'**ir**ais

parler – to talk / to speak	
je parler**ais**	nous parler**ions**
tu parler**ais**	vous parler**iez**
il / elle / on parler**ait**	ils / elles parler**aient**

The subjunctive

The following expressions are followed by a form of the verb called the subjunctive:

avant que	before
bien que	although
à condition que	provided that
il faut que	we / you / one must / it is necessary that

The most commonly used of these phrases is *il faut que*.

The subjunctive form is usually the same as, or similar to, the present tense, so it is easy to recognise.

*Il faut que vous **parliez** avec le patron.*
You must **speak** to the owner.

Some exceptions are *faire, aller, avoir* and *être* – these are different, and you need to be able to recognise them.

*Il faut qu'on **fasse** des économies d'eau.*
We must **save** water.

*Bien qu'il **ait** 25 ans, il habite toujours chez ses parents.*
Although he **is** 25, he still lives with his parents.

*Avant qu'elle **aille** à l'université, nous allons passer une semaine en Espagne.*
Before she **goes** to university, we're going to spend a week in Spain.

*Mon père m'a promis un nouveau vélo, à condition que mes résultats **soient** bons.*
My father has promised me a new bicycle, provided that my results **are** good.

parler (regular -er verb)	faire	aller
que je parle	que je fasse	que j'aille
que tu parles	que tu fasses	que tu ailles
qu'il / elle / on parle	qu'il / elle / on fasse	qu'il / elle / on aille
que nous parlions	que nous fassions	que nous allions
que vous parliez	que vous fassiez	que vous alliez
que ils / elles parlent	qu'ils / elles fassent	qu'ils / elles aillent

avoir	être
que j'aie	que je sois
que tu aies	que tu sois
qu'il / elle / on ait	qu'il / elle / on soit
que nous ayons	que nous soyons
que vous ayez	que vous soyez
qu'ils / elles aient	qu'ils / elles soient

The passive

The passive is used to say what is done to someone or something. It is formed from a part of *être* and a past participle. The past participle must agree with the noun:

active form: *Il lave la pomme.*
He washes the apple.

passive form: *La pomme **est lavée**.*
The apple **is washed**.

The passive can be used in different tenses:

present: *Les lits **sont faits**.*
The beds **are made**.

imperfect: *Les murs **étaient peints**.*
The walls **were painted**.

perfect: *J'**ai été invité**.*
I've **been invited**.

future: *La maison **sera vendue**.*
The house **will be sold**.

The passive is used less often in French than in English, as most sentences can be turned round:

- either by using *on*:

  ***On parle** français au Québec.*
  French **is spoken** in Quebec.

- or by using a reflexive verb:

  *Les tickets **se vendent** par carnets de 10.*
  Tickets **are sold** in books of 10.

en + present participle

The English present participle ends in '-ing', and the French present participle ends in -*ant*. Take the *nous* form of the present tense, remove -*ons* and replace it with –*ant*: *arriver* ➡ *arrivons* ➡ *arrivant*

En + present participle can be used when two actions happen together:

*Il fait ses devoirs **en chantant**.*
He does his homework **while singing**.

***En travaillant** le soir, je gagne de l'argent.*
By working in the evening, I earn money.

Useful verbs

avoir – to have

Use *avoir* to say how old someone is:

> *J'ai 15 ans.*   I **am** 15 years old.

Use *avoir mal* to talk about a pain or an ache:

> *J'ai mal à la tête.*   I **have** a head**ache**.

Use *avoir envie* to talk about feeling like or wanting to do something:

> *J'ai envie de courir.*   I **feel like** running.

Use *en avoir marre* to talk about being fed up with something:

> *J'en ai marre des examens.*
> I'**m fed up** with the exams.

Some more useful expressions with *avoir*:

avoir chaud	to be hot
avoir faim	to be hungry
avoir froid	to be cold
avoir mal au cœur	to feel sick
avoir peur	to be afraid
avoir raison	to be right
avoir soif	to be thirsty
avoir tort	to be wrong

il y a – there is, there are

Il y a une banque.	**There is** a bank.
Il y a beaucoup de cafés.	**There are** lots of cafés.
Il n'y a pas de piscine.	**There isn't** a swimming pool.

faire – to do

This verb can mean 'to do', 'to make' or 'to go' (when talking about activities):

faire du judo	**to do** judo
faire la vaisselle	**to do** the washing up
faire le lit	**to make** the bed
faire de la natation	**to go** swimming

This verb is also used with *il* to talk about the weather:

*Il **fait** beau.*	The weather is nice.
*Il **fait** mauvais.*	The weather is bad.

jouer à and *jouer de* – to play

To talk about playing games and sports, use *jouer + au / à la / à l' / aux*:

> *Je **joue au** basket.*   I play basketball.

To talk about playing a musical instrument, use *jouer + du / de la / de l' / des*:

> *Je **joue des** percussions.*
> I play percussion instruments.

se trouver – to be found, *être situé(e)* – to be situated

These verbs can be used in place of *être* to talk about where things are located:

> *La gare **se trouve** au centre-ville.*
> The station **can be found** in the town centre.

Make sure that *situé* agrees with the gender of the subject.

> *La ville **est située** au bord de la mer.*
> The town is **situated** by the sea.

Modal verbs: *devoir, pouvoir, vouloir*

Modal verbs are usually followed by an infinitive.

Use *devoir* (to have to) + infinitive to say what you must / mustn't do:

> *Je **dois porter** un uniforme.*
> I **have to wear** a uniform.

> *On **ne doit pas jeter** de papiers par terre.*
> You **mustn't drop** litter on the ground.

Use *pouvoir* (to be able to) + infinitive to say what you can / can't do:

> *On **peut faire** des randonnées.*
> You **can go** hiking.

> *Elle **ne peut pas sortir** pendant la semaine.*
> She **can't go out** during the week.

Use *vouloir* (to want to) + infinitive to say what you want and don't want to do. Adding *bien* changes the meaning:

> *Je **veux partir**.*   I **want to leave**.
> *Je **veux bien partir**.*   I **am quite happy to leave**.

The conditional of *vouloir*, *je voudrais*, means 'I would like':

> *Je **voudrais** partir en vacances.*
> I **would like** to go on holiday.

Note that *j'aimerais*, the conditional form of *aimer*, means the same as *je voudrais*:

> *J'**aimerais** faire de la planche à voile.*
> I **would like** to go windsurfing.

Impersonal verbs: *il neige, il pleut, il faut*

These verbs are only used with *il*:

> *Il neige.*　　**It**'s snowing.
> *Il pleut.*　　**It**'s raining.

Il faut can have different meanings depending on the context:

> ***Il faut*** *boire beaucoup d'eau.*
> **You must** drink a lot of water.

> *Il **ne faut pas** fumer.*
> **You mustn't** smoke.

> *Il **me faut** un kilo de tomates.*
> **I need** a kilo of tomatoes.

> *Il **faut** trois heures pour aller là-bas.*
> **It takes** three hours to get there.

G Negatives

To make a sentence negative, you normally put *ne* before the verb and *pas* after it:

> *Je parle espagnol.* ➡ *Je **ne** parle **pas** espagnol.*
> 　　　　　　　　　I **don't** speak Spanish.

Shorten *ne* to *n'* if the word that follows begins with *h* or a vowel:

> *C'est difficile.* ➡ *Ce **n'est pas** difficile.*
> 　　　　　　　　It's **not** difficult.

In negative sentences, use *de* instead of *un, une* or *des*:

> *Il y a un cinéma.* ➡ *Il **n'**y a **pas de** cinéma.*
> 　　　　　　　　　There is **no** cinema.

> *J'ai des frères.* ➡ *Je **n'**ai **pas de** frère.*
> 　　　　　　　　I **don't** have **any** brothers.

Other common negative phrases:

ne ... plus – no more	*Il **n'**y a **plus de** savon.* There is **no more** soap.
ne ... jamais – never	*Je **ne** fume **jamais**.* I **never** smoke.
ne ... rien – nothing / not anything	*Il **ne** fait **rien**.* He doesn't do **anything**.
ne ... personne not anybody	*Je **ne** vois **personne**.* I don't see **anybody**.
ne ... que – only	*Je **n'**ai **qu'**une sœur.* I **only** have one sister.
ne ... ni ... ni – neither ... nor	*Il **ne** parle **ni** français **ni** espagnol.* He speaks **neither** French **nor** Spanish.

Negatives in the perfect tense

In most negative phrases in the perfect tense, the phrase goes around the part of *avoir* or *être*.

> *Je **n'**ai **pas** dormi.*　　I **didn't** sleep.

But the negative phrases *ne ... que* and *ne ... ni ... ni* go around *avoir / être* and also the past participle:

> *Je **n'**ai mangé **que** du pain.*
> I **only** ate some bread.

Direct and indirect object pronouns are included within the negative phrase:

> *Je ne **l'**ai pas vu.*　　I didn't see **it**.
> *Il ne **me** parle plus.*　　He no longer speaks to **me**.

With reflexive verbs, the *ne* goes before the reflexive pronoun (*me, te,* etc.):

> *Il **ne** s'est **pas** lavé.*　　He **didn't** have a wash.

H Questions

You can turn statements into questions by adding a question mark and making your voice go up at the end:

> *Tu joues au tennis.* ➡ *Tu joues au tennis**?***
> 　　　　　　　　　**Do you** play tennis?

You can also add *est-ce que ...* at the beginning of the question:

> *Je peux vous aider.* ➡ ***Est-ce que*** *je peux vous aider?*
> 　　　　　　　　　**Can I** help you?

In more formal situations, you can change the word order so that the verb comes first:

> *Vous pouvez m'aider.* ➡ ***Pouvez**-vous m'aider?*
> 　　　　　　　　　**Can you** help me?

In the perfect tense, the auxiliary verb comes first:

> *Vous avez aidé la dame.* ➡ **Avez-vous** *aidé la dame?*
> 　　　　　　　　　**Did you** help the lady?

Many questions start with *qu'est-ce que ...*

> ***Qu'est-ce que*** *c'est?*　　**What** is it?

> ***Qu'est-ce qu'**il y a à manger?*
> **What** is there to eat?

> ***Qu'est-ce que*** *vous avez comme journaux?*
> **What** kind of newspapers have you got?

Other question words

combien (de)	how much / how many	*Tu as **combien** de chats?* **How many** cats have you got?

comment	how	***Comment** vas-tu?* **How** are you?	
où	where	***Où** habites-tu?* **Where** do you live?	
pourquoi	why	***Pourquoi** est-ce que tu n'aimes pas ça?* **Why** don't you like it?	
quand	when	*Il vient **quand**?* **When** is he coming? *\n**Quand** a-t-il commencé?* **When** did he start?	
quel / quelle / quels / quelles	which / what	*Ça commence à **quelle** heure?* **What** time does it start?	
que / qu'	what	***Que** veux-tu?* **What** do you want?	
qui	who	*C'est **qui**?* **Who** is it?	
quoi	what	*Elle fait **quoi**?* **What** is she doing?	

▌ I ▐ Prepositions

à, au, à la, à l', aux

À can mean:

in	*J'habite **à** Nice.*	I live **in** Nice.
at	*Je me lève **à** sept heures.*	I get up **at** seven.
to	*Je vais **à** l'école.*	I go **to** school.

Some special expressions with *à*:

à pied	**on** foot
à vélo	**by** bike
à gauche	**on** the left
à droite	**on** the right
*aller **à** la pêche*	to go fishing

masculine	feminine	nouns which start with a vowel or silent *h*	plural
à + le = au	*à + la = à la*	*à + l' = à l'*	*à + les = aux*

au théâtre	at / to the theatre
à la piscine	at / to the pool
à l'hôtel	at / to the hotel
aux États-Unis	in / to the USA

Use *au, à la, à l', aux* to talk about flavours and fillings:

*un sandwich **au jambon***	a **ham** sandwich
*une glace **à la vanille***	a **vanilla** ice cream
*un gâteau **à l'orange***	an **orange** cake

Use with *avoir mal* to talk about a part of the body that hurts:

*J'**ai mal à** l'oreille.*	I've got ear ache.
*Il **a mal aux** genoux.*	His knees hurt.

de

De is shortened to *d'* before a vowel or a silent *h*.

De can mean 'of':

*la mère **de** ma copine* (the mother of my friend) my friend's mother

*le prof **d'**histoire* (the teacher of history) the history teacher

Note that the word order can be different from English:

*un jus **d'**orange*	an orange juice
*un match **de** foot*	a football match
*la maison **de** mes grands-parents*	my grandparents' house

De can also mean 'from':

*Elle vient **d'**Écosse.*
She comes **from** Scotland.

De is sometimes part of an expression:

près de	near
*Il habite **près de** Lyon.*	He lives **near** Lyon.
de … à …	from … to …
*de neuf heures **à** cinq heures*	**from** nine **to** five

De is used for expressing contents and quantities. Some examples are:

beaucoup de	a lot of
une boîte de	a jar / tin of
une bouteille de	a bottle of
cent grammes de	100 grammes of
un kilo de	a kilo of
un peu de	a little / a bit of
*une **bouteille d'**eau*	a **bottle of** water
*un **kilo de** poires*	a **kilo of** pears
*un **peu de** sucre*	a **little** sugar

In a different context, *venir de* can mean 'to have just ...'

> *Il **vient de** retourner de vacances.*
> He **has just** returned from his holidays.

en, au / aux

En is used to introduce most names of countries. It means both 'to' and 'in':

> *Je vais **en** Allemagne.*   I am going **to** Germany.
> *Il habite **en** France.*   He lives **in** France.
> *Elle part **en** Angleterre.*   She's going **to** England.

A few names of countries are masculine. These are introduced with *au* or *aux*:

> *Il va **au** Portugal.*
> He's going **to** Portugal.

> *Elle habite **au** pays de Galles.*
> She lives **in** Wales.

> *Nous partons **aux** États-Unis.*
> We're going **to** the USA.

More prepositions

à côté de	next to	**à côté de** la salle de bains **next to** the bathroom
avec	with	*Je me dispute **avec** ma sœur.* I argue **with** my sister.
chez	at / to someone's house	*Je suis **chez** ma copine.* I'm **at** my friend's house. *Je vais **chez** mon copain.* I'm going **to** my friend's house.
dans	in	*Il est **dans** sa chambre.* He is **in** his bedroom.
derrière	behind	**derrière** l'hôtel **behind** the hotel
devant	in front of	*On se retrouve **devant** le théâtre?* Shall we meet **in front of** the theatre?
en face de	opposite	**en face du** parking **opposite** the car park
entre	between	**entre** la salle à manger et l'ascenseur **between** the dining room and the lift

pendant	during	*Qu'est-ce que tu fais **pendant** les vacances?* What are you doing **during** the holidays?
près de	near	*Mon chien est **près de** moi.* My dog is **near** me.
pour	for	*C'est super **pour** les jeunes.* It's great **for** young people.
sous	under	*Le chat est **sous** le lit.* The cat is **under** the bed.
sur	on	*Il y a des livres **sur** les étagères.* There are books **on** the shelves.

Expressions of time

depuis – for / since

To say how long you've been doing something, use the present tense with *depuis*:

> *J'apprends le français **depuis** quatre ans.*
> I have been learning French **for** four years.

> *J'ai mal à la gorge **depuis** hier.*
> I have had a sore throat **since** yesterday.

> To say how long you had been doing something, use the imperfect tense with *depuis*:
>
> > *J'attendais **depuis** une heure.*
> > I had been waiting **for** an hour.

pendant – for / during

To talk about a completed activity in the past and say how long it went on for, use the perfect tense and *pendant*:

> *J'ai joué au squash **pendant** deux ans.*
> I played squash **for** two years.

> #### Il y a
> You can use *il y a* with the perfect tense to mean 'ago'; not to be confused with *il y a* meaning 'there is' or 'there are'.
>
> > *Il a commencé à travailler **il y a** trois mois.*
> > He started working three months **ago**.

J Conjunctions

Conjunctions are words used to link parts of sentences together:

alors	so	*Je suis fatiguée, **alors** je me repose.* I am tired, **so** I'm having a rest.
car	because / as	*J'ai faim, **car** je n'ai pas mangé à midi.* I'm hungry **as** I didn't eat at lunchtime.
donc	therefore	*Je pense, **donc** je suis.* I think, **therefore** I am.
et	and	*J'ai 15 ans **et** j'habite en France.* I am 15 **and** I live in France.
et puis	and then	*Je me lève **et puis** je prends mon petit déjeuner.* I get up **and then** I have breakfast.
mais	but	*J'ai deux frères, **mais** je n'ai pas de sœur.* I've got two brothers, **but** I haven't got a sister.
ou	or	*Je joue au foot **ou** je vais à la patinoire.* I play football **or** I go to the ice-rink.
parce que	because	*J'aime la géographie **parce que** c'est intéressant.* I like geography **because** it's interesting.
quand	when	*Je prends le bus **quand** il pleut.* I take the bus **when** it rains.
si	if	*Samedi, je vais à la plage, **s'il** fait chaud.* On Saturday, I am going to go to the beach **if** it is hot.

Certain linking expressions are used with particular tenses:

- *au moment où*   just as

This expression is useful for linking a perfect tense phrase with an imperfect one:

> *Je suis arrivé **au moment où** mon père préparait le déjeuner.*
> I arrived **just as** my father was preparing lunch.

- *pendant que*   while

The expression is useful for linking an imperfect tense phrase with a perfect one:

> ***Pendant que** je nageais, ma copine a joué au volley.*
> **While** I was swimming, my friend played volleyball.

- *quand*   when

+ future: when talking about future intentions in English, the present tense is used after 'when', but in French the future is needed:

> ***Quand** j'irai à Boulogne, je mangerai du poisson.*
> **When** I go to Boulogne, I will eat fish.

+ imperfect: when talking about continuing or regular events in the past, the imperfect tense is used in both French and English:

> ***Quand** j'habitais à Paris, j'allais souvent au cinéma.*
> **When** I was living in Paris, I often used to go to the cinema.

- *tandis que*   while / whereas

This construction means 'whereas' when comparing an event in the past with an event in the future.

> *L'année dernière, j'ai fait de la voile, **tandis que** cette année je ferai du kayak.*
> Last year I went windsurfing, **whereas** this year I will go kayaking.

K Numbers

1	*un*	16	*seize*
2	*deux*	17	*dix-sept*
3	*trois*	18	*dix-huit*
4	*quatre*	19	*dix-neuf*
5	*cinq*	20	*vingt*
6	*six*	21	*vingt et un*
7	*sept*	22	*vingt-deux*
8	*huit*	23	*vingt-trois*
9	*neuf*	24	*vingt-quatre*
10	*dix*	25	*vingt-cinq*
11	*onze*	26	*vingt-six*
12	*douze*	27	*vingt-sept*
13	treize	28	*vingt-huit*
14	*quatorze*	29	*vingt-neuf*
15	*quinze*	30	*trente*

40	*quarante*	100	*cent*
41	*quarante et un*	101	*cent un*
42	*quarante-deux*	102	*cent deux*
50	*cinquante*	200	*deux cents*
51	*cinquante et un*	201	*deux cent un*
52	*cinquante-deux*	202	*deux cent deux*
60	*soixante*	300	*trois cents*
61	*soixante et un*	301	*trois cent un*
62	*soixante-deux*	302	*trois cent deux*
70	*soixante-dix*	1000	*mille*
71	*soixante et onze*	1001	*mille un*
72	*soixante-douze*	1002	*mille deux*
80	*quatre-vingts*	2000	*deux mille*
81	*quatre-vingt-un*	2001	*deux mille un*
82	*quatre-vingt-deux*	2002	*deux mille deux*
90	*quatre-vingt-dix*		
91	*quatre-vingt-onze*		
92	*quatre-vingt-douze*		

80, *quatre-vingts,* loses the final *s* before another digit or to give a page number or a date:

quatre-vingt-sept	eighty-seven
page quatre-vingt	page eighty
l'an mille neuf cent quatre-vingt	the year 1980

The same applies to 200, *deux cents,* and other multiples of *cent*:

deux cent dix	two hundred and ten
page trois cent	page three hundred

Ordinal numbers: *premier, deuxième*, etc.

The French for 'first' is *premier* in the masculine and *première* in the feminine:

mon **premier** *cours*	my **first** lesson
mes **premières** *vacances*	my **first** holiday

To say 'second', 'third', etc., simply add *-ième* to the original number:

deuxième	second
troisième	third

To say 'fifth', add a *u* before *-ième*:

cinquième	fifth

To say 'ninth', change the *f* of *neuf* to a *v*:

neuvième	ninth

If the original number ends with an *-e*, drop the *-e* before adding *-ième*:

quatrième	fourth
onzième	eleventh

To revise how numbers are used in dates and telling the time, see the reference section, pages 11 and 13.

Verb tables

L Verb tables

infinitive	present	perfect	imperfect	future
Regular -*er* verbs				
parler to speak	*je parle* *tu parles* *il / elle / on parle* *nous parlons* *vous parlez* *ils / elles parlent*	*j'ai parlé* *tu as parlé* *il / elle / on a parlé* *nous avons parlé* *vous avez parlé* *ils / elles ont parlé*	*je parlais* *tu parlais* *il / elle / on parlait* *nous parlions* *vous parliez* *ils / elles parlaient*	*je parlerai* *tu parleras* *il / elle / on parlera* *nous parlerons* *vous parlerez* *ils / elles parleront*
Regular -*ir* verbs				
finir to finish	*je finis* *tu finis* *il / elle / on finit* *nous finissons* *vous finissez* *ils / elles finissent*	*j'ai fini* *tu as fini* *il / elle / on a fini* *nous avons fini* *vous avez fini* *ils / elles ont fini*	*je finissais* *tu finissais* *il / elle / on finissait* *nous finissions* *vous finissiez* *ils / elles finissaient*	*je finirai* *tu finiras* *il / elle / on finira* *nous finirons* *vous finirez* *ils / elles finiront*
Regular -*re* verbs				
vendre to sell	*je vends* *tu vends* *il / elle / on vend* *nous vendons* *vous vendez* *ils / elles vendent*	*j'ai vendu* *tu as vendu* *il / elle / on a vendu* *nous avons vendu* *vous avez vendu* *ils / elles ont vendu*	*je vendais* *tu vendais* *il / elle / on vendait* *nous vendions* *vous vendiez* *ils / elles vendaient*	*je vendrai* *tu vendras* *il / elle / on vendra* *nous vendrons* *vous vendrez* *ils / elles vendront*
Reflexive verbs				
se laver to have a wash	*je me lave* *tu te laves* *il se lave* *elle se lave* *on se lave* *nous nous lavons* *vous vous lavez* *ils se lavent* *elles se lavent*	*je me suis lavé(e)* *tu t'es lavé(e)* *il s'est lavé* *elle s'est lavée* *on s'est lavé(e)(s)* *nous nous sommes lavé(e)s* *vous vous êtes lavé(e)(s)* *ils se sont lavés* *elles se sont lavées*	*je me lavais* *tu te lavais* *il se lavait* *elle se lavait* *on se lavait* *nous nous lavions* *vous vous laviez* *ils se lavaient* *elles se lavaient*	*je me laverai* *tu te laveras* *il se lavera* *elle se lavera* *on se lavera* *nous nous laverons* *vous vous laverez* *ils se laveront* *elles se laveront*

infinitive	present	perfect	imperfect	future
aller to go	je vais tu vas il va elle va on va nous allons vous allez ils vont elles vont	je suis allé(e) tu es allé(e) il est allé elle est allée on est allé(e)(s) nous sommes allé(e)s vous êtes allé(e)(s) ils sont allés elles sont allées	j'allais tu allais il allait elle allait on allait nous allions vous alliez ils allaient elles allaient	j'irai tu iras il ira elle ira on ira nous irons vous irez ils iront elles iront
avoir to have	j'ai tu as il / elle / on a nous avons vous avez ils / elles ont	j'ai eu tu as eu il / elle / on a eu nous avons eu vous avez eu ils / elles ont eu	j'avais tu avais il / elle / on avait nous avions vous aviez ils / elles avaient	j'aurai tu auras il / elle / on aura nous aurons vous aurez ils / elles auront
boire to drink	je bois tu bois il / elle / on boit nous buvons vous buvez ils / elles boivent	j'ai bu tu as bu il / elle / on a bu nous avons bu vous avez bu ils / elles ont bu	je buvais tu buvais il / elle / on buvait nous buvions vous buviez ils / elles buvaient	je boirai tu boiras il / elle / on boira nous boirons vous boirez ils / elles boiront
connaître to know	je connais tu connais il / elle / on connaît nous connaissons vous connaissez ils / elles connaissent	j'ai connu tu as connu il / elle / on a connu nous avons connu vous avez connu ils / elles ont connu	je connaissais tu connaissais il / elle / on connaissait nous connaissions vous connaissiez ils / elles connaissaient	je connaîtrai tu connaîtras il / elle / on connaîtra nous connaîtrons vous connaîtrez ils / elles connaîtront
croire to believe	je crois tu crois il / elle / on croit nous croyons vous croyez ils / elles croient	j'ai cru tu as cru il / elle / on a cru nous avons cru vous avez cru ils / elles ont cru	je croyais tu croyais il / elle / on croyait nous croyions vous croyiez ils / elles croyaient	je croirai tu croiras il / elle / on croira nous croirons vous croirez ils / elles croiront
devoir to have to	je dois tu dois il / elle / on doit nous devons vous devez ils / elles doivent	j'ai dû tu as dû il / elle / on a dû nous avons dû vous avez dû ils / elles ont dû	je devais tu devais il / elle / on devait nous devions vous deviez ils / elles devaient	je devrai tu devras il / elle / on devra nous devrons vous devrez ils / elles devront

infinitive	present	perfect	imperfect	future
dire to say	je dis tu dis il / elle / on dit nous disons vous dites ils / elles disent	j'ai dit tu as dit il / elle / on a dit nous avons dit vous avez dit ils / elles ont dit	je disais tu disais il / elle / on disait nous disions vous disiez ils / elles disaient	je dirai tu diras il / elle / on dira nous dirons vous direz ils / elles diront
dormir to sleep	je dors tu dors il / elle / on dort nous dormons vous dormez ils / elles dorment	j'ai dormi tu as dormi il / elle / on a dormi nous avons dormi vous avez dormi ils / elles ont dormi	je dormais tu dormais il / elle / on dormait nous dormions vous dormiez ils / elles dormaient	je dormirai tu dormiras il / elle / on dormira nous dormirons vous dormirez ils / elles dormiront
écrire to write	j'écris tu écris il / elle / on écrit nous écrivons vous écrivez ils / elles écrivent	j'ai écrit tu as écrit il / elle / on a écrit nous avons écrit vous avez écrit ils / elles ont écrit	j'écrivais tu écrivais il / elle / on écrivait nous écrivions vous écriviez ils / elles écrivaient	j'écrirai tu écriras il / elle / on écrira nous écrirons vous écrirez ils / elles écriront
être to be	je suis tu es il / elle / on est nous sommes vous êtes ils / elles sont	j'ai été tu as été il / elle / on a été nous avons été vous avez été ils / elles ont été	j'étais tu étais il / elle / on était nous étions vous étiez ils / elles étaient	je serai tu seras il / elle / on sera nous serons vous serez ils / elles seront
faire to do / to make	je fais tu fais il / elle / on fait nous faisons vous faites ils / elles font	j'ai fait tu as fait il / elle / on a fait nous avons fait vous avez fait ils / elles ont fait	je faisais tu faisais il / elle / on faisait nous faisions vous faisiez ils / elles faisaient	je ferai tu feras il / elle / on fera nous ferons vous ferez ils / elles feront
lire to read	je lis tu lis il / elle / on lit nous lisons vous lisez ils / elles lisent	j'ai lu tu as lu il / elle / on a lu nous avons lu vous avez lu ils / elles ont lu	je lisais tu lisais il / elle / on lisait nous lisions vous lisiez ils / elles lisaient	je lirai tu liras il / elle / on lira nous lirons vous lirez ils / elles liront

infinitive	present	perfect	imperfect	future
mettre to put	je mets tu mets il / elle / on met nous mettons vous mettez ils / elles mettent	j'ai mis tu as mis il / elle / on a mis nous avons mis vous avez mis ils / elles ont mis	je mettais tu mettais il / elle / on mettait nous mettions vous mettiez ils / elles mettaient	je mettrai tu mettras il / elle / on mettra nous mettrons vous mettrez ils / elles mettront
partir to leave	je pars tu pars il part elle part on part nous partons vous partez ils partent elles partent	je suis parti(e) tu es parti(e) il est parti elle est partie on est parti(e)(s) nous sommes parti(e)s vous êtes parti(e)(s) ils sont partis elles sont parties	je partais tu partais il partait elle partait on partait nous partions vous partiez ils partaient elles partaient	je partirai tu partiras il partira elle partira on partira nous partirons vous partirez ils partiront elles partiront
pouvoir to be able to	je peux tu peux il / elle / on peut nous pouvons vous pouvez ils / elles peuvent	j'ai pu tu as pu il / elle / on a pu nous avons pu vous avez pu ils / elles ont pu	je pouvais tu pouvais il / elle / on pouvait nous pouvions vous pouviez ils / elles pouvaient	je pourrai tu pourras il / elle / on pourra nous pourrons vous pourrez ils / elles pourront
prendre to take	je prends tu prends il / elle / on prend nous prenons vous prenez ils / elles prennent	j'ai pris tu as pris il / elle / on a pris nous avons pris vous avez pris ils / elles ont pris	je prenais tu prenais il / elle / on prenait nous prenions vous preniez ils / elles prenaient	je prendrai tu prendras il / elle / on prendra nous prendrons vous prendrez ils / elles prendront
recevoir to receive	je reçois tu reçois il / elle / on reçoit nous recevons vous recevez ils / elles reçoivent	j'ai reçu tu as reçu il / elle / on a reçu nous avons reçu vous avez reçu ils / elles ont reçu	je recevais tu recevais il / elle / on recevait nous recevions vous receviez ils / elles recevaient	je recevrai tu recevras il / elle / on recevra nous recevrons vous recevrez ils / elles recevront
savoir to know	je sais tu sais il / elle / on sait nous savons vous savez ils / elles savent	j'ai su tu as su il / elle / on a su nous avons su vous avez su ils / elles ont su	je savais tu savais il / elle / on savait nous savions vous saviez ils / elles savaient	je saurai tu sauras il / elle / on saura nous saurons vous saurez ils / elles sauront

infinitive	present	perfect	imperfect	future
sortir to go out	je sors tu sors il sort elle sort on sort nous sortons vous sortez ils sortent elles sortent	je suis sorti(e) tu es sorti(e) il est sorti elle est sortie on est sorti(e)(s) nous sommes sorti(e)s vous êtes sorti(e)(s) ils sont sortis elles sont sorties	je sortais tu sortais il sortait elle sortait on sortait nous sortions vous sortiez ils sortaient elles sortaient	je sortirai tu sortiras il sortira elle sortira on sortira nous sortirons vous sortirez ils sortiront elles sortiront
venir to come	je viens tu viens il vient elle vient on vient nous venons vous venez ils viennent elles viennent	je suis venu(e) tu es venu(e) il est venu elle est venue on est venu(e)(s) nous sommes venu(e)s vous êtes venu(e)(s) ils sont venus elles sont venues	je venais tu venais il venait elle venait on venait nous venions vous veniez ils venaient elles venaient	je viendrai tu viendras il viendra elle viendra on viendra nous viendrons vous viendrez ils viendront elles viendront
vivre to live	je vis tu vis il / elle / on vit nous vivons vous vivez ils / elles vivent	j'ai vécu tu as vécu il / elle / on a vécu nous avons vécu vous avez vécu ils / elles ont vécu	je vivais tu vivais il / elle / on vivait nous vivions vous viviez ils / elles vivaient	je vivrai tu vivras il / elle / on vivra nous vivrons vous vivrez ils / elles vivront
voir to see	je vois tu vois il / elle / on voit nous voyons vous voyez ils / elles voient	j'ai vu tu as vu il / elle / on a vu nous avons vu vous avez vu ils / elles ont vu	je voyais tu voyais il / elle / on voyait nous voyions vous voyiez ils / elles voyaient	je verrai tu verras il / elle / on verra nous verrons vous verrez ils / elles verront
vouloir to want	je veux tu veux il / elle / on veut nous voulons vous voulez ils / elles veulent	j'ai voulu tu as voulu il / elle / on a voulu nous avons voulu vous avez voulu ils / elles ont voulu	je voulais tu voulais il / elle / on voulait nous voulions vous vouliez ils / elles voulaient	je voudrai tu voudras il / elle / on voudra nous voudrons vous voudrez ils / elles voudront

Glossaire

A

à chaque fois each time
à côté de next to
à mon avis in my opinion
à une époque at one time
aboyer to bark
l'abricot (m) apricot
accompagner to accompany
acheter to buy
l'activité (f) physique physical activity
les actualités (f) the news
actuel(le) present
admis admitted
l'ado (m / f) adolescent / young person
l'agneau (m) lamb
agresser to attack / to assault
l'agriculteur / agricultrice farmer
aider to help
ailleurs elsewhere
aîné(e) older
l'aire (f) de repos stopping area (off the motorway, with basic facilities)
l'aire (f) de jeux playground
l'alcool (m) alcohol
alcoolisé(e) alcoholic (drinks)
l'alcoolisme (m) alcoholism
l'alimentation (f) diet
aller to go
aller à la pêche to go fishing
aller chercher to fetch
allergique allergic
alors so
l'alpinisme (m) mountaineering
l'alto (m) viola
améliorer to improve
l'ampoule (f) bulb
s'amuser to enjoy yourself / to have fun
ancien(ne) former
l'anglais (m) English
animé(e) lively
l'année (f) sabbatique gap year
l'anniversaire (m) birthday
l'annonce (f) advert

annuler to cancel
l'anorexie (f) anorexia
août August
l'appareil (m) camera / machine
l'appareil numérique (m) digital camera
l'appartement (m) apartment / flat
apprécier to appreciate
apprendre (appris) to learn
l'apprentissage (m) apprenticeship
après after (that)
l'arbre (m) tree
l'argent (m) money
l'argent (m) de poche pocket money
l'armoire (f) wardrobe
l'arrêt (m) (d'autobus) bus stop
arrêter to stop
l'arrondissement (m) administrative district of Paris
arroser to water
l'aspirateur (m) vacuum cleaner
assez quite
assis(e) sitting down / seated
assister à to be present at / to take part in
l'association (f) caritative charity / charitable organisation
l'athlétisme (m) athletics
l'Atlantique (m) the Atlantic
attaquer to attack
attendre (attendu) to wait
atterrir (atterri) to land
attirer to attract
au secours! help!
l'auberge (f) de jeunesse youth hostel
augmenter to increase
autant que possible as much as possible
l'automne (m) autumn
l'automobiliste (m) car driver
l'autoroute (f) motorway
l'avenir (m) the future
l'averse (f) (rain) shower

avertir to warn
en avion by aeroplane
l'avis (m) opinion
l'avocat / avocate lawyer
avoir to have
avoir … ans to be … years old
avoir besoin de to need
avoir chaud to be hot
avoir du mal à to have difficulty (doing something)
avoir envie de to want to / to feel like
avoir faim to be hungry
avoir froid to be cold
avoir l'intention de to intend
avoir l'occasion de to have the chance to
avoir mal à la tête to have a headache
avoir mal au cœur to feel sick
avoir peur to be afraid
avoir raison to be right
avoir soif to be thirsty
avoir tort to be wrong
avril April

B

le bac an exam equivalent to A-levels
les bagages (m) luggage
la bague ring
se baigner to bathe / to swim
baisser to lower
la bande dessinée comic book / cartoon strip
la banlieue suburb
barbant(e) boring
bas(se) low
le basket basketball
les baskets (f) trainers
la bataille battle
le bateau ship / boat
en bateau by boat
la batterie drums
bavarder to chat
le bazar chaos
le beau-père stepfather (also means father-in-law)

la Belgique Belgium

beaucoup (de) a lot (of)

la belle-mère stepmother (also means mother-in-law)

le / la bénévole volunteer

la bêtise something stupid

bien équipé(e) well equipped / with good facilities

bien payé(e) well paid

bien s'amuser to have a good time

bienvenue welcome

les bijoux (m) jewellery

la biologie biology

bio / biologique organic

la biscotte biscuit (like toast)

blanc(he) white

bleu(e) blue

le bloggeur blogger

le bœuf beef

boire (bu) to drink

la boisson drink

la boîte box / tin

la boîte aux lettres électronique (email) inbox

la boîte de nuit night club

bon anniversaire! happy birthday!

une bonne ambiance a good atmosphere

le bonnet hat

à bord on board

le bord de la mer seaside

la botte boot

la bouche mouth

le boucher / la bouchère butcher

la boucherie butcher's

bouger to move

le boulanger / la boulangère baker

la boulangerie (f) baker's (bread)

boulimique bulimic

le boulot work (informal)

la boum party

la bouteille bottle

la boutique shop

le bras arm

la Bretagne Brittany

briller to shine

bronzer to sunbathe / to get a tan

se brosser les dents to brush one's teeth

le brouillard fog

la brousse bush / bushes

le bruit noise

brûler to burn

bruyant(e) noisy

le bureau office / desk

en bus by bus

le but goal

C

la cabane shed / hut

le cabinet vétérinaire vet's

cacher to hide

le cadeau present

le cahier notebook

la caisse cash register / till

le caissier / la caissière cashier

le calcul (m) sums / arithmetic

calme quiet / placid

le camion lorry

la campagne countryside

le camping campsite

le canapé sofa

le candidat candidate

la canne à sucre sugar cane

le canoë-kayak canoeing

la cantine dining hall

la capuche hood

car because / as

en car by coach

le car de ramassage school bus

caresser to stroke

le carrefour crossroads

le carton cardboard

le casque helmet

casse-pieds infuriating / a pain

la cathédrale cathedral

la cave cellar

le CDI (centre de documentation et d'information) library

la ceinture belt

célèbre famous

célibataire single

le centre centre

le centre commercial shopping centre

le centre culturel cultural centre

le centre de recyclage recycling centre

le centre sportif sports centre

le centre-ville town centre

les céréales (f) cereal

le cerveau brain

la chaîne channel (TV)

la chaleur warmth, heat

la chambre bedroom

la chambre d'hôte bed & breakfast

le chameau camel

le champ field

le champignon mushroom

le changement climatique climate change

la chanson song

chanter to sing

le chanteur / la chanteuse singer

le chapeau hat

chaque each

la charcuterie pork butcher's / delicatessen

le chat cat

chaud hot

chauffer to heat

les chaussettes (f) socks

les chaussures (f) shoes

le chef du personnel personnel manager

la chemise shirt

le chemisier blouse

cher(-ère) dear / expensive

chercher to look for

les cheveux (m) hair

chic smart

le chien dog

la chimie chemistry

chimique chemical

chinois(e) Chinese

le choix choice

le chômage unemployment

choquant(e) shocking

chrétien(ne) Christian

le cidre cider

le ciel sky

le cimetière cemetery

le cinéma cinema

la circulation traffic

la cité housing estate

le citron   lemon
le citron vert   lime
le clavier   keyboard
le / la client(e)   customer
le climat   climate
la climatisation   air conditioning
le cœur   heart
collecter (de l'argent)   to collect / raise (money)
collecter des fonds   to collect funds
le / la collègue   colleague
combattre   to combat / to fight
combien (de)   how much / how many
la comédie   comedy
comme d'habitude   as usual
comment   how
le / la commerçant(e)   shopkeeper
la commode   chest of drawers
compréhensif(-ve)   tolerant / understanding
le comprimé   tablet
compris(e)   included
le / la comptable   accountant
le compte bancaire   bank account
compter   to count
le concombre   cucumber
le concubinage   living together (without being married)
conduire (conduit)   to drive
la confiance   confidence
la confiance en soi   self-confidence
se confier à   to confide in
la confiserie   sweet shop
le congélateur   the freezer
la connaissance   knowledge / consciousness
consacrer   to devote (time)
le conseil   council / advice
conseiller   to advise
la console de jeu   games console
la consommation   consumption
consommer   to consume
construire (construit)   to build
contaminé(e)   contaminated
le contrôle   test
le corps   body

la correspondance   change (on train journey)
la Corse   Corsica
la côte   coast / rib
la côtelette   chop / cutlet
la Côte d'Ivoire   the Ivory Coast
le coton   cotton
en coton   (made of) cotton
se coucher   to go to bed
la couleur vive   bright colour
le coupable   culprit
la cour de récréation   playground
le cours   lesson
le coût   cost
coûter   to cost
la couture   high fashion
le couturier   fashion designer
couvert   overcast
le crayon   pencil
créole   creole
la crêpe   pancake
la crevette   prawn
la crise cardiaque   heart attack
la croisière   cruise (holiday)
en cuir   (made of) leather
la cuisine   kitchen / cooking / cuisine (national)
le cuisinier / la cuisinière   cook / chef
cultiver   to grow

D

dans   in
le danseur / la danseuse   dancer
le déboisement   deforestation
au début   at the beginning
décembre   December
la décharge publique   rubbish dump
les déchets (m)   rubbish / waste
décider   to decide
décoller   to take off (plane)
décontracté(e)   relaxed
découvrir (découvert)   to discover
défavorisé(e)   disadvantaged
le défilé (de mode)   fashion show
dégoûtant(e)   disgusting
le degré   degree
dehors   outside

le déjeuner   lunch
délicieux(-ieuse)   delicious
le deltaplane   hang-gliding
déménager   to move house
et demi(e)   half past
le demi-frère   half brother
le / la demi-pensionnaire   day boarder (someone who has lunch at school)
démodé(e)   out of date
les dents (f)   teeth
dépendant(e)   addicted
dépenser   to spend (money)
se déplacer   to get around
déprimé(e)   depressed
derrière   behind
désagréable   unpleasant
désespéré(e)   desperate
le dessin   art
dessiner   to draw
le dessin animé   cartoon (film)
se détendre (détendu)   to relax / to calm down
la détente   relaxation / chilling out
détruire (détruit)   to destroy
la dette   debt
deux fois par mois   twice a month
la deuxième rue   the second street
devant   in front of
devenir   to become
le déversement   dumping
les devoirs (m)   homework
le dictionnaire (bilingue)   (bilingual) dictionary
difficile (à croire)   difficult (to believe)
dimanche   Sunday
le dîner   dinner
le directeur / la directrice   headteacher
diriger   to direct / to manage
discipliné(e)   disciplined / punished
disparaître (disparu)   to disappear
se disputer   to argue
divorcé(e)   divorced
les données (f) personnelles   personal details
donner sur   to look out over

dormir to sleep
le dortoir dormitory
le dos back
doucement gently
se doucher to have a shower
doué(e) gifted / clever
la douleur pain
doux / douce mild / soft / gentle
se droguer to take drugs
les drogues (f) douces soft drugs
les drogues (f) dures hard drugs
le droit law
à droite on / to the right
drôle funny
dur(e) hard
durer to last

E

l'eau (f) water
l'éboueur (m) refuse collector
échapper to escape
les échecs (m) chess
échouer à to fail
l'éclair (m) lightning
l'éclaircie (f) sunny spell
écologique ecological, green
l'écran (m) tactile touch screen
l'effet (m) de serre the greenhouse effect
l'égalité (f) equality
l'église (f) church
l'électricien(ne) (m / f) electrician
l'élève (m / f) pupil
l'emballage (m) packaging
embaucher to recruit
l'embouteillage (m) traffic jam
émettre (émis) to emit
l'émission (f) de télévision TV programme
empêcher to prevent / to get in the way of / to stop
l'emplacement (m) place / site
l'emploi (m) emloyment
l'employé(e) (m / f) employee
emporter to take (with you)
emprunter to borrow
en avoir marre de to be fed up of
en bonne forme in good shape
en ce moment at the moment
en ligne online

en version originale in the original language (films)
l'endroit (m) place
l'ennemi (m) enemy
l'ennui (m) worry / problem / boredom
s'ennuyer to get bored / to be bored
l'enquête (f) enquiry / investigation
enregistrer to record
enrichissant(e) rewarding
l'enseignement (m) teaching / education
enseigner to teach
ensemble together
ensoleillé(e) sunny
ensuite then
s'entendre (avec quelqu'un) (entendu) to get on (with someone)
entouré(e) surrounded
s'entraîner to train
l'entraîneur (m) trainer
entre between
entre … et … between … and …
l'entreprise (f) business / firm
l'entreprise (f) de logiciels software business
l'entretien (m) interview
environ about
l'environnement (m) the environment
envoyer to send
épicé(e) spicy
l'épicerie (f) grocery shop
l'épouse (f) wife (spouse)
épouser to marry (someone)
l'époux (m) husband (spouse)
l'EPS (f) PE
épuiser to exhaust
l'équilibre (m) balance
équilibré(e) balanced
l'équipe (f) team
l'équitation (f) horse riding
l'escalade (f) rock climbing
l'espace (m) vert park
l'espagnol (m) Spanish
l'espoir (m) hope
l'essence (f) petrol
l'est (m) east

et and
l'étage (m) floor
l'étagère (f) shelf
l'été (m) summer
éteindre (éteint) to switch off / to turn off
l'étranger (m) / l'étrangère (f) stranger / foreigner
à l'étranger (m) abroad
étranger(-ère) foreign
être accro to have a habit (addiction)
être hors d'haleine to be out of breath
être en train de to be in the middle / process of
étroit(e) tight / narrow
l'étude (f) study
l'événement event
éviter to avoid
excessif(-ve) excessive
s'excuser to apologise
l'explication (f) explanation
expliquer to explain
exprimer to express
à l'extérieur outside
extraverti(e) extrovert, outgoing

F

fabriquer to manufacture
se fâcher to get cross
la faculté university
faire (fait) to do / to make
faire attention to pay attention
faire beau to be nice weather
faire de la planche à voile to go windsurfing
faire de la voile to go sailing
faire des économies (f) to save up
faire des randonnées to go hiking
faire des recherches to do research
faire du cyclisme to go cycling
faire du jardinage to do the gardening
faire du lèche-vitrine to go window shopping
faire la cuisine to cook
faire la grasse matinée to have a lie in

faire la lessive   to do the washing

faire la vaisselle   to do the washing up

faire le ménage   to do the housework

faire les achats   to do the shopping

faire les courses   to do the shopping

faire les magasins   to go shopping

faire mauvais   to be bad weather

faire partie de   to belong to

faire une cure   to take a course of treatment

il fait beau   the weather's nice

il fait chaud   it's hot

il fait froid   it's cold

il fait mauvais   the weather's bad

la famille nombreuse   large family

le / la fana   fan / enthusiast

fatigué(e)   tired

le fauteuil   armchair

le fauteuil roulant   wheelchair

la femme   woman / wife

la femme au foyer   housewife

la femme de ménage   cleaning lady

la fenêtre   window

la ferme   farm

la fête   party / celebration

la fête de l'Aïd el Kebir   Eid Ul Fitr festival

fêter   to celebrate

le feu   fire

feuilleter   to flick through

le feuilleton   soap (TV series)

les feux (m)   traffic lights

les feux (m) rouges   red lights (traffic lights)

février   February

les fiançailles (f)   engagement (to be married)

fidèle   loyal / faithful

fier / fière   proud

la fièvre   fever

le fils   son

la flûte   flute

le foie   liver

fondre   to melt

la fontaine   fountain

la forêt   forest

la forêt tropicale   rainforest

la formation professionnelle   professional training

se former   to train (for a job)

fort(e)   strong

le foulard   scarf

les frais (m)   expenses

le français   French

frapper   to hit

le froid   cold

le fromage   cheese

la frontière   border (between countries)

la fumée   smoke

fumer   to smoke

le fumeur   smoker

G

gâcher   to waste / to spoil

gagner   to win / to earn

garder   to look after / to keep

garder la forme   to keep in shape

la gare   railway station

la gare routière   coach station / bus station

à gauche   on / to the left

les gaz (m) d'échappement   exhaust fumes

geler   to freeze

gênant(e)   inconvenient / annoying

gêné(e)   embarrassed

gêner   to be a nuisance

en général   generally

le genou   knee

le genre   type

la géographie   geography

le gigot d'agneau   leg of lamb

le gilet   cardigan

le gîte   self-catering accommodation / holiday cottage

la glace   ice

la gomme   eraser

la gorge   throat

le goût   taste

goûter   to taste

le grain de café   coffee bean

la graisse   fat

grand(e)   large

la grand-mère   grandmother

le grand-père   grandfather

la grasse matinée   lie-in

gratuit(e)   free (no cost)

gratuitement   free

le grenier   attic

la grippe   flu

gris(e)   grey

gros(se)   fat

la guerre   war

le guichet   ticket office

la guitare   guitar

le gymnase   gym

H

l'habillement (m)   clothes

s'habiller   to get dressed

l'habitant(e) (m / f)   inhabitant

habiter   to live

d'habitude   usually

l'habitude (f)   habit

la haie   hedge

les halles (f)   food hall

les haricots (m) verts   green beans

l'herbe (f)   grass

à l'heure   on time

le héros (m)   hero

heures   o'clock / hours

l'heure (f) d'affluence   rush hour

l'heure (f) d'étude   study period

historique   historical

l'hiver (m)   winter

le / la HLM   block of high-rise council flats

l'homme (m) au foyer   house husband

l'horaire (m)   timetable

l'hôtel (m) de ville   town hall

l'hôtesse (f) de l'air   air stewardess

humide   humid

humiliant(e)   humiliating

I

il y a   there is / there are / ago (time)

il y a des nuages   it's cloudy

il y a du brouillard   it's foggy

il y a du soleil   it's sunny

il y a du vent   it's windy

il y avait   there was / were

l'île (f) island

l'immeuble (m) building / block of flats

l'immigré(e) (m / f) immigrant

inciter à to stir up / to incite

l'incivilité (f) rude behaviour

des inconnus (m) strangers

l'infirmier (m) / infirmière (f) nurse

l'informatique (f) information technology / ICT

l'ingénieur (m) engineer

injuste unfair

l'inondation (f) flood

inondé(e) flooded

(s')inquiéter to worry

l'instruction (f) civique citizenship

l'instruction (f) religieuse RE

interdit(e) forbidden

l'interprète (m / f) interpreter

intitulé(e) entitled

introduire to introduce

islamique Islamic

isolé(e) isolated

ivre drunk

J

j'en ai marre! I'm fed up!

jaloux(-se) jealous / possessive

jamais never

la jambe leg

janvier January

le jardin garden

le jardin public park / public garden

le jardin zoologique zoo

le jardinier / la jardinière (paysagiste) (landscape) gardener

jaune yellow

le jean jeans

jeter to throw (away)

le jeu (les jeux) game / game show

le jeu vidéo computer game

jeudi Thursday

les jeunes délinquants (m) juvenile delinquants

joli(e) pretty

jouer to play

jouer à la pétanque to play (French) bowls

le jour de l'an New Year's Day

le jour férié public holiday

juif(-ve) Jewish

juillet July

juin June

la jupe skirt

le jus juice

L

le laboratoire laboratory

en laine woollen

le lait milk

la langue vivante modern language

large loose-fitting / broad

le lavabo washbasin

se laver to have a wash

le lecteur DVD DVD player

le lecteur mp3 mp3 player

léger(-ère) light

le légume vegetable

se lever to get up

la librairie bookshop

la licence degree

le / la licencié(e) university graduate

lier to link

le lieu place

le lieu de travail workplace

la ligne line / route

lire (lu) to read

le lit bed

les lits (m) superposés bunk beds

le livre book

le logement housing / accommodation

loger to live / to stay

logique logical

la loi law

les loisirs (m) leisure activities

louer to rent / to hire

loyal(e) loyal / faithful

le loyer rent

la lumière light

lundi Monday

lutter to struggle

le lycée high school (for students aged 16–18)

M

mâcher to chew

le magasin shop

le maçon builder

mai May

maigre thin

le maillot de bain swimming costume

la main hand

la mairie town hall

mais but

la maison house

la maison de couture fashion house

le mal de mer seasickness

la maladie illness

malgré in spite of

la manche sleeve

manger équilibré to eat a balanced diet

la manifestation (public) demonstration

le mannequin fashion model

le manque lack

manquer to miss / to be lacking

le maquillage make-up

se maquiller to put make-up on

le marché market

marcher to work (of a machine)

mardi Tuesday

le mari husband

le mariage marriage / wedding

se marier to get married

le Maroc Morocco

marquer un but to score a goal

marron brown

mars March

les maths / mathématiques (f) maths

la matinée morning

de mauvaise humeur in a bad mood

de mauvaises notes (f) bad marks

le / la mécanicien(ne) mechanic

méchant(e) nasty / naughty

la médaille medal

la Méditerranée the Mediterranean

la méduse jellyfish

même same

mener to lead
la menthe mint
mentir (menti) to lie
la mer sea
mercredi Wednesday
la mère mother
le métier job / profession
le métro the underground (in Paris)
en métro on the underground
la météo weather forecast
mettre (mis) to put (on)
mettre à jour to update
se mettre en colère to get angry
mettre la table to set / lay the table
midi midday
mignon(ne) cute
le milieu rural rural environment
mince slim
minuit midnight
la mode fashion
moins le quart quarter to
mondial(e) global
le moniteur / la monitrice sports trainer / instructor
la monogamie monogamy
monoparental(e) single-parent
la montagne mountain(s)
montrer to show
se moquer de to make fun of
la moquette carpet
mort(e) dead
le moteur de recherche search engine
motiver to motivate
à moto by motorbike
mouillé(e) wet
le moyen de transport means of transport
multinational(e) multinational (company)
la municipalité local council
musclé(e) muscular
la musculation weight training
le / la musicien(ne) musician
le / la musulman(e) Muslim

N

nager to swim
naïf(-ve) naive, unsuspecting

la naissance birth
naître (né) to be born
la natation swimming
ne … aucun not any / none
neiger to snow
nettoyer to clean
le nez nose
le niveau level
Noël (m) Christmas
noir(e) black
la noix nut
le nord north
normalement usually / normally
la nourriture food
nouveau (nouvelle) new
le Nouvel An New Year
les nouvelles (f) news
novembre November
le nuage cloud
nuageux cloudy

O

l'obésité (f) obesity
obligatoire compulsory
s'occuper de to be busy with / to look after
octobre October
l'œil (m) / les yeux eye / eyes
l'oeuf (m) egg
l'offre (f) d'emploi job advert / job offer
offrir (offert) to give (e.g. a present)
l'oignon (m) onion
l'ombre (f) shade
l'oncle (m) uncle
l'orage (m) thunderstorm
orageux(-euse) stormy
l'ordinateur (m) computer
l'ordinateur (m) portable laptop
les ordures (f) rubbish
l'oreille (f) ear
l'organisation caritative (f) charity / charitable organisation
ou or
où where
oublier to forget
l'ouest (m) west
l'ouvrier (m) / ouvrière (f) worker

P

le pantalon trousers
Pâques (f) Easter
le paquet packet
par by
par contre on the other hand
par terre on the ground
le parc à vélos bicycle park
le parc d'attractions theme park
parfois sometimes
le parking relais park-and-ride
partager to share
pas tellement not much
le passage à niveau level crossing
le passager / la passagère passenger
passer to spend (time)
se passer de to do without
passer l'aspirateur to do the vacuuming
passer un examen to take an exam
passif(-ve) passive
la pâte (à pain) (bread) dough
les pâtes (f) pasta
le patinage ice skating
la patinoire ice skating rink
la pâtisserie baker's (pastries, cakes)
le / la patron / patronne boss / manager
la pause-déjeuner lunch hour
pauvre poor
la pauvreté poverty
le pays étranger foreign country
le pays voisin neighbouring country
le paysage landscape / scenery
la pêche fishing
la peinture painting
la pelouse lawn
pendant during
pénible annoying / a nuisance
les percussions (f) percussion instruments
le père father
perfectionner to improve
permettre (permis) to allow
petit(e) small
le petit ami boyfriend

le petit déjeuner breakfast
la petite amie girlfriend
la petite annonce small advert / classified advert
le pétrole oil
un peu de a bit of
peut-être perhaps
la photocopieuse photocopying machine
la physique physics
la pièce room
à pied on foot
le pied foot
la piscine swimming pool
la piste cyclable cycle path
pittoresque picturesque
le placard cupboard
la plage beach
plaire (plu) to please
le plaisir pleasure / enjoyment
la planète planet
le plat dish
plein(e) de vie lively
pleurer to cry
pleuvoir (plu) to rain
la pluie rain
le plombier / la plombière plumber
la plongée sous-marine scuba diving
la plupart de most of
pluvieux(-euse) rainy
le point de vue viewpoint
la poire pear
le poisson rouge goldfish
pollué(e) polluted
la pompe pump
la pom-pom girl cheerleader
la porte door
poser sa candidature to apply
le poste job / post
la poubelle (dust)bin
le poumon lung
le pourboire tip
pourquoi why
pourtant however
pousser to grow
pratique practical
le premier / deuxième étage first / second floor
la première rue the first street

prendre (pris) to take
prendre une douche to have a shower
presque almost
la pression pressure
prêter to lend
prévenir (prévenu) to prevent / to inform / to warn
le printemps spring
la prise électrique electric socket
privé(e) private
le prix price
le problème problem
produire (produit) to produce
le produit de beauté beauty product
des produits bio (m) organic products
le / la professeur teacher
le professeur principal form tutor
le programmeur / la programmeuse programmer
promener le chien to walk the dog
promettre to promise
la promotion promotion / special offer
propre clean
le / la propriétaire owner
protéger to protect
les provisions (f) groceries
provoquer to provoke
le pull à capuche hoodie
punir (puni) to punish

Q
le quai platform
quand when
quand même all the same
et quart quarter past
le quartier area of a town
que that / what
qu'est-ce que what
qu'est-ce que c'est? what is it?
quel(le) which / what
quelquefois sometimes
qui who
quoi what

R
le racisme racism

raciste racist
ramasser to collect / to pick up la randonnée hike (on foot) / ride (bike or horseback)
ranger to tidy / to put away
ranger sa chambre to tidy one's bedroom
se rappeler to remember
rarement rarely
rater to fail
recevoir (reçu) to receive
recyclable recyclable
le réchauffement de la planète global warming
la récréation break (in school day)
redécouvrir to rediscover
le redoublement repeating a school year
redoubler to repeat a school year
la réduction reduction
réduire (réduit) to reduce
le régime diet
la règle rule / ruler
le règlement rules
rejeter to discharge / to pour
remarquer to notice
rembourser to pay back
remercier to thank
remplacer to replace
rencontrer to meet
rendre (rendu) to give back
renoncer to give up
renouveler to renew / to update
rénover to renovate
les renseignements (m) information
renvoyer to sack
repasser un examen to resit an exam
répondre to reply
réservé(e) reserved / quiet
résister à to resist
résoudre to solve
respirer to breathe
rester to stay
le retard delay
retenir (retenu) to keep
la retenue detention
se réunir (réuni) to meet up
la réunion meeting

réussir (réussi) to pass (an exam) / to succeed

le rêve dream

se réveiller to wake up

le réveillon Christmas Eve / New Year's Eve party

réveillonner to celebrate on Christmas Eve or New Year's Eve

révéler to reveal, disclose

le rez-de-chaussée ground floor

le rhum rum

le rhume cold

rien à voir avec nothing to do with

rigolo(-te) fun / funny

rire to laugh

le risque risk

le riz rice

la robe dress

le robinet tap

le roman novel

le rond-point roundabout

rose pink

rôti(e) roast

rouge red

la route road

la rue street

S

le sable sand

le sac bag

sain(e) healthy

la Saint-Sylvestre the festival on 31st December

la Saint-Valentin Valentine's Day

saisonnier(-ière) seasonal

le salaire salary

sale dirty

salé(e) salty

la salle à manger dining room

la salle d'attente waiting room

la salle d'informatique ICT room

la salle de bains bathroom

la salle de séjour living room / sitting room

la salle des profs staff room

le salon living room / sitting room

samedi Saturday

sans domicile fixe homeless

sans plomb unleaded

le / la sans-abri homeless person

sauf except

le saumon salmon

sauver to save

les sciences (f) science

scolaire school / to do with school

le / la SDF (sans domicile fixe) homeless person

sec (sèche) dry

le sèche-cheveux hair-dryer

le / la secrétaire secretary

le séjour stay (in a place)

le sel salt

selon according to

le sens de l'humour sense of humour

le sens interdit no entry

se sentir (senti) to feel

septembre September

la série series

le serveur / la serveuse waiter / waitress

seul(e) alone

le short shorts

le sida AIDS

le siècle century

le sirop (cough) syrup

le site site (internet)

le skate skateboarding

la société company / business

la sœur sister

le soir (in) the evening

le soldat soldier

les soldes (m) the sales

le soleil sun

la solitude solitude / being on one's own

le sommeil sleep

sonner to ring (phone, bell)

le souci worry / problem

souffrir (souffert) to suffer

souhaiter to wish

souriant(e) cheerful / smiley

sous under

le sous-sol basement

les sous-titres (m) subtitles

le souvenir memory

souvent often

spacieux(-euse) spacious

le sparadrap plaster

le sport d'hiver winter sport

le stade stadium

la station balnéaire seaside resort

la station de métro underground station

la station de ski ski resort

la station de taxi taxi rank

la station thermale spa resort

stationner to park

stressant(e) stressful

le stylo pen

les sucreries (f) sweets / sweet things

le sud south

la Suisse Switzerland

suivant(e) following

sur on

le sweat sweatshirt

sympa nice / kind

T

le tabac tobacco

le tabagisme addiction to smoking

le tableau blanc interactif interactive whiteboard

la tablette tablet computer

la tâche task

la taille size

la taille zéro size zero

les talons (m) heels

tard late

tardif(-ve) late

le taux rate / level

le / la technicien(ne) technician

la technologie D and T

tel(le) such

la télé connectée smart TV

télécharger to download

le (téléphone) portable mobile (phone)

la température temperature

la tempête storm

le temps weather

de temps en temps from time to time

à temps partiel part-time

à temps plein full-time

tenir to hold

le terrain de camping campsite

la Terre (the) Earth
le terroir local area
la tête head
le texto text (message)
en TGV (train à grande vitesse) by high-speed train
le thé à la menthe mint tea
le théâtre theatre
le Tiers-Monde developing world
les toilettes (f) toilet
la tombe grave
le tombeau grave
tomber amoureux(-euse) to fall in love
le tonnerre thunder
le / la touriste tourist
tous les jours every day
la Toussaint All Saints Day
tout droit straight on
tout le temps all the time
en train by train
le traitement de texte word processing
le trajet journey / trip
en tram by tram
tranquille quiet / calm
les transports (m) en commun public transport
le travail work
le travail bénévole voluntary work
travailler to work
travailleur(-euse) hardworking
la traversée crossing (e.g. the Channel)
tremper to soak
très very
le tricheur cheat
triste sad

la troisième French equivalent of Year 10
trop too
trop de monde too many people
le trottoir pavement
le trouble alimentaire eating disorder
la trousse pencil case
le tuba snorkel

U

une bonne ambiance a good atmosphere
une fois par semaine once a week
l'usine (f) factory
utiliser to use

V

la vague wave (water)
varié(e) varied
la vedette star / celebrity (male or female)
végétarien(ne) vegetarian
la veille eve / the day before
en veille on stand-by
à vélo by bike
le vendeur / la vendeuse sales assistant
vendre (vendu) to sell
vendredi Friday
le vent wind
le ventre stomach
vérifier le montant to check the balance (of an account)
le verre glass
vers towards
vert(e) green
les vêtements (m) clothes
le / la vétérinaire vet

le veuf widower
la veuve widow
la viande meat
la victime victim
la victime éventuelle potential victim
vider la poubelle to empty the bin
la vie life
vieux (vieille) old
la ville town / city
violet(-te) purple
le violon violin
la visite guidée guided tour
vivre (vécu) to live
vivre en concubinage to live together (without being married)
la voie path
la voile sailing
voir to see
voisin(e) neighbouring
le / la voisin(e) neighbour
en voiture by car
le vol flight
voler to fly / to steal
le volet shutter
vomir to vomit
le vomissement vomiting
le voyage journey
le voyage scolaire school trip
voyager to travel
la vue view

Z

la zone piétonne pedestrian zone

Acknowledgements

Kathy Baxendale p60; Mark Draisey p13, 16, 69, 101, 117 (reporter), 150, 157, 161; Russ Cook p164; Robin Edmonds p116; Stephen Elford p26; Tony Forbes pp36, 77, 98, 135; Celia Hart pp11, 12, 19, 21, 22, 27, 28, 35, 39, 63, 73, 79, 83, 97, 103, 107, 109, 117 (5), 138, 141, 149, 153, 159; Abel Ippolito pp40, 48, 108, 117 (3a A-C), 143, 148; Andy Keylock pp64, 65

The authors and the publisher would also like to thank the following for permission to reproduce material:

p7, Design Pics Inc./Alamy; p9, Shutterstock; p10, A: BigStockPhoto.com, B: iStockphoto, C: Shutterstock, D: BigStockPhoto.com, mobile phone screen: iStockphoto; p16, topic banner: iStockphoto; p16 - 17, Shutterstock; p18, A: Picture Partners/Alamy, B: Shutterstock, C: Juanmonino/Getty Images; p20, A and B: iStockphoto, C: 123rf.com; p23, Yannick Agnel: Getty Images, swimmer: Shutterstock; p24, banner: iStockphoto, girl: BigStockPhoto.com; p25, beer and cigarette: Shutterstock, tablets: Image Source/Alamy; p27, BigStockPhoto.com; p32, topic banner: iStockphoto, Pierre: iStockphoto, Amélie: BigStockphoto.com, Julien: Fotolia, Estelle: 123rf.com; p34, iStockphoto; p38, A, B and C: Shutterstock; p42, Kamarulzaman Russali/Alamy; p43, David Hoffman Photo Library/Alamy; p56, topic banner: Fotolia, girl with popcorn: 123rf.com, girl on horseback: BigStockPhoto.com; p58, Charlotte: iStockphoto, Alexis: BigStockPhoto, Marine: iStockphoto; p62, BigStockPhoto.com; p66, A: Fotolia, B: Shutterstock, C and D: Fotolia, E: iStockphoto; p72, topic banner: iStockphoto, A: Fotolia, B: BigStockPhoto.com, C: iStockphoto, D: Fotolia, E: iStockphoto; p74, beach: 123rf.com, countryside: iStockphoto, snow: Fotolia; p76, boy with rucksack: Alan Dawson Photography/Alamy, girl on beach: Fotolia; p78, boat: iStockphoto, climber: BigStockPhoto.com; p80, A: Stock Connection Blue/Alamy, B: Shutterstock, C: Chris Howes/Wild Place Photography/Alamy, D: Vespian/Alamy; p82, 1: Durand Patrick/Corbis Sygma, 2: Fotolia, 3: iStockphoto; p88, 123rf.com; p96, topic banner: Fotolia.com, A: 123rf.com, B: iStockphoto, C: BigStockPhoto.com, D: 123rf.com; p100, A: Peter Phipp/Getty Images, B: Natureworld/Alamy, C: Bloomberg/Getty Images, D: Blickwinkel/Alamy; p102, A and B: Fotolia; p104, Sally & Richard Greenhill/Alamy; p106, Keith Morris/Alamy; p112, topic banner: iStockphoto, Martin Jenkinson/Alamy; p113, whale and forest: 123rf.com; p114, iStockphoto; p118, iStockphoto; p119, iStockphoto; p120, A: iStockphoto, B: Shutterstock, C: Fotolia; p124, litter on beach: iStockphoto, factory: BigStockPhoto.com; p125, geogphotos/Alamy; p132, topic banner: iStockphoto, girl: BigStockphoto.com; p134, girls on grass: Sally and Richard Greenhill/Alamy, student group: David R. Frazier Photolibrary, Inc./Alamy; p136, iStockphoto.com; p138, Mark Burnett/Alamy; p140, Photo Alto/Getty Images; p148, topic banner: Shutterstock; p154, model: BigStockPhoto.com, man with headphones: Fotolia; p156, iStockphoto, Fotolia, BigStockPhoto.com, iStockphoto; p158, girl with books: Fotolia, boy with laptop: iStockphoto, woman in garden: iStockphoto; p165, classroom: Greenshoots Communications/Alamy, Desert: iStockphoto.

Every effort has been made to trace the copyright holders but if any have been inadvertently overlooked the publisher will be pleased to make the necessary arrangements at the first opportunity.